I've Been Thinking
Or, the Secret of Success

by
A. S. Roe

I've Been Thinking
Or, the Secret of Success
by A. S. Roe

Copyright © 2024

All Rights reserved.

ISBN: 978-93-65781-12-0

Published by

DOUBLE 9 BOOKS
2/13-B, Ansari Road
Daryaganj, New Delhi – 110002
info@double9books.com
www.double9books.com
Tel. 011-40042856

This book is under public domain

ABOUT THE AUTHOR

A. S. Roe, an influential figure in the realm of self-help and personal development, is best known for his motivational and inspirational writing. His works, including *I've Been Thinking Or, The Secret of Success*, have left a significant mark on readers seeking practical advice for achieving personal and professional success. Roe's writings focus on the principles of positive thinking, goal setting, and self-discipline, providing readers with actionable strategies for self-improvement and empowerment. Roe's approach combines motivational insights with practical advice, aiming to inspire individuals to take control of their lives and reach their full potential. His emphasis on the power of mindset and perseverance resonates throughout his work, reflecting a deep understanding of the challenges and opportunities faced by those striving for success. Through his books, A. S. Roe has contributed to the broader self-help genre, influencing countless individuals to adopt more effective strategies for personal growth and achievement. His legacy lies in his ability to provide clear, actionable guidance that empowers readers to pursue their goals with confidence and determination.

CONTENTS

CHAPTER I

'Where is the use, Jim, of our working and working to raise so many vegetables? we never can use them all. Mother said last year there was no necessity for raising more than we could eat, and now this potato patch is larger than ever.' And as he said this, the little speaker threw himself upon the soft ground, struck his hoe into the soil, and looked up at his brother to see how he would take it.

Jim, as he was called, rested a moment on his hoe, eyed his brother closely, and then, with something of a smile, replied:

'Come, Ned, don't give up to lazy feelings; the things will do somebody good; and you know my father always told us, that it was better to be at work, even if we got no pay for it: and besides, I have been thinking of a plan by which we may do something with what we raise, if we have more than we can use.'

'What plan, Jim?' and Ned raised himself from his prostrate position, and sitting with both hands resting on the ground, looked very inquiringly at his brother.

'Why, suppose we should try to sell some of the things we raise?'

'Try to *sell*, Jim? ha, ha, ha!' and the little fellow threw himself upon the ground, and indulged in a hearty fit of laughter. Jim laughed a little himself, resuming his work, and hauling the dirt up faster around the potatoes he was hilling.

'Come, Ned, you had better go to work; the sun will soon be down, and we shall not get our task done.'

'Well, tell me then *where* you are going to sell the things; that's all.'

'I shall say no more about it now, at any rate; you will only laugh at it. So come, take up your row.'

Ned, perceiving that Jim was working upon both rows, was ashamed to waste any more time, and inspired by his brother's kindness, sprang to his feet, and the two boys worked away with alacrity.

The sun had gone down, the cow had been milked and the pigs fed, the hens had all gone to roost, and the two brothers had sauntered towards the river which ran before their dwelling, and taken a seat together on a rock under the branches of a huge oak, of which there were several around the premises. Before them lay, *first*; a gentle slope of short greensward, part of what was known as the town commons, where every body's cow, or pig, or goose, could roam unmolested; beyond *this* lay a smooth sandy shore, washed by a river, whose waters had not far to go before they mingled with the ocean, or with a large arm of the ocean; along the shore, as far as the eye could reach, was the same, or nearly the same, strip of green commons, dotted here and there with small rude dwellings, the abodes of a few fishermen, who existed on the products of the river that rolled before them; a few small boats lay drawn up on the shore, and occasionally a row of stakes running out into the water, told where the fishermen had planted their nets. The only house in sight that had any appearance of comfort was the one these brothers called their home—a plain one-story building, with a little wing to it; a paling ran in front and around three sides, enclosing the patch of ground used as their garden; a few fine old trees threw their shadows over and around the premises, adding much to the domestic aspect of the place; a pleasant country spread back from the river, and in the distance could be seen here and there the chimney top, or the peaked roof of some obscure dwelling, making no greater pretensions than those described.

'I wonder what Sam Oakum is doing along shore there?'

'Where, Jim?'

'Down by that clump of rocks. Don't you see him?'

'Oh, he is picking up horse-shoes; he has not fed his pigs yet; I suppose his father is drunk to-day, and the pigs are squealing, and Sam has gone to look for something for them to eat; poor fellow!'

'Sam is a clever fellow; I do wish his father would act differently. I cannot see what is to become of him. They who have no father are bad enough off, but I think poor Sam is worse off still.'

'Do you think, Jim, if father had lived, that we should have stayed here?'

'I cannot say—I suppose we should. Why do you ask that question, Ned?'

'Because I think it is a poor place to get a living in; nor do I see how we are going to get along here; it is hard hoeing for it any how.'

'*Hard hoeing?* I don't think so, Ned; it is a great deal harder doing nothing.'

'Perhaps it is; I should like to try it once, and see.'

'I believe it to be true what father often said, that "hard work made short nights and sweet food," and if we should give up work, what would become of mother and Ellen?'

'I will work for them, Jim, as long as I have got any fingers to work with; but we may hoe and hoe here all our lives, and what will it amount to?'

'I have been thinking a great deal about that, Ned, and therefore I spoke to you as I did to-day when you laughed so at me.'

'Well, tell me *now*, Jim; I promise you I will not laugh any more.'

'I have been thinking for some time, just as you say, Ned, "that we must hoe and hoe all our lives," and without much hope of making our condition any better.'

'Why you see, Jim, if there was any one here to buy what we raised, more than we wanted to eat, there would be some use in raising all we could.'

'I know it, Ned; and the great trouble is, that the folks all round here are as poor as we are, and the most of them not so well off; they live from hand to mouth, and would never want any thing we could raise.'

'Why, I suppose they would like our strawberries and peaches well enough, if we would give them away; but they will never take the trouble to raise any for themselves, and I am very sure they will never have any money to buy them with.'

'That is it, Ned; you are right now. Father has taught us to raise such things, you know, and if we had any way to dispose of them, we could raise many more than we do.'

'Then you would see how I could work, Jim, and we would stuff the old garden full of every thing.'

'I have been thinking—now, you won't laugh again?'

'No, I won't, I promise you.'

'Well, I have been thinking—you know, just over the other side of the island is that large fort; sometimes there is quite a company of soldiers, and always some officers and their families there; the grounds about there are so rocky and sandy, that they cannot raise any thing if they would; they no doubt get their provisions in large quantities from a distance, but the officers and their families might like some of our fruits and vegetables, as we could supply them fresh; the only thing is, how to get there?'

'Yes, Jim, that would be the trouble; we have no boat, and we should not know how to manage one if we had it, and mother would be so afraid to let us go such a distance on the water.'

'I have thought of these difficulties, Ned, but I believe we can get along with them. I know it will be difficult getting to the fort sometimes, in rough weather; and then, as you say, we have no boat, and we should not be able to manage one if we had it; but how would it do to ask Sam Oakum to join us?'

'Sam Oakum is the very fellow, just the very fellow; but stop, Jim, Sam has not got a boat.'

'I know that; but no doubt he can borrow one for the first trip, and then, if our plan should succeed, perhaps we could hire it until we were able to buy one for ourselves.'

Ned could stand it no longer; he jumped from the rock, clapped his hands, huzzaed, caught hold of Jowler, who had sprung up, and was barking away in answer to Ned's huzza, and down they went on the green sward together.

'Don't go crazy, Ned, we may be disappointed after all; mother may not give her consent, Sam may be unwilling to go, or not able to get a boat.'

'Do stop, Jim, bringing up difficulties; I don't want to hear them now. I know mother will let us go, and I know Sam will like dearly to join us; he can get a boat, I am sure he can.'

'Well, Ned, the first thing we must do is, to get mother's consent.'

'Yes, and you will speak to her this very night, won't you, Jim? I will put in a word once in a while, just to help along.'

Twilight was past; the stars were shining through a clear bright sky, when these two brothers retraced their steps towards home. It is pleasant to see them so cheerfully complying with that command, 'Honor thy father and thy mother, that thy days may be long in the land which the Lord thy God giveth thee.'

And now I suppose my readers may be anxious to know some particulars about our boys, and the place where they lived.

Their father, Mr. James Montjoy, who had died a few months before the period at which our story commences, was rather a plain man in his appearance and manners, and lived on a small pension just enough to sustain his family, so that he left nothing for their support but the house and garden. I think he must have been a good man, for his boys revered his name, and often repeated his sayings to each other; and on no account would they deviate from what they believed would have been his will.

As to the place where they lived, I have already partly described it; it was a very retired spot, a few farm-houses were scattered about at irregular intervals, but all wearing the same general aspect. A want of enterprise was manifest on every side; poor roads, poor fences, broken barns, patched windows in almost every house, miserable-looking waggons and horses, and people in appearance as uncouth and woe-begone as their teams.

There was but one store in the place, and how that was supplied was somewhat mysterious; for no boats sailed from or to this lone spot. I have heard, that once in a year a large lumber waggon, that came from a distance, brought a load of casks and boxes, which contained all the goods necessary to supply the few wants of its customers, a little tea, and sugar, and molasses, and a few coarse dry goods, with an undue proportion of whiskey. The storekeeper looked no better than his customers; he was a dried-up, wrinkled little man, with a very red nose; always clad in a suit of grey clothes, with a broad-brimmed greasy hat, turned up in front, and a pair of iron spectacles, through which stared two very large eyes, somewhat the worse for the use of cider and whiskey.

The store itself was a long, low, tumble-down-looking place, with a shed running along its front, under which might almost always be seen a certain number of miserably dressed persons, the customers of the store.

It will be of no use to any of my readers to be told the real name of this place, nor its exact locality. I have mentioned that it was on a river, and not far from where that river emptied itself into a sound, or arm of the sea; but as there are a great many rivers and sounds in our beautiful country, I must leave you all to guess the right one. And perhaps many of you will pass this place, or have already passed it many times, and when you have seen, or shall see, the beautiful church spire that now rises from the midst of the trees which embower it, and the neat white houses along the shore, and the trim vessels that line the wharves, and hear the lively—'Yo, heave yo!' of the sailors, as they hoist the white sail to the breeze, you will little dream that it was once as I have described it.

And now we must see how Jim gets along in gaining the consent of his mother.

Mrs. Montjoy was a good mother, and loved her three children most tenderly; but as all mothers who truly love their children must sometimes deny their wishes, Jim and Ned had learned some lessons, which made them feel less and less confident the more they thought of the matter. At length the former, taking up the candle, whispered to his brother.—

'Perhaps, Ned, we had better not say anything about it until to-morrow.'

'I think so too, Jim.'

So, kissing their mother and little Ellen, up they went to their garret room, talking and laughing in great spirits.

'The poor dear children,' thought Mrs. Montjoy, 'it makes my heart ache to hear them; they think not of the future. May God, in his mercy, open some way, for I see but a poor prospect before them. And it may be that prayer was heard, and the God of the widow and the fatherless was preparing the means by which these unprotected children would prove the light of their native place, and her stay and comfort. Had she seen them as they knelt down by the bedside together, she would have felt that her children were not fatherless.

The next morning the boys had a long conference with their mother; and after she had listened to their plans, and stated to them, more particularly than she had ever before done, the straitened circumstances to which they were reduced, and expressed many fears on account of their exposure on the water, she finally agreed that they might try what they could do.

No sooner had they reached the door, after thus accomplishing their wishes, than Ned started on the full run, jumped over the first thing that stood in his way—which happened to be old Jowler—caught up his hoe from under the shed, and entering the garden by a cross cut, began tearing the dirt around the potato hills with all his might.

Jim walked very leisurely to his work, and for some time permitted his brother to go on, thinking that he would soon become tired, and relax his efforts; but seeing that Ned was coming back on *his* row,—

'You had better keep your own row, Ned; I shall get along soon enough with mine, and you will only tire yourself by working so fast.'

'Well, I am in such a hurry, Jim; I want to get these potato hills finished, so that we can go and talk with Sam Oakum about the boat.'

'I am as much in a hurry as you are, Ned; but we have quite a patch to hill yet, and we shall get through sooner, by working steadily, besides doing our work better; we can get along with them by the middle of the afternoon, and that will give us time enough to see Sam.'

And as Jim had said, by the middle of the afternoon the last hill of potatoes was finished; and, having made all their arrangements, and agreed upon all they would say to Sam, they had nothing to do but go to the tree where they placed their tools, and hang up their hoes for that day.

As Sam Oakum will be a prominent character in our story, I must introduce him more particularly to my reader. His father lived in one of the huts which I have said were scattered along the shore of the river for some distance, and followed the occupation which *his* father had followed before him, that of a fisherman; or, in other words, that of catching a few fish or clams, sufficient to satisfy the cravings of hunger for the day, and spending the rest of it in idleness and drinking, without enterprise or ambition. As their fathers had done for generations back, so did they; they seemed to feel that it was their luck to be poor, and, to all appearance, felt willing that their children should follow in their steps.

Sam Oakum's father was rather a superior man to his neighbors; he had some knowledge, too, of boat-building; he had never learned the trade, but, being ingenious, could put together a small craft quite decently, and the few poor boats which the fisherman owned were the work of his hands; but he also exceeded many of his neighbors in the use of strong drink, and too frequently it was feared that his wife and children suffered for the necessaries of life, because the father was away, and in no condition to get home. For a few years past, however, since Sam had become able to manage a boat, he would see that there was food for his mother and sisters, although there had been as yet no opening for him by which he could do any more than this. There was no ground attached to their poor house for him to cultivate; there was no work in the vicinity that he could get; and the boat, by means of which he could procure their supply from the water, he was obliged to borrow.

Sam was now about sixteen years of age; a good-looking fellow he was too, although his clothes were old and patched; his hair was black as a coal, and very much disposed to curl; he had a good open countenance, very bright black eyes, and a fine nut-brown complexion. As we shall learn his character in the progress of our story, it will not be necessary to describe him any closer at present.

On the day that Jim and Ned had been so successful in obtaining the consent of their mother to put their plan into execution, Sam had experienced a severe trial: his father had indulged more freely his dreadful appetite, and although in general kind to his family, had begun to manifest a morose and sullen temper.

Sam's mother was a good-natured, inoffensive woman, always endeavouring to make the best of things; managing as well as she could with what was in the house, and although sorely pinched sometimes, never finding fault with her husband.

'It would do no good,' she said, 'to be dinging at Oakum; it would only make him worse.'

So the poor soul went on from day to day, doing her best, and always hoping, woman like, that he would be different one of these days; but on this eventful morning her accumulated grievances could no longer be repressed, and as her husband was about to leave the house, only to return at evening in a wretched condition, she ventured to say to him—

'Oakum, don't you think you'd better not go up to the store to-day?'

'Don't I *think* I'd better *not*? *No*, I don't—what makes you ask me?'

'Oh well, I didn't mean no harm; only you have been away so much lately.'

'Well, supposing I have, whose business is *that*, I want to know?'

'Why nobody's, I suppose; only you know, Oakum, we ain't got nothing in the house but them two fish you brought in this morning; there ain't no meal nor nothing.'

'No meal nor nothing; yes, there is meal: didn't I bring home some yesterday?'

'Well, you know how that was, the pigs got at it.'

'The pigs got at it—then why didn't you take care of it, and not let the pigs get the children's bread?'

'It wasn't mother's fault,' said Sam, who was by at the time, and knew all the circumstances.

'Whose fault was it then, you little vagabond?'

'I ain't a vagabond yet; but we shall all be soon, if you keep going to Grizzle's every day.'

Sam's father was utterly confounded; he took off his hat and sat down.

'What, are my children going to rise up against me? Go out of the house, sir.'

Poor Mrs. Oakum was in great trouble. Sam had said what was true; his father had, in a state of unconsciousness, left the flour at the mercy of the pigs; but she felt sorry that he had spoken, and Sam soon felt very sorry for it too; his conscience upbraided him; he went out of the house and kept as busy as he could, but he could not feel happy.

By little and little Oakum found out from his wife all about the meal; he was thoroughly ashamed, asked for another bag, and immediately took his hat and departed.

About the middle of the afternoon Sam sauntered along the shore to a large flat rock that stood just at the water's edge. He took a seat upon it, and with his eye stretched far over the beautiful bay, mused on his sad condition and hopeless prospects. Was life to be as it had ever been—a scene of idleness and want, a waste, with nothing to cheer or stimulate his youthful mind? without education (not being able even to read), without a trade, or the prospect of one, or any employment that offered the least inducement to exertion? His conscience sorely troubled him also on account of the disrespect he had shown to his father that morning; and as he mused, his excited feelings started the tears down his sunburnt face, and in the agony of the moment he exclaimed,

'I wish I was—'

'What do you wish?' said Ned Montjoy, as he stole up behind, and put his hands over Sam's eyes.

'But what is it, Sam?' you are in trouble; tell us right away. 'Can Jim and I help you?'

Sam wiped away his tears as he best could, but was unable at once to make any reply.

'Come, Sam, tell us, has anything happened to day?'

'Oh, nothing particular, Ned; only sometimes I get tired of living as I do.'

'Oh well, Sam, if that is all, come cheer up; for Ned and I have a plan in view, and if you will join us, perhaps things will be better for us all.'

'I'll join you and Ned in any thing, but I don't see what use I can be to you.'

'So much use, that we can do nothing without you *do* join us Sam. Can we, Jim?'

'No, I fear we cannot.'

'Well, what is it, boys? Come, I'm ready for any thing.'

'You tell him, Jim, all about it. I say, Sam, it's the best thing you ever heard of. I tell you *what*, won't it be nice though?'

And Ned kicked up his heels, ran a few steps, caught up a smooth flat stone, and away it went skimming the surface of the water, and in plunged Jowler, as he had often done before, on a fruitless search after it. Jim took a seat alongside of Sam, and soon unfolded his scheme for adventure. Sam's countenance brightened as Jim went on, and he was too impatient to wait until the whole was regularly told.

'And you want me to manage the boat, and you will sell the things?'

'That is it, Sam.'

'I tell you what, Jim, who put all this in your head? I wonder why I never thought about taking clams and oysters there! I am sure they will buy them: I might try some, couldn't I?'

'Certainly—but how are we to get a boat? your father has none, has he?'

'No, not now, but I know where I can borrow one; it has a sail to it—it is old and leaky though, but a little calking will make all tight.'

No sooner had Sam said this, than Ned started off again on another gallop; he took quite a circuit this time, and coming back caught Sam by the back of his collar, and pulled him over flat upon the rock.

'Didn't I tell you, Jim, that Sam Oakum was the fellow for us?'

'Don't, Ned, act so crazy; let Sam go.'

'Oh let him alone, Jim; he is so full, he must let out a little.'

Sam rolled himself off from the rock, and picked up his little tarred hat, which had fallen upon the sand.

'Well, boys, when shall we go,—to-morrow?'

'Why, can you get the boat ready by that time, Sam?'

'Yes, that is, if old Andrews will let me have it; I guess there will be no fear of that.'

'Well, how shall we know? for if we go to-morrow, we must be up early and pick our strawberries. Shall we come down here to-night, Sam?'

'No; I tell you what we'll do—if I can get the boat, and father will let me go, I won't come up; so, if you don't see me, you may conclude we shall go.'

'Agreed, Sam.'

Sam was on good terms with the old man from whom he expected to get the boat, and found no difficulty on that score; it occupied him, however, the remainder of the afternoon in putting her in a condition suitable for their voyage, and even then it was but a frail concern to venture in, where at times the winds were strong and the waters rough. But Sam knew no fear; so taking the oars and thanking his old friend very heartily for his kindness, 'lay to,' and the little skiff flew through the smooth water like a bird.

He had accomplished, however, but one part of his work; he had yet to meet his father and obtain his consent, and his heart sunk within him when he thought of home, and the probable condition of things there. He had resolved what course to pursue—he had done wrong, he had spoken improperly to his parent, he must ask his forgiveness before he could be happy. But he knew not in what condition he might find that parent. He rowed his boat up to the rock where he had held the conversation with Jim and Ned—hauled her up on the shore as far as he was able, carried the stone anchor on land, and walked directly towards home, strong in good resolutions, and with some faint hope that things might be better than he feared. He gathered up the horse-shoes as he went along which he had collected on the beach in the afternoon, enough to make a good supper for his pigs; and throwing them over into their pen as he passed, was just entering the door of his dwelling when he met his father, who had his hat on and was going out. Sam saw at a glance that all was right—he cast his eyes down:

'Father, I'm sorry I spoke so this morning.'

'Oh, never mind now, Sam.' And as he saw Sam wiping his eyes, for the tears came fast, 'Never mind now, my boy; it has gone by, and a good many other things I hope too—go in and get your supper.'

Sam entered the room, happier than he had been for many a day; his mother's countenance was lighted up with a smile, and his little sister came up and whispered,

'Father ain't been to Grizzle's to day.' Sam looked at his mother and she at him—tears were glistening in both their eyes, but they told only of joy and hope.

He soon communicated to his mother his plan for the next day; she made no objections, only she hoped he would take care of himself.

'And may be you'd better speak to your father, Sam.'

Just then Mr. Oakum came in, and Sam proceeded at once to tell him what had been proposed, and what he had done about it.

'I thought I saw a boat laying up by the rock there, and I couldn't think where it came from—is that Andrew's skiff? don't it leak badly?'

'Oh, I've calked her, Father, she is tight as a whistle now.'

'Well, Sam, you must take care of yourself, you know it's rough sometimes round the point; you most keep close to shore, that skiff won't stand much. I don't think it will be of much use for you to go there, but you may try.'

Early the next morning—so early that a faint streak of light was barely visible in the east—Sam was off with his skiff, raking for clams and oysters as his share of the freight; and by the time Jim and Ned were at the shore with their baskets, he was ready to receive them.

CHAPTER II

It was a bright and beautiful morning, the water as calm and peaceful as it was possible for water to be so near the restless ocean. Ned stood on the shore, delighted to see the little skiff cut her way through its glassy surface, and to hear the sound of Sam's oars reverberating for a great distance along the opposite shore.

He watched as it receded, until thinking it was about as far as he could make them hear, hallooed with his loudest call, 'Good bye, boys!' He saw them both look towards the shore, and heard in return, 'Good bye, Ned!' coming as from a great distance. He took off his hat and waved it, then went on his way to his daily task.

Sam, although not experienced in long excursions, knew enough of the labor of rowing, not to expend his strength at starting. They had ten miles to pass over before they could reach their place of destination, and the latter part would require much more exertion than the commencement of their voyage; so, like an experienced mariner, he made but little effort at first, and suffered his boat to flow along with the tide. Jim was quite a novice in such matters but Sam had placed him at the helm, and given him sundry directions how to steer.

'The tide is just beginning to fall, and I guess it will bring me up with the point without much rowing, if you will just keep her head right there?'

'I'll try, Sam; but don't you think I had better help you to row?'

'Oh, no; it's easy work now. She goes a pretty good jog; and I only just dip my oars and take them out again. I guess, though, there will be some pulling when we get round the point; but perhaps we shall have a little breeze, and then we can put up our sail.'

Sam's guessing turned out to be very correct; it required but little effort to make the point; and as they turned their course in the opposite direction to that in which they had been steering, and were no longer sheltered by the island which formed their beautiful harbor, but were fairly in the outer bay, across whose waters they could see the haze of the ocean and the white beacon that lighted its weary voyagers to their desired haven, the wind blew gently, and Sam lost no time in taking advantage of it; there was just enough to carry them along against the tide, which was no longer in their favor.

The fort to which our little voyagers were steering had been erected about ten years. It was intended to command the channel through which vessels of ordinary size must pass, in their way from the ocean to one of our most valuable cities. It was built with two tiers of ports, and of sufficient strength for heavy guns; and as our foreign relations were in an unsettled state, it had, at the period under consideration, its full complement of men. It was erected at some distance from the shore on a ledge of rocks which, at low water, formed a passage to the main land; but when the tide was in, a few only of the highest rocks could be seen.

The nearer they approached the place of their destination, the more serious did the matter appear to them.

'Do you think, Sam, there is danger they won't let us in?'

'I don't know; I hope not, Jim. It would be too bad, after all our trouble, not to get even a chance to sell any thing.'

'Well, Sam, we can but try, you know. We have only to tell them what we've come for;—but I *say*, Sam, it makes my heart beat to look at it: what high walls it has; and see, there are the sentinels walking up and down—how their guns glitter in the sunshine!'

'Halloo! halloo! where are you bound, my hearties?'

The boys were startled by the gruff tones in which they had been accosted; and, turning their eyes toward the shore from whence the sounds seemed to come, saw an elderly man dressed in a sailor's habit, seated on a rock, and beckoning to them, or rather, by a motion, endeavouring to stop their progress.

'Halloo! my boys; don't go ahead there, or you'll be foul of the rocks.'

Sam immediately turned the skiff toward the shore, and they were soon in close contact with the stranger. He was sitting on the rock, with one leg swinging backwards and forwards, and the stump of the other sticking straight out. His dress was a true sailor's rig, of blue originally, but now much soiled, and of many colors. Spots of tar were pretty well sprinkled over both, coat and trousers; vest he had none; but instead thereof, a dark blue shirt, trimmed around the collar and bosom with something that had once been white. On his head sat (for the crown was too low to permit much of any thing to enter into it) a glazed hat, which, from its bright appearance, had lately received a fresh coat of tar; large bushy locks of sandy-colored hair stood out from beneath, based by a thick mat of whiskers, extending under his chin, and covering his whole neck; while down his back hung a queue of enormous size, reaching nearly to the rock on which he sat. His features, what could be seen of them, were not forbidding, although very much doubled and twisted by the wear and tear of time and rough weather.

'We were going to the fort,' said Jim; 'and can you tell us, good man, if they will let us in!'

'That's accordin' as to what your business is—if you got an arr'nd to the major or his lady, or any of his folks, or to the lieutenant and his lady, or so on—why the case is, they'll have to pass you right in; but if it's only one of the privates you see, that's another thing.'

'But we have no particular errand to anybody; we have got a few things to sell, and would be glad to dispose of them at the fort.'

'Ay, ay, that's a new case—things to sell, ha! I guess it will depend upon what things you've got. If it's contraband goods, and you're thinking to git the better of Uncle Sam, you've come to the wrong market; the major'll make short work with you.'

'I don't know what you mean by contraband goods or trying to get the better of anybody,' said Jim; 'we only thought they might be in want of a few fresh vegetables and some strawberries.'

'Ay, ay, that's clean another case, there's no contraband in them; but where under the blessed heaven have you come from? these things can't grow nowheres round here.'

'I shouldn't think they could,' said Jim, looking significantly at the dreary waste of sand and stunted pine that spread as far as he could see; 'strawberries might grow up in the pines there, but I guess not such as these.' With that Jim stopped, and taking up a basket, pulled off the covering of green leaves, and held them out for the old man to look at.

'Of all sights my eyes ever looked at! ——'

'I think you'll find them as good as they look,' taking a double handful, and holding them out towards the old man.

'No, no,' shaking his weather-beaten face, 'I've no money to buy 'em; you must go to the major.'

'Take them and welcome, sir; I had no thought of asking you for pay; you're very welcome to them.'

'God bless your young heart!' and holding out his hands he soon showed that he knew how to dispose of them; as soon as he had finished he jumped down on his one leg, and adjusted his crutches.

'Now, my hearties, I tell you what do you do; steer that craft o' your'n right straight across to the fort, and just where you see that ledge of rocks ends, you'll come foul of a pair o' stairs; haul up there, and wait till I hobble round to my boat, and I'll be with you afore you've made all fast.'

Away went the old man, his crutches making the sand fly in his haste to get to his boat, which lay a short distance from where he had been sitting.

The boys obeyed his directions, and had scarcely made their boat fast, ere the old man was alongside.

'Now, my hearties, you just hold on awhile here, till I see the major.'

The moments seem long when we are in suspense, and our boys, in their anxiety, began to fear that they should see no more of the old sailor; it appeared so long, so very long that he stayed. After gazing intently at the gate until their eyes were aching, all at once the sentinel stopped, made a peculiar motion with his musket, and put his hand to his cap; a gentleman of fine appearance passed out, followed at a respectful distance by the crutches. He came directly to the stairs, and accosting the boys in a very pleasant manner, inquired where they had come from, and what they had for sale. Jim, in a straightforward, manly way, answered his queries.

'But, my little fellow, what ever put it into your head to come so far as this in search of a market?'

'We could think, sir, of no other place where there would be the least chance to sell any thing; the people in this region are too poor to buy such things.'

'You may well say so, my lad, and they are like to be so; for a lazier set I never saw; but I am glad to find that you, boys, are disposed to do something. Peter tells me that you have some choice things for sale.'

Peter, as we must call him hereafter, touched his hat when his name was mentioned, but otherwise remained perfectly still, at a respectful distance, saying nothing.

Jim immediately uncovered the different articles, and with his hat off, looked up at the officer, who smiled as he surveyed the little stock of goods.

'You have made out a pretty good assortment—those strawberries are fine, indeed; are there plenty such raised in your area?'

'None, sir, but in our garden; my father used to be very fond of fruit, and he taught us to raise it.'

'Is your father living?'

'He is not, sir.'

A shade of sadness at once passed over the countenance of the officer, and his eye settled more intently upon the boy.

'Well, my lad, have you fixed upon a price for your articles?'

'I leave that to yourself, sir, as I am entirely ignorant of their value.'

Major Morris then ordered the different articles to be measured, and putting down prices to them such as he was accustomed to pay, handed the paper to Jim.

'Not reckoning the strawberries, which I must pay something extra for, the amount is one dollar and a half.'

Jim looked up with astonishment.

'I have calculated them at city prices, but if that is not enough— —'

'Oh yes, sir; yes, sir. I was not thinking of that; it is much more than I expected.'

'And now for the strawberries, what shall I say for them? they are finer than those I usually purchase.'

'Oh, sir, I cannot think of taking any thing for them, since you allow me so much for the others; if you will only let me take some out and give that good man there (pointing to Peter), you are welcome to the rest.'

'Certainly, certainly, here Peter.' But Peter had other views of the matter, and instead of advancing to receive them, made two or three retrograde steps with his crutches, at the same time putting his hand upon his long queue and smoothing it down—a custom of his when at all confused, and rolling a tremendous quid from one side of his mouth to the other.

'The young gentleman wishes to give you some of these, Peter.'

'Thankee, sir, thankee;' nodding his head very fast all the time; 'no occasion at all.'

'Well, Peter, since you refuse them, take this basket and hand it to Mrs. Morris yourself.'

'Ay, ay, sir;' and away went Peter in double-quick time.

In the meanwhile, Sam manifested no impatience, although somewhat anxious as to what would be *his* fate; the moment Jim could with propriety, he directed the attention of the gentleman to Sam's little heap of clams and oysters.

Sam took off the seaweed which he had thrown over them, and blushed deeply as he met the keen black eye of Major Morris, which having glanced a moment at *them*, was scrutizing with apparent interest the appearance of their owner.

As Sam had no more idea of fixing a price than Jim had, the buyer was obliged to pay for them on his own terms; so handing him fifty cents, he said,

'I fear it will not compensate you for the trouble of bringing them so far, but it is the rate for which I buy them.'

Sam expressed his perfect satisfaction the best way he could; for the eye of the major was so long fixed upon him, that it quite took away his self-possession.

Having made arrangements to bring such articles as their garden afforded twice a week, with light and happy hearts, lighter and happier than can be well described, they pointed their sail and bent their course for home. The rock was to be their landing-place, and long before they reached it, Ned could be seen throwing stones and cutting capers with Jowler.

'Well, boys, how are you? what luck—sold any thing? I know by your looks you haven't!'

'How are you, Ned? any thing happened? You look sober.'

'No, nothing.'

All this was said while the boat was nearing shore, the moment it touched the land Ned was on board; he looked at the empty baskets, and then at Jim and Sam. Jim smiled, and held out his hand, full of silver pieces, and Sam held out his; and then they told him of their success, and what arrangements they had made for the future.

Ned was somewhat confounded at the good news; but no sooner did he comprehend it fully, than he took hold of both of them at once, shaking them, and pushing them about, and hallooing.

'How are you, boys? huzza! huzza!'

'Do, Ned, stop your noise, and don't carry on so; you'll have us all in the water.'

'Never mind, Jim, we'll soon work ourselves dry. Huzza! huzza!'

'I'm afraid you'll set the old boat a leaking, Ned.'

'Well, Sam, I'll stop; but how can you fellows keep so still when you've had such good luck?'

Sam would have been perfectly contented with the product of his clams and oysters for his day's work, but Jim would insist upon giving him a certain proportion of what *he* had received, which was finally fixed at one quarter; so that Sam was to have, besides all he could procure from the sale of his own articles, one-fourth of whatever other things were sold, as his pay for the boat, and his labor in rowing.

And when Sam took the money which Jim handed to him, and put it with what he had already received, and looked at it, a crowd of thoughts rushed into his mind. Parents, sisters, home, the past, the present, and the future—and that future bright with prospect of employment, and the means of making those he loved as happy as himself. He could make no answer to the cheerful 'Good bye' of Ned and Jim, but he turned his bright and glistening eye towards them; and they went on their way the happier that they saw how full of joy Sam was.

Sam kept his money in his hand until he reached home, and, going directly to his mother, put the whole of his treasure into her lap.

'Why, Sam, where did you get all this?'

'Earned it, mother;' and then he told her all about it, and what he was expecting to do in future.

'Oh,' said his mother, laying down her work, and clasping her hands together in strong emotion, 'isn't this good! And now, Sam, you'll have something to do all the time, and may be, your father will help you; and may be he'll feel encouraged to do different; and may be— —.' But the hope of what might be, was too bright for her to utter it; and so she sat and looked at Sam, and then she turned and looked out at the window; and who can tell what a pleasing picture was painted out before her on the sandy shore and the glassy river.

Sam had designed that his mother should keep the money, and use it for their need; but she refused.

'No, no; keep it yourself, Sam; or, if you please, hand it to your father. I see he's coming yonder, and all seems to be right with him.'

And so it proved; he had been to work for a neighbor where no restraint would have been placed upon his appetite; but, strange to say, he had not indulged. He had received no money for his services, for there was seldom any of that to be got; but he had a bunch of fish in one hand, and a kettle with flour in the other.

'Why, Sam, you got back? that is clever. What luck? not much, I guess.'

Sam made no reply, but as soon as his father had laid down his things he handed out his little store.

'Here, father, please to take this.'

'Why, Sam, you didn't sell your things for all this, did you?'

And then Sam told him all the story, while his father looked in amazement at the money, and at Sam, and then at his wife; as soon as he had finished he held out his hand.

'Here, my boy, go give it to your mother; it's better with her than with me.'

'No, father, I'd rather you would take it, and do what you please with it.'

Blessings on you, Sam, that you had the good sense and good feeling to answer as you did. You have poured a cordial into that father's heart, which will do more to heal his weaknesses, and strengthen his good resolutions, than could have been done by all the world beside. He feels that he is yet a father, all is not lost—his *children yet* trust in him—the bright happy look of that boy has accomplished a work which an angel would gladly have been commissioned to perform. God bless you, Sam, for this one act, to your latest day.

'Well, Sam, then keep it yourself, and add as much to it as you can; for you are a good boy.'

'They shall have it tho' yet, in some way or other,' said Sam to himself, as he put it into his little chest. 'I shan't keep it for myself; that *I shan't.*'

It would have required two smart talkers to have answered all Ned's questions as fast as he put them; and as Jim never talked fast, he was not half through answering when they reached home: their lively conversation brought their mother out to meet them as they were entering the front yard.

'Oh mother, what *do* you think? Jim has sold all the things for ever so much; see the empty baskets, and (striking Jim's pocket) hear that—hear the money jingle.'

Both smiled at Ned's earnestness; and entering the house, a little circle was soon formed around Jim, who went through with his story in his own way.

'And now, mother,' said Ned, as soon as his brother had finished, 'you'll see how I can work; and if you will only give me a little bite of something, I will go at once and finish my hoeing, for I was so anxious to see the boys come back, that I have done nothing all the afternoon but look over to the point.'

'You now feel, boys, the benefit of having been taught to work; it is no hardship to you now.'

'Why, mother, I would rather work than play.'

'You thought differently the other day, Ned.'

'I know that, Jim; but you see the case is altered—that plan of yours which I laughed so much about, makes altogether a great difference. I don't believe any body would want to work just for the sake of it, would they, mother?'

'No doubt, my dear, we need some stimulus to make us exert ourselves cheerfully; but your father always said that it was better to be at work, even if it did not amount to much; it was impossible, he said, for an idle person to be happy.'

Mrs. Montjoy said but little by way of encouragement, for she saw that the boys were both highly elated with their success and the prospect before them; but she secretly admired and gratefully acknowledged the overruling of that kind Providence, which had opened a way for her children's usefulness and the supply of their wants.

The next morning Jim and Ned did not need to be awaked; there was real business on their hands now, and they must use their time to the best advantage; so at it they went while the sun was but just rising, and by the time their breakfast was prepared, had completed hilling their cabbages: as they ceased work, Jim leaned on his hoe, and looking at his brother,—

'I've been thinking, Ned, what we've got to do.'

'I knew you'd been thinking, for you haven't spoken a word this half hour; twice I asked you about old Peter, and you only answered, "Ha!"'

'Did I, Ned? well, I was thinking what we are going to do about these cabbages.'

'I don't see any thing to do about them; ain't they well hoed?'

'Yes, they are doing well enough; but what will the cow do!'

'Why, eat them; I am sure none of us wants them.'

'Yes, but Ned, how can the cow have them if we sell them?'

'That, to be sure; but where can we put any more—the garden is full?'

'We can put one here, and another there, and there in those vacant spots; there will be room for one hundred heads and more.'

'Well, Jim; any thing more?'

'Yes, I've been thinking where we could plant some more potatoes.'

'There is no use of thinking about that, Jim; for when these cabbages are planted, every spot will be occupied; you don't think of digging up the walks, do you?'

'No, not exactly that, Ned; but there is that strip of turf, south of the path running to the barn; the grass is of no value, and if mother would let us take it, we might turn it over with our spades, and raise twenty bushels of potatoes there.'

'Any thing else, Jim?'

'That will do for to-day, won't it, Ned?'

'I think we shall find it will—it makes my back ache already to think about that digging. I wish it was a little cooler.'

The pleasant voice of their little sister was now heard calling them to breakfast, for which they were both well prepared by their early labors.

CHAPTER III

Sam's first care after awaking on the morning which succeeded the scenes in the last chapter, was to make some arrangement with old Mr. Andrews for the boat. The old man was of the easy sort; he had never done much when young, and now in advanced life depended entirely for the few clams he wanted upon his son, who lived a short distance from him, and was growing up in his father's likeness.

'You're welcome, Sam, to use the boat as long as you're amind to, and I won't ax you nothin' for it; only once in awhile you may bring the old woman a few clam.'

'I thank you very much, Uncle John; I will take good care of the boat, and will bring you some clams every day.'

'Oh, no, no, no, Sam; I don't want no sich thing as that; only once in a while, you see. Jack, he's a gettin' lazy like, and sometimes the old woman gets tired of fish, and then a few clams is a kind of change for her.'

Sam's next business was to visit Mr. Grizzle's store, that he might purchase some article his mother needed.

'There shan't be no more trust, if I can help it,' said he, as he took up his money-box, and put some of its precious contents into his pocket. It was quite early in the day, yet several of Mr. Grizzle's customers were already assembled when Sam reached the store; he had a great reluctance to enter it, associated as it was in his mind with all that had been dark and sorrowful in his past experience; but nowhere else could supplies be obtained. Old Mr. Grizzle was busy behind his counter, twirling the toddy-stick, saying smart things, or what he took to be so, for he laughed very heartily at his own wit; and his customers, poor souls! were so much in his debt that they were obliged to laugh too.

Sam glanced his eye over them all—some were bald with age; some in the prime of life; and one, he knew him well, a lad but two years older than himself, was draining the last sweet drop from the cup of poison as Sam stepped up to the counter.

'Mr. Grizzle, what do you charge for seven pounds of flour?'

'What do I charge?' At the same time putting his spectacles upon his forehead.

'Yes, sir, what is the price?'

'The price, boy? Why, how does your father want it? for fish or for trust?'

'We don't want it for neither, sir, but for the money.'

'Ah!—the money. Well, I s'pose we must try to let you have it a little less; but flour is plaguy dear any how, and I aint got none but rye.'

Sam succeeded in procuring a small deduction, and with that he purchased some tar.

'I shall tar my boat with what I have saved by paying the money,' said Sam to himself, as he laid down his cash on the counter; then taking up his goods went straight on his way.

'That seems to be rather a 'cute boy, Mr. Grizzle—that young Oakum.'

'The younker, I guess, will go ahead of the old man,' said Grizzle, as he dropped the money Sam had given him through a little hole in the counter.

An old man, with his thin white locks dangling on his shoulders, placed his half-emptied tumbler on the bench beside him, and turning his head very emphatically on one side, said, 'Oakum is naturally a smart man, and he has got a clever wife, but somehow he don't get along much—no better than the rest of us.'

'And what is the reason, Uncle John,' said another, addressing the last speaker, 'that we are all so poor?'

'Why, I s'pose it's to be so—it's our luck, as I take it.'

'Our *luck*?' said the young man, who stood by the door with his hands in his pockets, looking at the receding form of Sam Oakum, whose light steps were carrying him far on his way—he laid a strong emphasis on the word luck.

'Yes, as I take it, it's our luck; a man may work ever so hard, but if luck is agin him, it's no use.'

'Yes, it is use,' said the same young man; 'that is, if a man would let rum alone—that makes the bad luck; I wish there had never been a drop made.'

'What's that you say, Bill? I guess your bitters is gone down the wrong way this morning.' And old Grizzle laughed heartily, and so did his customers. Bill, as he was called, laughed a little too, but not as the rest did.

'S'pose you mix Bill another glass, Mr. Grizzle, and see how that will go?' And they all laughed again; and to carry the joke through, Grizzle did prepare another glass, and placing it on the counter,

'There, try that, Bill; but may be you darsen't, you seem to be so afraid all at once.'

Bill hesitated a moment; the fear of ridicule was too powerful. He seized the glass, and pouring its contents hastily down his throat, left the store amidst the uproarious laughter of his companions.

Jim and Ned had collected a much larger quantity of vegetables for their second trip, and to the baskets of strawberries which they designed as gifts, added a beautiful nosegay of the earlier flowers.

'Strawberries and flowers,' said Sam, as he was pushing the boat from the shore; 'your things look tempting indeed; I guess old Peter will hop round when he sees these.'

'I have brought that small basket on purpose for him; and the flowers I thought the ladies might be pleased with—I don't think they see many where they are.'

'It almost makes me feel bad, Jim, to think that I have nothing to carry worth looking at.'

'Why, it is all one concern, you know, Sam; and I mean to have you hand them the flowers.'

'I shan't do it, Jim—I should make a pretty figure, with my old patched clothes and bare feet, handing flowers to ladies and gentlemen!'

'Sam Oakum, if you talk so, you'll make me feel bad; who cares for your clothes?'

'*You* don't Jim, I know; but all don't feel as you and Ned do—Keep her head to the point, Jim, straight as you can.'

Sam had much more rowing to do than on the former trip, the wind not coming quite so soon to their aid.

Peter was on the look-out for them, and hailed them before they reached the landing.

'Halloo, my hearties! keep her jist about so—there—ease up—in with your oars; you've had a long pull to-day—but you'll learn to take it sailor-fashion after a while.'

The boys were very busy fastening their boat and taking down their sail, and did not at the moment perceive that any one was present but the old sailor, until attracted by the bunch of flowers lying on one of the baskets, he exclaimed,—

'Susie, Susie, look here! did you ever see such posies as these?'

Sam at once seated himself in the stern of the boat, as far out of the way as possible; while Jim, taking up the flowers, handed them to Peter, and blushing very much,—

'These are for the lady, if you will be so good as to give them to her—and this basket of strawberries; and here is one for yourself, sir, if you will please accept it.'

'Bless your young hearts, to think of the old sailor. I thank you kindly, boys; but'—putting his face down to Jim, and whispering—'you won't mind my giving them to this little pet of mine;'—then raising himself up—'Here, Susie, you carry these flowers to your Ma, and I'll carry the strawberries;'—then stooping down again, and speaking in a low voice—'the Major will be here pretty soon; he's busy now—you won't be none the loser for these, I tell you. He's a real gentleman, and a liberal soul, and he's got plenty to do with.' And the old man shook his head very knowingly, making his long queue, as it stuck out in the air, perform some strange manoeuvres; the boys, however, were diverted from observing its wonderful gyrations by a sudden attraction towards the flowers. It must have been that Peter's rapturous praises, or the delight which they seem to have afforded Miss Susan, had unfolded new beauties to our boys, for their eyes followed *the flowers*, even when the young lady buried her pretty face among them to enjoy a fulness of their fragrance—it could not possibly have been any thing else, Sam was so very bashful, and Jim so very discreet—but their eyes followed the flowers, even until the lovely little maiden that carried them was lost to their view, and entered the castle gate.

Major Morris appeared well pleased with the variety Jim had brought, and arranged every thing, as to price and measurement, in the same business manner as before. He then proceeded to speak with him in reference to a supply for the ensuing winter, enumerating a variety of articles, and among them beans and potatoes.

'Potatoes we shall have, sir, and perhaps a few beans.'

'I wish to engage three hundred bushels of potatoes, to be well selected, and of good size, and fifty bushels of beans. If you choose to make a contract to deliver me these articles in the fall'—at the same time handing to Jim a strip of paper with the prices annexed—'on these terms, you can do so; and if you have not so many of your own, you can doubtless purchase them of your neighbors, so as to pay you well for your trouble.'

The boys were so confounded by the magnitude of the business proposed to them, that when the Major ceased speaking, Sam looked at Jim and he at Sam, and neither of them the wiser for any thing gained from the countenance of the other—until Sam, as though it was more than he could stand under, sat down; in doing so, however, he stumbled over his clams and oysters, which attracted the notice of the Major to them.

'Ah, what have you got there? clams and oysters? I had like to have forgotten to inquire for them.'

This brought Sam to his senses again; clams and oysters, almost in any quantities, were familiar to him, but where three hundred bushels of potatoes and fifty bushels of beans were to come from, was beyond his comprehension. He soon had his part of the cargo on shore, and as Major Morris handed him the money, thanked him in a very civil manner.

It was some time before Jim gave any reply to the proposal which had been made to him, he was so absorbed in thinking; his mind had to run over all the names of persons likely to have such articles for sale, and the probable quantity each might be willing to spare. At length, after thanking Major Morris for giving him such a chance—for he had sense enough to perceive that it was all in kindness that the offer had been made—he agreed to accept it.

'And now, my lads, you must go with me, as Mrs. Morris wishes to thank you personally for the flowers and fruit.'

Again the boys looked at each other, and Sam turned very pale and then very red, and finally sat down, and made signs to Jim to go along.

Jim knew that it would not be proper to hesitate under such circumstances, so he prepared at once to follow; while Peter, who always observed the most perfect silence in the presence of the Major, as soon as he saw him on the way to the fort, began to make the most furious gestures imaginable, motioning with his head so violently, that his queue flew round behind him like a fly-brush; and when he thought there was no danger of being overheard,—

'Go along; go along, I say! he's axed you himself—go along; it will be the makin' of you.'

But it was of no avail. Sam shook his head and sat still, until the old man, having exhausted his means of persuasion, took a seat beside him, muttering something about 'dumb-founded perverseness.'

Jim had a great curiosity to see what was within the walls of the fort; but he had only time to catch a glimpse of large guns on wheel-carriages, and soldiers with glittering muskets; for Major Morris passed quickly on, and opening a side door in the hall, was at once in an elegantly furnished apartment, and in the presence of several fine-looking ladies and the little girl, who still held the bunch of flowers in close contact with her face.

Jim was not allowed to suffer the least embarrassment; for immediately on his entrance Mrs. Morris arose, and coming toward him with a pleasant smile and kindly salutation, thanked him so heartily for the present he had sent to her, and talked so familiarly with him about his home and his garden, that he felt as much freedom as though he had been long acquainted.

'I regret exceedingly,' said Mrs. Morris, 'that I have nothing to offer you in return for such beautiful fruit; but you must not refuse to taste some of my cake. Susie, lay down your flowers, if you can part with them so long, and hand that plate to our young visitor.'

Susie did at once as she was bidden: but she looked so very serious about it, and walked so very slowly, that Jim would just at that moment have preferred being in the boat by the side of Sam. She came directly towards him with the silver plate in her hand, and some rich-looking cake lying on it; so he had no alternative but to step towards her, and in the politest manner he could, select a piece. His attention was, of necessity, directed to the plate; but he could not help giving a glance at other things. And indeed, Jim, you are not to blame for blushing as you did, when you encountered the gaze of those sweet blue eyes, which, in all the unaffected simplicity of youth, were fastened upon you. Her golden-colored hair, parted smoothly from the fair forehead, and hung in such a cluster of curls upon her snow-white neck— the rich color that painted her parting lips, just tinged with the slightest blush her dimpled cheek. She meant nothing by her gaze; it was only the expression of an innocent curiosity in reference to the young gentleman she was waiting upon. His clothes, to be sure, were coarse, and such as well became the work in which he was engaged; but his collar was very white, and neatly tied with a black ribbon; and his light-brown hair, so soft and silky; his fair complexion, his pleasant voice, and good manners, all made a contrast which she did not understand; and it would seem that some of the company present, much older than Susie, were equally surprised.

'What a fine, manly-looking boy! and how well he behaves,' said Mrs. Morris, as soon as Jim had retired, to an elderly lady richly dressed, and who, from the peculiar glance she gave to another lady much younger than herself, while Mrs. Morris and Susie were paying so much attention to our Jim, felt anything but satisfied at the scene.

'I say, aunt, what a fine little fellow that is!'

'Well, Lettie,' said the elderly lady, shaking her sides a little, as though it was something so ludicrous that she must laugh—she could not help it, 'I didn't see anything very extraordinary. Where is he from? who is he? a son of some of the gentlemen down in the pines here? Mary and I saw some specimens of their houses—a mansion or two;' and the old lady laughed so heartily, that she could say nothing more, and the young lady had to put her handkerchief to her face to hide the emotion which was agitating her. Mrs. Morris was aware of the peculiarities of this lady, an aunt of her husband's, and as she unintentionally had opened the way for a long lecture on the plebeian notions of herself and husband, she was much relieved by the entrance of the Major, who, full of praises of 'those manly little fellows,' as he called Jim and Sam, whom he had just parted with, drew upon himself the storm which Mrs. Morris came near enduring alone.

'I felt disposed to laugh, I must say, Philip,' addressing the Major, 'to see Lettie paying as much personal respect and attention to a little market boy, as it seems he is, as though he had belonged to one of our best and most respectable families. I say, I felt at first disposed to laugh, but I must say, Philip,' and the old lady straightened herself in a very decided manner, and began fanning herself very earnestly—'I must say, that when I saw that dear child, at her mother's bidding, waiting upon a young clown as though he had been a very gentleman, and when I thought what blood ran in her veins, it fired my indignation. Such things ought not to be, Philip; you will demolish all distinctions in society, or at any rate, bring your own family to feel that it is no matter whom they associate with, and that one is as good as another.'

The Major suffered his aunt to 'say her say out,' and, knowing as he did what reason he had personally to set a high estimate on the pedigree to which she seemed to think it was such an honor to be allied, was designing some palpable hits for the special benefit of his kindred, drawn from his own experience; but being a wise man, as well as a noble-hearted one, he concluded to treat the matter as he saw his wife was doing, and laugh it off.

'Why, aunt! I thought you had given me up long ago as an incorrigible boy, who would have his own way. You know, aunt, I began very early in life to do as I pleased; and having worked my own way up the ladder so far, it is not strange if I should be a little headstrong, or my notions of such matters as you have touched upon somewhat peculiar.'

His good aunt had heard enough to refresh her memory on a matter that, now the subject of it had, as he reminded her, raised himself to distinction, she, as well as the rest of his kindred, would have been willing should pass into oblivion; and was well satisfied when the Major invited her and the other ladies to walk with him upon the ramparts to witness a fine sight, the passing of a ship of the largest class, under full sail.

This lady and her daughter will not be subjects of our story; so I will not trouble the reader with any farther description of them. They belong to a class often met with in the common walks of life, who, because of some imaginary value which they attach to the ancestry from which they have descended, gauge their estimate of others by what they think to be the equality, or inequality, of their station to that which they suppose themselves to occupy. Major Morris estimated society by a different standard; and, as we shall have much to do with him, it may be well to trace the causes which led him thus to judge.

He was born in a part of our country where the distinctions which formerly prevailed between the classes of society were still kept up. His parents were allied to those who claimed the higher ranks of life as theirs by birth, and struggled hard to maintain their station; but poverty and death are great levellers, and young Morris found himself, at twelve years of age, an orphan, without a home, or the means of support, except that which was afforded him by the charity of his kindred. He was invited by an uncle to make his house a home, and for a while enjoyed the privilege of dwelling within a splendid mansion, and faring sumptuously, and mingling amongst the gay youth that thronged where abundance flowed. But he soon found that poverty was thought to be a disgrace, even in nearest kin, by those who would have scorned the idea of his engaging in any lawful calling whereby he could have earned his bread, if that calling was not one which, in their view, his peculiar class could engage in. Young Morris knew nothing of such distinctions; but he knew that he was poor, and was made, on more than one occasion, to feel his dependence. His high spirit rebelled; he left his place of refuge, and took shelter beneath the roof of a poor family, with whom he labored for a time most cheerfully in earning his daily bread. From thence he obtained employment in one of our large cities in the mercantile line; but as he reached the age in which generally a choice is made of an occupation for life, his feelings prompted to the military profession. Through the influence of a friend, whom his own correct deportment had gained, he obtained a commission. His strict attention to all the rules of the service, his entire devotedness to every duty committed to him, and his well-established reputation as a noble-minded and chivalrous officer, gave him favor in high places, and he rose rapidly to the grade he then held. To a commanding appearance and most polished manners, he united a kind and benevolent heart, warm in its sympathies towards every object of distress; and he would have poured out full streams to every child of want, to the very extent of his ability. But well for him, as for those he would aid, he had learned not only to bring others under wholesome discipline, but himself also; he had learned that some of our best feelings must be under subjection to prudent counsel, and that he who scatters in profusion, even from the promptings of a noble heart, is as likely to do evil as good. He had abundance to bestow, for he had married a lady of great wealth, and the whole responsibility of its proper use was devolved on him; his lovely wife had not only committed herself, but all she possessed, entirely to him. 'She wanted nothing to call her own,' she said, 'but her husband's heart.'

Nothing could have been more gratifying to Major Morris than his introduction to our boys. He could sympathise in their feelings; he could value properly their enterprising spirit, and he had an opportunity of indulging his kindness of heart in a way that would stimulate them to exertion.

It would be no easy task to describe the happiness which our boys Jim and Sam enjoyed, as they drew their skiff to shore that evening, and separated, each for their several homes. Sam found every thing as peaceful as his heart could wish, while the wonderful story which he had to tell excited the astonishment of his parents.

'I don't believe tho', Sam,' said his father, 'you will find so many beans and potatoes to sell in all this place; and then I don't see how you are goin' to carry them, nor how you are goin' to pay for them.'

'I don't know much about it, father; but I guess Jim will work it out some way. He didn't hardly speak a word all the way home; he was thinking, I know.'

'Perhaps he may manage it, somehow; but I don't well see through it all, Sam. I can't do much for you myself; only if I had the stuff, I might build you a bigger boat, and one that would stand the waves better than the old one you've got.'

'Oh, would you, father?' and Sam's eyes began to glisten; and his mother, good soul, had to wipe away the tears that her joyful heart could not restrain—some of the *may-bes* which had so lately played in pleasant vision before her, were indeed realised.

CHAPTER IV

The place where the scene of this story is laid, I have said was a lone village; it had no communication with other places by means of boats, although its water privileges were abundant; and between it and neighbouring towns intervened an extent of country, consisting of pine-barrens, where no settlements could exist, or at least any that deserved the name. There were those, however, who dwelt amid its dreary solitudes, and called it home. Scattered here and there upon an area of ten to fifteen miles square, might be seen, sometimes alone and sometimes in clusters of three or four, a few miserable dwellings, made principally of logs. A door, and one window without glass, were the only openings to these abodes; and a rude chimney running up against the outside, formed a receptacle for the pine logs, which blazed often through the long winter nights, the only light they could afford, as well as almost their only protection from the searching cold.

Poverty and wretchedness generally make sad havoc with the human frame; the haggard countenance, the dry and skinny hands, the stoop, the feeble, tottering gait, we expect and look for, when visiting abodes that betoken destitution. But miserable as was the appearance of these dwellings, the aspect of their inhabitants was generally that of health and sufficiency; their swarthy complexions, and fine athletic forms, almost compelled the traveller through these lonely regions to believe that he had alighted upon a tribe of those sons of the forest who once called our country all their own.

The moral character of this people was in keeping with the aspect of their dwellings. Having no regular religious instruction, seldom hearing the voice of a living teacher, with scarce a Bible to be found within their gloomy houses, they were but little in advance of the heathen as to religious knowledge, and far too near allied to them in many of their vicious habits.

They earned their daily bread by laboring amid the lofty and dense forests, in levelling the majestic pines, cutting them into lengths suitable for transportation, and conveying them to the outskirts of the barrens: their hire was but a pittance when considered as a remuneration for their toil, but it enabled them to live; it procured for them food, coarse indeed, but enough to satisfy their appetite, and the plain and simple clothing which necessity demanded, or to which perhaps their taste aspired.

The owners of these forests lived at some distance, and employed an agent to attend to all the various labors of preparing the timber and conveying it to market.

Cross, the individual employed for this business, had grown up amid these solitudes, and labored with his axe for some years. Gifted by nature with shrewdness, and not very particular on the score of morality, he had managed to obtain the post he occupied, and with most of the proprietors stood on good terms; he was active, prompt, and efficient, and perhaps, for the business intrusted to him, did as well as any one could. But he was, beyond measure, grasping and avaricious; and as he could not well gain undue advantage from those who employed him, being bound by contracts not easily evaded, he made up such deficiency by 'grinding the faces' of the poor laborers.

Without any means of gaining a livelihood besides, they had become entirely dependent on the good-will of Mr. Cross. He fixed their wages, supplied them from his store with the necessaries of life at his own price, and in that way managed to bring them, at the close of every month, either without any surplus, or most generally a trifle in debt.

On the border of these barrens, and near the principal scene of our story, lived the widow Mary Brown; her husband had been one of the woodcutters, an intemperate man, who had caused her much trouble while he lived, and when he died left her with two orphans. She had to struggle hard to support herself and little ones. But as a light in a dark place, so was this widow among these outcasts. She was generally known throughout the region where she lived, and the wildest and most abandoned never brought against her a railing accusation—they never spoke lightly of her not her religion; for the garb of piety she wore was so unassuming, the light that shone around her humble path was so mild and unobtrusive:—

> Like the soft fleecy cloud at the close of day,
> That far in the west where the sun's last ray
> Rests bright on its bosom—its mellow light
> Steals to our heart, as we gaze in delight;
> No glare to dazzle, we love to view
> Its changing tints and its golden hue.

Having a very humbling view of herself, she felt great pity for the deluded ones around her; she never chid them for their follies, but would weep and pray in secret, and when called to watch at their dying bed, she had such a quiet, happy way of holding up before the weak and guilty spirit the Saviour in his love and pity, that many a poor wanderer took courage from her message of mercy, and ere the spirit fled, it was enabled to look in faith, and go its lone way in peace. Wherever sorrow or sickness visited, there was she sent for, as one who carried with her a charm that could neutralize their power.

Her dwelling was a log hut like those in that vicinity, but it had an air of comfort the others had not. Her plain door was white-washed, and a little curtain hung across the window; and there was a box of flowers by the step, and every useless thing was removed from around the house, and the ground swept neatly, and beneath some of the large pines that afforded a grateful shade to her lonely abode, were rude seats, as though made for the wayfaring man, on which to rest and be refreshed.

Her children, though helpless little ones when their father died, had now grown up to an age when each of them, in different ways, could materially aid her. She felt no longer a dread of want, although often sighing in secret that her son was compelled to labor with those whose example could only lead astray, and that her daughter had no brighter prospect than a residence among these uncultivated foresters. But she had done what she could. Of worldly wisdom she knew nothing; but she had a Bible, and could read it. Its requirements and its doctrines were all plain to her, she loved them, and taught them to her children; they learned passages from them on the long, still Sabbath days, and as she sat in the shade of the large pines by her door, they would come and sit near her, to hear and listen to some story she would tell them of those whose names have been recorded, and their history handed down for the benefit of every coming generation. But other influences have now begun to exert a counteracting power; William is eighteen, a man in size and strength, a hardy laborer, and much from home. He still brings all he earns, or nearly all, to the common stock; he still reverences his mother, and listens to her instructions, and treats with kindness his only sister; but rumours have reached his home that his chosen associates were some whose names had become by-words for rude and evil doings, and any heart but a mother's would have given up his chance for any future good.

'She had hope for William,' she said, 'although he might be led astray by evil companions.'

And she had good cause for hoping—for she had fastened to his heart that golden chain, each link of which a mother's prayers and gentle teachings and untiring love had formed. He felt its power even in his hours of revelling, and although he never met with an upbraiding word or look from her, his conscience had no rest.

The daughter was all that her mother could ask; she had no desire to depart from the beautiful precepts of the Bible—because she loved them.

Her mind was active, thoughtful, and discerning beyond her years; of kind and generous disposition, ever ready for any work of love, and cheerful and happy in the consciousness of good-will to all. Her moral character was well matched with a beauty of person rarely found, even under every advantage. Hettie had no ornaments to set off her beauty, and no graces imparted by culture to heighten the natural ease of her movements; her complexion, though dark, was brightened by the rich color which adorned her cheeks, and her jet-black eyes were softened by the long dark lashes that gave to their expression almost the languor of a southern clime, while her dark hair dangled in luxuriant curls, very much to her annoyance, for she often said:—

'She did wish her hair was straight like other girls; it was always getting into such a tangle.'

As Mrs. Brown—or the Widow Brown, as she was universally called—lived nearer to the open and more cultivated settlement than any of the other inhabitants of the barrens, she was well known among the farmers' families, although intimate with very few. Hettie had some associates there, which her mother preferred for her to those in her own immediate vicinity. Of these, the family of the Widow Andrews was one to which they were peculiarly attached. They could sympathize with each other; the mothers were both widows, and each had two children of about the same age. They both loved good things; they could converse bout their past trials, and present hopes and fears. But while many things in their circumstances were similar, there were others in which they were very unlike to each other; for the Widow Andrews was much under the power of strong natural feelings, easily excited by joy or grief, and her passions when aroused seemed at times to know no bounds: no sooner was a chord struck that touched a tender point in her heart, than she would begin to talk very rapidly and to weep freely; her words flowing faster and faster, and louder and louder, until, between weeping and talking, she would finally break into a flood of tears, and all was over.

The Widow Brown was aware of this weakness in her neighbor, and lamented it, for she knew that at times it did real evil; but there were so many things that she loved her for, this she considered as a mere weakness, for which she should be pitied.

In reference to worldly goods, too, there was a dissimilarity. The Widow Andrews had a much better house, although a very plain one; still it was called a house, and not a log hut; and she had a few acres of land attached to it, and a small barn, old and shackling to be sure, and a few head of cattle, and had been enabled, hitherto, to make out to live in a very frugal way from her own resources.

Mary, her daughter, was not pretty, like Hettie Brown, nor was she so intelligent; but she had a kind heart, and was obedient to her mother, and being about Hettie's age, the two girls became much attached.

The son had promised fair to be a support to his mother, and a good member of society, but a dark cloud had arisen upon all such prospects—bad company had now begun to have attractions for him. He neglected his work, disobeyed his mother, lost his ambition, and was in a fair way to make a wreck of body and soul. His mother had been proud of her William—of his good behavior, of his efficiency at work, of his industrious habits; and not a little proud was she of his fine appearance—it was a mother's weakness; but we will not judge her harshly. He had, indeed, a very pleasant expression to his countenance; his lively eye looked so kindly at you; there was such a play of roguishness and good-nature about his mouth; and when he spoke, a musical voice brought out the words so soft and clear—all tended to interest both friends and strangers. But all the love which his mother bore towards him, and all her pride in him, caused her to be more violent in her rebukes. She poured out such a torrent of invective at him, that much as he felt he deserved her displeasure, he could not stand the violence of it. Every bad feeling of his heart was aroused; he began to dread his home and his mother's voice, and sought refuge where, alas! ruin alone could be the end thereof.

He was now eighteen years of age, and as my reader was first introduced to him at Mr. Grizzle's store, we will follow him as he left that den of evil. His conscience was troubled; there was something in the appearance and behavior of Sam Oakum that morning, that revived the memory of what he himself had once been. We saw how he watched Sam when he left the store, as far his eye could follow him; how madly he poured down the offered glass, and rushed from the scene of his shame.

Whither to direct his steps he knew not, but onward he went; he was glad to be in the open air, it was so much better than the poisonous atmosphere he had just left. Soon his attention was arrested by the appearance of a dwelling and its precincts that he was about to pass. It was a scene of desolation—the house and all its accompaniments; the windows stuffed with every variety of color and substance to supply the places of broken panes; the door hung sideways by one hinge, the boards loose and flapping against the timbers of the house, the roof broken in, and apparently ready to fall upon the inmates, and the inclosures around the place lying prostrate or scattered about the grounds. A woman was outside, picking up what rubbish she could meet with to replenish the fire; sorrow was plainly marked upon her withered features; and as she walked into the house with a few faggots in her hand, there was such a deadness in her step, such a bowing down under the weight of some too heavy burden—ambition, comfort, hope, all seemed to have departed, and left her in her misery with a broken spirit.

William halted in his rapid course; he looked upon the scene and considered it well.

This was the house of one of those whom he had just left; the one most forward to complain of bad luck, and who joined most heartily in the laugh which had been excited at his expense. He had been familiar with this place; often had he seen it, just as it then appeared, but never had its desolate condition affected him before;—a light from heaven seemed pouring upon it, and singling it out from all other objects. He could look at nothing else. 'It was the vineyard of the man void of understanding, and the field of the slothful; the stone wall thereof was broken down; it was all grown over with thorns, and nettles covered the face thereof.'

William looked upon it, and received instruction: slowly and sadly he passed along.

A little by-road now crossed the public highway. Instinctively almost, he turned into it; the trees which lined it formed a grateful shade, and seemed to invite him therein to cool his heated, feverish frame.

Near to this path, and not far from the highway he had left, was a pure, bright, bubbling spring; it came up through the clean white sand, and the green turf formed its only curb. On one side it had cleared an opening, and meandered away through a little bed of fine gravel stones, which sparkled in the sunbeams as they stole through the branches of the willows which encircled the fountain. His throat parched with thirst, and his mind and body in an excited condition, he threw himself upon the velvet turf, and allayed his thirst from the pure stream. He tried to think, but his thoughts ran wild into each other; he turned his head towards the roots of one of the willows, and rested it there. It throbbed against the cool green turf; its coolness was refreshing to him, and there he slept.

Hettie Brown had that morning left her home in the barrens to do an errand for her mother in Mr. Grizzle's store; she stopped at the Widow

Andrews', and found the mother and daughter in tears, and had to listen to a long tale of William's delinquencies.

'And he's gone off to Grizzle's, now again, I *know* he has; and there he'll sit and drink, and he'll come home drunk yet one of these days, and he'll be a drunkard and a vagabond.'

And the good woman went off into another hard crying spell. Hettie made no reply; she was not in the habit of talking much, nor did she shed any tears—she was not given to that either. A few expressions of sympathy she dropped as she parted from Mary, telling her to hope for the best, and making a short call, went on her way to the store.

She was anxious to see William, and therefore she hastened her steps. She seemed to feel a consciousness of power to lead him away from the path of ruin. He had been her playmate when a little child; nor had he ever, by word or deed, done aught to offend her. The intimacy of childhood had indeed passed away—her wise mother had cautioned her on matters referring especially to William, and of late she had seldom seen him; but she felt that she possessed an influence over him, and she meant now to exert it.

As she crossed the by-path we have already mentioned, she thought of the little spring, and how refreshing it would be to drink of its cool water. She turned, and followed the path towards the willows which marked the spot.

When William Andrews awoke, it was from a troubled dream, and the quiet which surrounded him was grateful to his spirits. He arose and drank freely from the spring—the birds were singing sweetly in the hedges and on the trees; there was no sound beside, but the rippling of the little rill that stole gently away from the fountain where he had slaked his thirst. His feelings, late so hurried and disturbed, were calm—the storm had lulled, a dark and dreadful gulf seemed to have been passed, and now he was upon a path where all above and around him combined to make it light and pleasant. This change, however, was but the effect of that rest which sleep had given to his frame; 'twas the pure fresh feeling which the soul enjoys when waked by morning's dawn, before the hopes and fears, the business and the cares of life, have time to urge their claims. Scarce had he quenched his thirst, and fully awaked to a consciousness of his situation, ere the scenes of the morning rushed back upon him. As the tumult of his thoughts arose, he stood and leaned against one of the willows, and cast his eye down at the little fountain, bubbling up so incessantly and with so little disturbance, that it came to the surface with no alloy of earth about it; and he saw how fresh and rank was the greensward all along its course—it not only gave from its little receptacle a full supply for all who needed, but virtue seemed to emanate throughout its meanderings, and to bless wherever it flowed.

'This spring,' said he, 'is like the life of one that is good—pure at the fountain, and the whole life a blessing, making things better and happier all around him; but *my* life—oh, what has it been?' And his cheek flushed, and tears of anguish fell fast, while with hands firmly clasped, and still leaning against the tree, he looked down at the bubbling water.

'Why William!'

He started at the well-knows voice.

'Oh, Hettie, is this *you*? how glad I am to see you.'

She extended her hand towards him, but there was something in the sight of Hettie that caused the cup, already full, to overflow; he did not take the offered hand, but covering his face, gave way to a passionate burst of weeping.

Hettie was much surprised, but she attempted not to interfere; nor did she weep with him, but waited silently until the violence of the storm had passed, and he was sufficiently composed to address her.

'I am very unhappy, Hettie, and have been so for a long time.'

'I have thought so, William, and I am very glad of an opportunity to say something to you about it. I was certain that you must be unhappy. There can be no peace for us when we have left the path of duty, until we return from our crooked ways: it would not be best for us that we should be happy when our doings are not right.'

'Well, mine are not right, and I am afraid they will never be any better.'

'Why not, William? are you willing still to be unhappy, and to break your mother's heart, and fill the minds of all your friends with sorrow?'

'I have been far astray, Hettie. I have sunk myself very low, and have struggled hard at times to break the charm that was leading me to ruin; but I feel now as I have not felt before; and if you will only not despise me, if you will let me hope that a new course of life may yet gain your respect, it will be a helper to me—a great helper to me. And oh! Hettie, you cannot tell how much I need your aid.'

Hettie was wise perhaps beyond her years. She felt much interest for the youth who had grown with her from childhood.

'I fear, William, that the struggle you will be compelled to encounter will need help greater than a creature can give. You must look to Him who made you, and relying on his strength, resolve to do your duty, cost what it may. All that I can promise is my feeble prayer; and whenever I offer it for myself, I will offer it for you too, William. And now I must leave you, for I have an errand to the store, and mother will be uneasy at my absence.'

And the happy girl, smiling a pleasant good-by, went on her way. William watched her until she turned into the public road, and then, with one strong cry to Heaven for help, turned towards his home, a happier person than he had been for many long months.

He had resolved to do right.

CHAPTER V

The difficulties which presented themselves to our boys in fulfilling the engagement they had made with Major Morris were of no trifling account, for it was a great question if so large a quantity could be found in the place, above what was pledged to Mr. Grizzle for debts already incurred. Again, if they should succeed in finding the quantity, how could they pay for them? and lastly, where was a boat to be procured, in which to carry them at a season of the year when storms and high winds were to be expected? But as difficulties are apt to vanish before a resolute mind, Jim felt not at all daunted by them.

He had resolved, first of all, to make a thorough trial as to the possibility of finding persons willing to engage specific quantities to him. And it was for this purpose that the boys were assembled early in the morning of a bright and beautiful day in June; Jim and Sam to go on the expedition, and Ned to see them off.

'Well, boys, I hope you'll find all you'll want; but it looks to me like a hard case.'

'So it does to me, Ned, too; but Jim has been thinking it all out, you know. I should feel better, however, if we knew where the *money* was to come from to pay for them; I do hate so to ask folks to trust us.'

'I have no idea, Sam, of doing any such thing; I mean to offer them the money down as soon as they deliver the potatoes.'

'Just hear *that* Ned,' said Sam, looking verily confounded.

'Well,' said Ned, kicking away a small stone that lay in reach of his foot, 'that is a good plan enough if one had the money; but it will take all of a hundred dollars: and it looks dark to me where such a sum as that is to come from.'

'That is the least of the difficulties, boys; we shall make, I hope, by our summer's work enough money to pay for twenty-five bushels of potatoes, which will be the most we shall be able to carry at a trip, and Major Morris will pay us for them as we deliver them to him.'

Ned and Sam looked at each other. 'I told you, Ned, that Jim would think it out somehow.'

'And besides,' continued Jim, 'I have great hope that our offering them the money on delivery, will induce them to sell to us in preference to Grizzle. But what troubles me the most is, how to get a boat sufficient for our purpose.'

'Supposing I should say'—and Sam's bright eyes sparkled as he looked from one to the other of his companions, while a smile played around the corners of his mouth—'I hope to have a good new boat, not very handsome, but tight and strong, and able to go in rough weather, and carry twenty-five bushels of potatoes at a load; what would you say to that?'

'Now, Sam Oakum, what do you mean?'

'I mean just what I say. My father told me last night, that as soon as he could get the stuff, he would go right to work and build a boat as large as that, and that it should be mine; and I am going to take my money as I can earn it, and buy the stuff. What do you think of that, Jim?'

'It is the best news I have heard this long while;—how strangely things work! but look out for Ned there.'

The warning was too late, for Sam was lying on his back, laughing heartily; and Jim was scolding Ned for his folly, and Jowler was barking at them all. As soon as matters were composed again, Jim and Sam started on their expedition; while Ned, with Jowler at his heels, went with right good-will to his work in the garden.

A blacksmith's shop is a very necessary article in all social establishments, as the place where persons are likely to be met with and news collected or circulated. The one which answered the demands of this place was not a very extensive establishment; it was a little dark-looking hovel, with an exceedingly high chimney. It was situated at the meeting of several roads, and was surrounded with a multitude of articles that had once seen better days, but *when*, the oldest inhabitant could scarcely remember. Mr. Cutter, the proprietor of this establishment, was now somewhat advanced in life, but by no means so old as his appearance indicated. From some cause not well ascertained, he had begun about his thirtieth year to increase in flesh, and had for more than twenty years been adding to his stock; neither wielding the sledge-hammer in his shop, nor the worrying of his good wife in the house, could keep it back; but I believe it was all the increase, of any consequence, that resulted from his labors, and yet he was, in comparison with his neighbors, 'well to do in the world.' He was, moreover, of a good disposition, ready to oblige, and of sound judgment, and as well acquainted with persons and things for many miles round as any other man in the place, and a little better.

Our boys had determined to make their first call at 'Uncle Sam Cutter's,' as he was generally styled.

'He's a clever man,' said Sam, 'and he knows every body, and all about every thing in the place; and it may save us a great many steps.'

It was a very warm day, and Uncle Sam was sitting outside his shop, on what had once been the hub of a large cart-wheel; there was a fine shade where he sat, a large apple tree which stood in an adjoining lot, extending its branches almost to his shop door. He had his hat in his hand, and was using it violently as a fan; the heat was making terrible work with him, for on his bald head and down his fat cheeks and sunburnt breast, the perspiration was running in streams.

'A pretty warm day, Uncle Sam, ain't it?'

'Here, you young rogue, take this, and blow a little wind on to me, if there's any to be got, for I'm most dead,' (handing Sam his great broad-brimmed chip hat.) 'I guess you'd think it warm, blowing them tarnel old bellows all day long, with such a lump of fat lugging to you as I've got; I can't hardly waddle under it, let alone handling them bellows.'

'Why don't you have the boys blow for you, Uncle Sam?'

'The boys! ah yes, the boys! I'd like any one to tell me what the hul kit on 'em is good for, but to eat mush and milk. Do blow away Sam, if there's any wind in all creation any more. I want to git this carcass o' mine cool a little, just so I shan't go *all* to soap-grease. Talk of the boys, they're wus than wild cats; I wouldn't give my old mare for all the boys between this and the barrens—don't talk to me about boys, Sam—don't stop blowing, or I'm a dead man. Here, Jim, my good fellow, spell him a little.'

'Yes, that I will, with pleasure, sir.'

'That's like a man, there's no boy about that—ah, Jim, I knew your father well, and a likelier man never came to this place; but what he came *here* for was more than I could ever see—it seems to me there's a cus on it; the men are bad enough, but the boys are the old Nick's property altogether. I tell you what, if we don't have a preacher, or something of that kind, along here pretty soon, we're a gone case; there'll be another sort of bellows blowin' than my old groaner, I tell you. Ah, Jim, that feels good, I won't touch a hammer agin' to day; if Grizzle wants his old plough mended, he may come and sweat away at it himself, it will do his old dry carcass good, won't it Sam? It won't hurt him, will it?' And the old man went off into a good hearty laugh, his whole body shaking like a lump of jelly—the idea of sweating Grizzle amused him so much, that he forgot about the heat, and taking his hat clapped it on his head.

'And now, boys, what are you up to? going crabbing down to the mill, I know; for my boys have been there this hul blessed morning.'

'Oh, no sir,' said Jim, 'we were not thinking about that this morning; but are wishing to find out who would be willing to engage some beans and potatoes for the fall.'

'Beans and potatoes? why, you blessed child, are you crazy? You ain't grown up here, not to know better than to try to sell sich things in this place. You must go to Grizzle with them, and he won't take them only for jist what you owe him.'

'Ah, but we don't want to sell, but to buy.'

'Want to buy!—you're wus off than I thought you was. Why, didn't you plant any? How did you think you was goin' to live? like Bill Moore and his brother down the lane here? eh?'

'Oh, no sir, we have plenty for our use; but we can sell quite a quantity of these articles, more than we shall have.'

'And pray tell me what you call a quantity, mister.'

'Why, we want two or three hundred bushels.'

'*Two or three hundred bushels!*' And the old man took off his hat and began to fan himself again very fast. '*Two or three hundred bushels!*—you boys wasn't neither on you brought up to lie, but I don't know but you've taken up the trade; it's pretty easy larnt, to be sure.'

'It's true, Uncle Sam, what Jim tells you; *true* as we stand here.'

'Sam Oakum, them eyes o' yourn warn't made to help a lyin' tongue; so don't stand there looking so honest, and telling me sich stuff as that.'

'It is true, Mr. Cutter, just as Sam says; we are telling you the truth, and no joke about it.'

But the old man kept shaking his head and fanning himself; so that Jim felt called upon to tell their whole story.

'Now boys, *is* this *true*, you're tellin' me? Sam, you're a smilin'; there's some catch about it, ain't there, you rogue?'

'No, there ain't, Uncle Sam, upon my honor.'

'Well, it's a queer story, any how; *three hundred bushels potatoes*; why you'll take all that's raised, and Grizzle won't have none for Cross this year; you know he sends all he takes in up to Cross, who keeps the store or tavern, or whatever they call it, in the barrens; but it ain't much matter, they're two precious rogues, both on 'em. And you say you want to know where you can find so many: I raally can't say; but the Widow Andrews would be like to have *some*. Bill tell'd me he had planted a considerable patch, beans and potatoes too; but whether they'll come to any thing I don't know, for he's got like the rest on 'em—he's round to Grizzle's too much, I guess. Sorry for it; Bill's a likely fellow if he'd mind his own business. And then there's my namesake, Cutter; he may have a few, not a great many. I tell you what, you'll have to hunt considerable, boys, afore you'll find all you want. And then there's Billy Bloodgood, deaf Billy, you know him; but you'll have to holler loud enough to wake the dead to make him hear—he ought to have a speakin' trumpet fastened into his ear, it's enough to give a man the consumption to talk with him. And may be I'll have a few myself, and I would as leave you'd have them as Grizzle, the old varmint; I don't believe I shall owe him much this year. What are you goin' to give, boys?'

Sam looked at Jim for an answer.

'Why, if they are fair-sized potatoes, we can give twenty-five cents a bushel.'

'I wish I had more on 'em, for that's double what Grizzle gives; and *beans* you want *too*; well, I guess I shall have three or four bushels. I can't say but they ought to be hoed now, and I can't do it, no how; for a man like me to work out in the sun, it's idle to talk about it. Why I should die in the operation, and the boys don't care for nothin'; but when they hear what a price you're givin', it may spur them up a little.'

The boys thanked him for his information, and started off at a good pace on their way to the Widow Andrews'. Bill was at work in the field, fighting manfully with a large growth of weeds; he greeted them kindly, but continued his labors.

'You will excuse me if I don't stop working; things are so behind-hand with me, that if I don't labor hard, I shall not catch up with my work, all summer.'

'By no means stop,' said Jim; 'we can say what we wish to, just as well while your hoe is going.' He made known their errand in few words, but no sooner did Bill hear what Jim had to say than he stopped hoeing, and looked with some surprise, first at one and then at the other of the boys.

'Yes, certainly, you shall have them; how many bushels do you want? Haven't you planted any this year?'

Jim then acquainted him with his reasons for wanting them, and the quantity he wished; stating also the price he could afford to give.

'And the money shall be paid to you when you deliver them.'

'You shall have every potato and bean I have for sale. I supposed I should be obliged to let Grizzle have them, but he may whistle for them, for all me; he allowed me last year but ten cents for potatoes, and fifty cents for beans. He will be angry, probably, but if I can have the money to pay, I shall not fear him any more than you seemed to the other day'—looking at Sam.

'No, I don't fear him; and all I wish is that father didn't owe him any thing.'

'Well, he is a very bad man, and will injure us all, if he can in any way, when he finds he is to be disappointed in getting things at his own price. He and Cross work into each other's hands, and they will not, if they can help it, have any one interfere with them; but I don't well see how they can.'

William Andrews was not mistaken in his views of the effect these things would have upon the minds of such men. But it will be time enough to meet trouble when it comes; at present we must hasten with our boys on their way to Billy Bloodgood's, much elated with their success, and with the change which seemed to have taken place in the views and feelings of young Andrews.

Mr. William Bloodgood—or Billy, as he was generally called—was the best to do of any of the folks for miles round, that is, he had more land, and a few more head of cattle, and managed a little better than his neighbors. But his house was rather a small concern, and his fences were in all sorts of shape, and his barn had far too many rents in it, and things lay in all directions around. Still, he did better than his neighbors, for Billy did not drink, and he kept himself busy, flying round on his farm, and made out almost always to raise quite a respectable quantity of one thing and another. He was a very good-natured man, and was blessed, as many good-natured men are, with a wife that could take his part, and her own too, sometimes. He had a peculiar way with him of going from one piece of work to another, without finishing either. Before his field of corn was half hoed, he would begin the potato patch, and leaving that unfinished, would be among the beans; and so on. This habit he carried with him into smaller matters, to his disadvantage, certainly, and very much to his discomfort; for his good woman was sorely annoyed by it, and whatever troubled her, he was sure to be obliged to bear a part of it. They lived happily however; for although Billy did not practise sound philosophy in his work, he did in that very delicate matter of conjugal relationship. He knew it would never answer for both to have their own way, one or the other must rule sometimes; and as he saw very soon that it would be a very difficult matter, if not an impossibility to get his better half to yield, unless she had a mind to it, he very properly decided to give up the reins to her. He was a wiser man than many took him to be.

As the boys entered the gate, Billy was coming out of the house, having just finished his dinner; he had a knife in one hand, and a piece of pigtail in the other, from which cutting a fair allowance, he put it into his mouth with a manifest relish. Without apparently noticing the boys who were walking towards him, he made directly to a great pile of brush which lay in the yard, and commenced chopping. They walked up to him, and endeavored to catch his eye, but he took no notice of them. After cutting a few sticks, he threw down the axe, and, looking at Jim, asked in a very loud voice,

'Did you speak to me?'

Jim shook his head in the negative, and then began to say something about his errand; he spoke, as he thought, in a pretty loud voice. But Billy only noticed his negative reply to the question he had put, and started for another corner of the yard, where lay a heap of farming utensils, and began dragging forth an old one-horse plough. After separating it from the rest, he commenced tinkering the rigging; Jim, in the meantime, trying to catch his eye, long enough to let him know that, although he had not yet spoken to him, he wished to do so. Twice, as he raised himself, Jim made a desperate effort, and called out as loud as he thought necessary,

'Mr. Bloodgood!'

But it availed nothing. He stared at him an instant, and then ran across to another side of the yard to a little old corn crib; and jumping into it, began to overhaul a box of old irons, for something probably that belonged to the plough. In the midst of all his hurry, however, he would find time every now and then to put his hand into his vest pocket, and taking out large pinches of snuff, would regale his olfactory sense, and apparently with great zest. The boys began to feel that it was a desperate case, and at the same time were so amused, that they could with difficulty refrain from showing it. In fact, Jim did once or twice give a kind of whine, just the beginning of a peculiar laugh he had, and Sam would go off with a very slight sneeze. As Billy appeared to be in no hurry to come out of the crib, they walked slowly across to where he was.

'You try him this time, Sam? see if you can make him hear.'

'I can't, Jim, no how. I should burst out laughing in his face.'

'I am afraid, then, we must give it up, for I can't get him to look at me.'

Mrs. Bloodgood, however, saw their dilemma, and out she came. The boys hardly knew whether she was for peace or war, for she advanced towards them with tremendous strides, muttering as she came. Her appearance was indeed rather dubious, for her hair was flying, and her face was very red, from the joint exercise of cooking and eating, and helping half a dozen children. And as to the dress, having great respect for the female sex we will say nothing about it; it was, moreover, very warm weather, and a Calamink petticoat was warm enough without the burden of its upper companion, the short gown—but she was just as she was, and we cannot help it. She had a little more nose than most women, that is, it was a very long, sharp, and crooked nose; but the good woman had use for it. And never were boys more astonished when they saw how well it answered her turn; it was a veritable speaking-trumpet, and, although the sounds which issued from it were rather of the nasal order, they were the better calculated to penetrate the very narrow passages to her husband's sounding-board. Having been so long accustomed to use a very high pitch in her communications with the good man, she made no allowance for the more delicate organs of other people, but so drove the sounds into them as truly made their ears to tingle, not only at the time, but a great while after.

'What is it you're wanting?'

Jim started; he could not help it.

'Do you want to speak to Bloodgood?'

'Yes, ma'am; I should like to speak with him about some beans and potatoes.'

With that she made off to the crib, where she met her good man coming out with a piece of old iron in his hand, and making for the other side of the yard where the plough was. He seemed as regardless of her as he had been of the boys; but as he was stooping over the plough, she put her hand on his shoulder, and gave such a blast in his ear that his soul must have stept out of his body not to have heard it; he immediately raised himself, and, looking at the boys, roared back to her in a strain scarcely less loud,—

'What do they want?'

'I don't know; something about potatoes and beans.'

'Bees? We 'aint got no bees;' and with that he took one of his tremendous pinches of snuff.

'Beans, beans! don't you hear *that*?' And then turning to Jim and Sam, who had walked up beside her—

'He grows wus and wus; and it's my candid belief that it's his snuffin' and snuffin' all the time so; his ears, I s'pose, is all stopped clean up; and the only way the sound can git into his head is through his nose, like; and when he stuffs that full, it's like hollerin' agin' a log.'

But he did hear *beans*, as she last spoke it.

'Beans? What of 'em?'

'Well, do tell *me*, boys, what you want on 'em, and I'll try to make him hear, for *you* never can.'

With that Jim communicated to her his business, and when she understood it clearly, appeared not a little pleased.

'I didn't know but you'd come from Grizzle's, and I don't like him; he's a good-for-nothin' old varmint, and he's spilin' all the men and boys in the place; and I told Bloodgood I'd rather throw the potatoes in the creek than let him have one on 'em.' So she went to work with a good will to tell their errand.

'Who sent 'em? Grizzle?'

'No, no; you think there is nobody in the whole creation world to buy anything but Grizzle.' And then raising her voice to the very loudest—

'Nobody sent 'em; they come o' themselves, and they'll pay you the money right down when you take 'em the things.'

'Well, well, that will do,'—and he smiled then, for the first time, as he looked at the boys—'that'll do; you shall have 'em; let me know when you want 'em.'

And now Mrs. Bloodgood would insist upon their going in, and taking something to eat. In vain it was they protested that they were not hungry, having eaten a lunch on their way.

'I know better than that. I know what boys are; they can always eat; so if you won't go in, don't either on you stir one step till I come out.'

In she ran, and in a moment appeared again with one-half of a large bread-cake, which she had just taken from the griddle, with a lump of butter on the top of it, and she with a knife spreading it on; but there was no occasion for the knife, for the butter was running like snow in summer, and dripping over the sides of the cake.

'Here, boys, take this;' breaking it in two, and giving each half 'I *know* it will taste good.'

CHAPTER VI

A few evenings after the events recorded in the last chapter, Sam started from home on his way to meet Jim and Ned. When but a short distance from his house, to his surprise he met William Andrews; he was on his way to visit the Montjoys, and designed calling upon Sam that he might accompany him to their house.

'I am going to see them,' said Sam; 'but they will not be at the house. Such fine evenings as this we meet at a large rock near by—they will be as glad to see you as I am.'

The rock was large enough to accommodate the whole of them; but Ned preferred the grass for his seat; he and Jowler had always some business of their own to attend to, and very frequently they would both be rolling together on the ground. The moon was rising beautifully, and a long streak of light played across the expanse of water at a distance, dancing on the waves that were formed by the fresh sea-breeze, and, nearer the shore, where the water lay smooth and unruffled, marking a line of clear silver light, as from the surface of a mirror.

There is always something peculiarly fascinating in the formation of youthful friendships—everything seems so fair; the interchange of confidence is so mutual, so whole-hearted—there is no secret standing on our guard—no cautious feeling of our way, to see whether we can safely trust. The heart has not yet been deceived, and therefore yields implicit confidence. One short hour, in our boyhood's days, will do more to knit our hearts in bonds strong and true, than months can accomplish, after the coldness and selfishness of the world have set us on our guard.

William Andrews had yielded to the impulses of a kind and social disposition, and thereby had been led sadly astray; but the charm was now broken, and he turned away with disgust and loathing from his past habits and companions. He had formed no friendships with those who were his partners in the idle hour, and the place of temptation. His heart was yet in its freshness, with a love of the pure and good, more intense for what he had seen of impiety and evil. His spirit panted for communion with those on whom it could confide, and longed to pour out its breathings into the ear of virtue and truth.

And now, under the great oak-tree, seated on the large flat rock, he confessed all his delinquencies, related the narrative of what he believed to be a change for life, and its happy influence upon his daily routine of duties.

'I can work, now, without being wearied; I can go home and meet my mother without the fear of rebuke; and I can lie down to rest at night without my head throbbing, or my body burning as in a fever; and when I awake in the morning, the stupor of deadness I used to feel is gone; I am happy, and ready for my business.'

Jim and Sam had no such personal experience of their own to tell. Sam might, indeed, have unfolded scenes of misery in his own past history; but in his own bosom must now for ever rest all that had been bitter in his own experience.

But there was no lack of subjects, and the evening was gone before they had said the one half they had to say; and long before the evening was spent, they were as intimate, and as much one in their feelings, as though they, had associated for years.

Sam's heart was full of happiness that night as he walked along the shore, and saw the water glistening in the moonlight, and heard the soft sound of the distant waves; and as he beheld the little light that twinkled in his lowly home, it seemed as bright to him—yea, brighter than does many an illuminated palace to its princely owner. Dark is the heart, Sam, that would bring a cloud over your pleasant sky; but such there are, sitting in council beneath the same pleasant moonlight which you are enjoying;— well for you that you see them, hear them not.

Had we the power of knowing what is going on at the same time in different places—could we look into the hearts of the actors in these various scenes—could we know how very near, sometimes, are the plotters of mischief and spite to the unconscious, inoffensive objects of their malice, it would be a cause of misery to us, unless our power was equal to our knowledge. Happy is it for us, that but one place, and one set of circumstances, can engross our minds.

Not far from where these happy youths held sweet counsel together, encouraging each other in the path of manliness and virtue, beneath the same clear sky and bright shining moon, sat two specimens of humanity, beneath the shed that ran along the front of Mr. Grizzle's store:—one of these the owner thereof, and the other a miserable-looking bloated youth, of about eighteen years of age.

'Do you say, Bill Tice, that they've been round buying up all the potatoes, and giving twenty-five cents a bushel?'

'Yes, it's fact. Old Sam Cutter told his boys on it, and they told me; and they said the old man wanted them to go to work and hoe 'em out, because they were goin' to bring sich a price, and he didn't mean to let old Grizzle have none on 'em.'

'He did, ha? Ay, ay, well, well.'

'And they'd bought all Billy Bloodgood's, and Bill Andrews', and ever so many more.'

'They have, eh? and gin' twenty-five cents a bushel, you say? that's a putty business, Bill.' And Grizzle turned his bleared and spectacled eyes full upon his companion. 'A putty business, Bill, ain't it? And who is to have potatoes and sich things to sell in the dead o'winter to poor folks, who may be ain't raised none? What would your folks have done last winter in sich a case?'

'Sure enough, we might starve; they wouldn't care.'

'And then if you was jist to help yourself a little,' (giving him a slight hunch,) 'why they'd be the first to complain on you; and away you must go another three months in the old cage.'

'I hate them Montjoy boys, they always look as if no one was good enough for 'em; goin' round with their shirt collars on their necks, and shoes on their feet.'

'And you say Oakum is with 'em, ha?'

'Why yes, Oakum's boy is with 'em, and you know it must be the old man that does it; the boy aint got nothin'.'

'No, nor the old one neither, when his debts is paid; but I'll see, I'll see. Folks musn't git in debt to me, and then come out agin' me; that won't do, Bill Tice.'

'I shouldn't think it would.'

'And you say Oakum is goin' to build a boat for his boy?'

'That's what Dick Cutter tell'd me.'

'To carry away everything we've got here, and make things so high, poor folks must starve or else work hard, one or the two.'

'They don't care.'

'I tell you what, Bill, you and I know one another; you've done some little jobs for me, and may be I've done some little things for you.'

'Yes, I know that.'

'Well now, Bill, this business must be stopped by fair means as foul.'

'That boat shan't never be built.'

'Whist, Bill, whist, don't be too fast; time enough yet.'

'What will you do, then?'

'What will I do—jist take the law on Oakum. Don't you see if I tie his hands the boat can't be built; and the old one they've got now, will only sink 'em to the bottom of the bay, if they try to take a load in her. I can make out a bill, I guess, that will keep him tight for three months at any rate.'

'That's a good idee.'

'Well, what I want of you is, to go some time to-morrow or next day, and jist ask Dick Tucker to come and see me, and may be I'll give him a job. You ain't afraid of Dick, now, are you?'

'No, I don't *care* nothin' for him; I should like just once to turn the key upon him, and see how he'd like it.'

'He'd rather turn it upon you and me, Bill; but you jist go there and tell him what I say. But keep mum, Bill.'

'No fear o' me.'

With that the old man patted Bill on the back.

'Come, come in and take something afore you go.' And in they went, and down went the fiery draught, and away went Bill Tice, a wretched victim to the hateful cup—a youth in age, but already old in ways of wickedness. Along the highway he plodded, his hat pulled down over his eyes, his head bent over, and his look fixed upon the path he was treading. He heeded not the beautiful moon that was lighting him on his way—brightly it shone upon him and his home, but only to expose wretchedness and vice waiting upon each other.

The path of duty is said to be the path of safety. When considered in reference to all final results, this is doubtless true; but to go steadily forward in our daily or weekly routine, we must expect to encounter more or less exposure to danger and disaster.

The little 'craft,' as Peter called the boat in which Jim and Sam made their voyages, was by no means suitable for the work; and again and again did the old sailor warn them, that 'they must look out for the southeasters, and never venture in no sich thing as that.'

It was the only one at present that they could procure, and they must either run the risk or give up their trade—a thing not to be contemplated for a moment.

It was early in July; the weather for some days had been oppressively warm. A dense fog covered the land and the water; and as our boys started upon their usual trip, they were obliged to lay their course as they best could, as there was nothing visible beyond a few lengths of their boat. The water was smooth without a ripple; not a breath of air could be felt from any direction. Sam's father had endeavored to dissuade him from venturing on the water at such a time.

'There's no telling what kind of weather we may have when this goes off, and I'm most sure I heerd it thunder a while ago.'

'I guess it wasn't thunder, father; and you know I can hardly miss my way in crossing the river; and when we get on the other shore, it will be easy to make the point; and by the time we get there, the wind will rise and the fog will go off.'

Sam's reasoning was well enough, but his father was not quite satisfied that it was best for them to go; however, as he saw their minds were set upon it, and all their things on board, he made no further objections.

As Sam had said, he was able to make the other shore without much difficulty; and that once reached, by keeping close to it, the point was also gained; but when about to turn into the open bay, Sam had some misgivings as to what was best to be done. The fog still surrounded them, as dense as ever, the shore could be seen only a few oars' length from it; and if they could keep within sight, they might proceed with their voyage, although by following the windings of the shore the distance would be greatly increased. This, however, would not have discouraged Sam, if he had not known that there were spots where close hugging the shore was impossible, as ledges of rocks ran off from it, which must be avoided. Thinking that he could keep the shore in sight until these were reached, and then venture out a little to avoid them, and not willing to turn back, he concluded to try the experiment. Jim knew nothing of the dangers to which they were exposed in being once out of sight of land, with no possible guide, in a small open boat, on the bosom of a bay that opened fair to the ocean. He therefore made no objections to any of Sam's movements. There was no wind, of course the sail was not up, and Sam handled the oars. Jim had his usual place at the helm, at which he had become quite expert.

'Keep her along shore, Jim, and don't lose sight of the land for any thing. Tell me when you see the large white rock, or the big tree; but I don't much think you will be able to see *that* to-day, but keep a sharp look-out for the rock.' The tree, as Sam expected, was not visible; but after half an hour's rowing, Jim pointed out the rock to which Sam had alluded.

'You remember, Jim, that near to this is the first ledge of rocks—turn her off shore a little—there, that will do; look sharp for the rocks, for if we lose sight of them and the shore too, we are gone.'

Jim did look sharp; for he perceived, from the anxious countenance of his companion, that there was some peculiar difficulty to be apprehended: in a few moments, however, they lost sight of the shore. This Sam expected; but instead thereof, anticipated making use of the large rocks, which usually protruded above the ledge or sunken reef, as his beacon. He exerted his utmost strength in the direction, as he supposed, they would be found, and the little boat skimmed rapidly through the water. Not a sign, however, of rock or shore could they discover; and, to add to their confusion, Sam, by accident, slipped an oar. Jim sprang to assist him in securing it, his tiller shifted, and the points of the compass were lost to them; the fog, too, evidently thickened around them—

'Don't you feel a breeze, Sam? I did just then.'

'Yes, and I think I know where it comes from; you see the fog grows thicker; it is driving in from the sea, and this wind must be from the east. Father said this morning he thought we should have the wind from that quarter—here it comes again, Jim.'

In a few moments a fresh and steady breeze came on; Sam, too, confident in the direction from which it came, hastened to spread his sail, and taking the helm into his own hands, put her head, as he supposed, in a direction that would carry them towards the fort, and at the same time bring them near the shore. For a while after the breeze sprung up, the fog was by no means diminished; but at length it began to recede, and as the circle of their horizon enlarged, anxiously they watched on the quarter where they were confident the land lay.

'We must be wrong, Sam, or we certainly could see the land by this time.'

Sam answered not, for other signs than the non-appearance of the land convinced him that he had mistaken his bearings. The wind had not increased much since it had at first sprung up, and, in fact, was giving tokens of ceasing or changing, by its frequent lulls; yet the water was becoming very rough; in fact, the waves were different from any they had ever encountered yet, threatening at times to fill their boat;—he began, indeed, to fear that he had been running out instead of nearing shore. At length the covering which had so long enveloped them rolled off, the distant points of land appeared, and their truly critical position was clearly exposed. Far off, in nearly an opposite direction to the one they were steering for, loomed up the fort; and the shore, which they had trusted was near at hand, could just be seen through the creeping vapors which yet clung to the land rising in patches slowly into the atmosphere. Before them was the open ocean, and the southeastern shores of the bay in a proximity to them, which in their present circumstances was any thing but agreeable.

Sam's first impulse, of course, was to steer directly for the haven they had started for; this, a moment's reflection upon the state of things convinced him would be madness.

Several times, while still enveloped in the fog, they had distinctly heard peals of thunder, which had by no means been a source of quietude; and now, far over the western sky, had gathered a dark and threatening mass of vapours, heaps on heaps rolling together, and spreading to the north, where the blackness of darkness seemed to have settled. Beneath that heavy mass, at the edge of the horizon, was a long light streak, showing where in the far distance the storm had already begun, and the winds lifting it up and bearing it towards them. In the direction of the storm was the shore they had left; to reach that or the fort, before it should burst upon them, was utterly impossible, and to be caught in their frail boat by such a tempest would be certain destruction. On the south and south-east lay a long line of shore, not much nearer than that on the west; yet from it, there ran out for a mile from the land, in a circular direction, a bar of sand; at high tide this bar was nearly covered, but when the tide was out, some acres of hard white sand were exposed, and afforded a firm landing-place. Sam knew of this; and, in fact, he could plainly discern its white surface in the distance, for the tide had been for some time running out, and was the main cause why he had, in so short a time, made so long a stretch.

'What shall we do, Sam? It looks black there, don't it?'

'Black enough—we must run away from it.'

At once, Sam tied up the sail as carefully as he could, and stowed it as near the bottom of the skiff as possible.

'Where will you run, Sam? we are most out to sea now.'

'We must go a little nearer yet, for all that I see;—quick, Jim, take the helm; you see that white streak, don't you, running out from the shore yonder?'

'Yes.'

'It is a mile nearer to us than any place we can get to; make for that—it is our only chance.'

Jim did as directed; for, on the water, he yielded implicitly to Sam. The oars were out, and Sam's utmost strength was tasked; their lives depended on the fact of his ability to reach that bar before the storm should overtake them. As they progressed, the waves sensibly increased; and occasionally, through Jim's inexperience in steering, water enough would be shipped, not only to wet them thoroughly, but to endanger the feeble craft.

Sam's eye was steadily fixed upon the rising gust; he heeded not the waves—death was behind them—if they reached not that landing-place in time, they must be his prey. Vivid streaks of lightning ran along the curling edges of the clouds, and heavy-rolling thunder, increasing in loudness at every clap; far off upon the distant land could be seen volumes of dust rolling high up in the air; and when the thunder ceased, the sullen roar of the tempest was distinctly heard.

'How fast it comes, Sam!'

'Keep her straight for that bar, Jim.'

'Do you hear the roaring, Sam?'

'Are we near the bar? Keep her as straight as you can—it's coming fast.'

Already had the storm reached the water. Sam knew now what they had to expect; for before it arose a mass of spray like a thick low mist. Rising on his feet, and throwing himself back with all his force, the little fellow did all that in him lay to reach the shore.

'Don't let go the helm, Jim.'

And Jim immediately braced himself upon the bottom of the boat, holding with main strength to the tiller. As the wind struck them, Sam was obliged to throw himself down in the boat; he could not face its fury. In an instant, all sights and sounds but that of the storm were lost; they were at its mercy, or more properly, at the mercy of Him who directed it. A few moments, their little boat tossed and floated amid the tumult, and then struck heavily upon the beach.

'Out, Jim! out, and hold on!'

The days when the little skiff was expected at the fort began to be looked forward to with much pleasure by old Peter and his little charge. Seated on the parapet which surrounded the fort, with a spyglass in his hand, he would watch a bend of the shore, around which the little boat could first be seen. Susie would be near him, looking at the play of the waters among the broken rocks which formed the foundation of the fort, or listening to marvellous stories of sea life, of which Peter had the usual supply.

This day they had watched until the storm came, and after it had cleared away; until giving up all expectation of seeing the boat, Peter had hobbled into the fort to attend to some little matters, and Susie sought for amusement in her usual play-ground—the narrow strip of land, about twenty feet in width, encircling them. It has been mentioned that a ledge of rocks connected with the main-land, being formed partly by nature and partly by a deposit of large broken stones—the design apparently was to have formed a passage to the shore without the aid of a boat, but for some cause or other it was not carried out. At low water, one acquainted with the locality might have made his way across it, from rock to rock, without much difficulty; but when the tide was in, all communication was cut off. At the rising and falling of the tide, the water flowed through the narrow passages with great rapidity; and a very expert swimmer would have needed much muscular strength not to have been swept away with it. Peter never ventured upon this rough causeway himself, for two very good reasons: first, because it was no place for crutches to travel over; and, secondly, considering it unsafe, he did not wish to set the little girl an example which might lead her into danger.

Tired, however, with her narrow promenade, when she reached the ledge spoken of, without any misgivings, she rambled across the rough pavement of broken stones, until she came to a large rock forming the terminus. On one side this rock was shelving. Fearless she walked down to the water's edge: the tide was running swiftly past, and this peculiar motion of the water being new to her, she laid herself down, and watched the coursing of the dark current with delight.

When Peter returned, he saw nothing of Susie; and thinking she had gone to the other side of the fort, was hobbling round to look after her; when to his surprise, on turning the first angle, he saw the little boat close at hand, and apparently coming from a very different quarter than usual.

'Hulloa, my hearties: where do you hail from now?'

'The Horse Shoe,' said Sam, putting his hand to his mouth, and making as grum a noise as old Peter did.

'The Horse Shoe! What! druv down there in the gale?'

'Got lost in the fog, and made for the sand-bar; when the storm came up, we had a hard time of it.'

Peter began to chew hard on his cud, and shake his head very violently; at the same time resting on his crutches, he doubled up his fist, and held it in a very threatening manner towards Sam.

'The fog—lost in the fog—and didn't you know better than to venture off shore, with no *pints of compass*, and *no reckoning* and *no nothing* to steer by, in *sich a craft* as *that*? That ain't fit to trust a man's life in on a mill pond.'

Sam smiled.

'It aint no laughing matter, my young man, to foller the water; I've tell'd you *that*, many a time; it ain't like the land, where you can lay to, and hold on jist as you likes. No, no; them that deals with the winds and the waves must keep a sharp look-out, and watch their chances; its nothin' more nor less but a temptin' o' Providence with your dumb-founded perverseness. But howsomever, I'm glad to see you; so jist haul up, and I'll call the Major.'

Peter hobbled towards the landing-place, to which Sam urged his boat. Just as she struck the stairs, a loud scream was heard. Sam sprang from the boat, and ran with lightning speed across the ledge of broken rocks. He had seen what those on the dock could not see. The little girl had caught a view of the boat, and rising to return, had ventured to tread upon a part of the rock which was covered with sea-weed; her foot had slipped, and when Sam beheld her, she was hanging just above the water, clinging to the rock, and screaming in her agony. Almost distracted, Peter called aloud for help; although he could see nothing, as yet, of the child. Sam felt that life or death depended upon his exertions; and none but one accustomed, as he had been, from infancy, to tread with bare feet the flinty shore, could have made such fearful haste over that rough pavement. One false step would, in all probability, have cost his life. He reached the rock—she was still clinging; he grasped at her—it was too late—and down she plunged into the deep water, and was borne swiftly along by the current. But Sam was with her; he waited not to calculate the chances against his own life—in an instant he plunged, and then arose a cry from the fort, that brought help and dear friends to witness the heart-rending spectacle; for there could be little doubt in the minds of all that both must perish. Major Morris, at the first alarm, rushed to the spot. His distress at seeing the idol of his heart sinking in the deep water, cannot be described. He flew with one or two attendants to his own boat, which lay near at hand; and made all the haste the most intense anxiety could urge, to reach the struggling children. But Peter was before him, in the little skiff with Jim; the moment he understood the case, he threw down his crutches, sprang into the boat, and like a master workman, made her fly through the water.

'Hold on, my darlings, don't be frightened; I'll soon be with you.'

But no answer was returned; Sam had not calculated his own strength, and had no idea of the desperate energy it would require to sustain himself with another clinging to him. His arms could afford him no assistance; the little girl had grasped them with such energy, that the most he could do, was just to keep her head from beneath the water. Every thing was done with the greatest speed from the moment their situation was observed; but it took some little time to reach them. Sam felt his strength failing, he could not even call for help—intent upon one only object, he struggled on; and when he could raise his head above water to speak, he tried to encourage her. But the powers of nature could do no more, and he felt the water rushing above his head, and was conscious that all was over with him; when a hand, strong and steady, grasped his arms, still extended, and bearing up their precious burden.

'She's saved! she's saved!' hallooed Peter, with his loudest voice. 'She's saved! God be praised!—she ain't hurt a bit.' With one hand he took Susie from her hold on Sam, and raised her into the boat; and with the other supported him, so that his head was above the water.

'Thank God!' exclaimed Major Morris—'But the *boy*—is he alive?'

'Oh yes,' said Peter; at the same time raising Sam, and laying him down in the boat.

'No, no, he ain't,' said Jim, throwing himself on the body of Sam. 'He's dead!—oh dear—he's dead! he's dead!'

'I tell you he ain't—he ain't; he's only swooned like—he ain't dead: no, no.'

But when Major Morris saw his pale and deathlike countenance, he was in great alarm.

'To shore, instantly; he has saved my child, but I fear with the loss of his own life.' And while he hugged the darling of his heart to his bosom, and thanked God for his mercy, he could not restrain the big tears as he looked at the pallid features, and felt the cold and clammy temples of the brave heart that had saved her. Frantic with grief and joy alternate, Mrs. Morris watched every motion, from the stairs to which she had flown, at the first summons of the danger of her child. Receiving her from the arms of the father, crying and kissing her in the wildness of her joy, surrounded by attendants, she hurried into the fort; while Major Morris took the lifeless body of Sam in his arms, followed by Peter and Jim, who was almost beside himself with grief and terror.

It seemed a long, long time to those who, under the direction of the surgeon of the garrison, were using means to resuscitate him; and scarcely less rejoiced was Major Morris when he received his own child alive in his arms, than when he perceived the signs of returning consciousness in Sam. At length he awoke as from a troubled dream. With an expression of deep anxiety he looked upon the circle which surrounded him. Mrs. Morris was bending over him, parting the wet and tangled locks from off his pale forehead; beside her stood the Major, holding his hands, and rejoicing in the warmth which he felt was returning to his system. Peter stood at the foot of the bed, chewing incessantly a tremendous quid of tobacco, which he had found leisure to slip into his mouth even in the midst of all the confusion. He had done great execution in the way of rubbing; his hands, very unlike his heart, were rough, and well calculated for such a purpose. He had, however, now ceased rubbing, and was looking alternately at Sam and at a short, red-faced personage, the Irish servant woman, who stood at his elbow. Endowed with all the feelings of her sex and her nation, she continued to be in great agitation. Her arms were crossed upon her breast, her eyes turned up to the ceiling, and with her body swinging to and fro, she was uttering certain groans and exclamations.

'Is the little girl safe?' said Sam, looking full into the face of Major Morris.

'Yes, my fine fellow, she is safe and well; thanks to you, under a kind Providence, for it.'

Sam shut his eyes again; he said nothing further; but there was a tremulous motion on his lips, and about the muscles of his face. Some cordial was administered, and he was allowed to fall asleep. As he slept, the powers of nature began to assume their natural energy, a gentle warmth spread over his frame, the color again glowed on his cheek, and his whole countenance told the story to those anxious watchers, that he was doing well. All breathed more freely; the scene so late full of terror and dismay, was changing, like the black clouds which bring the thunder storm, into beautiful visions for the eye to rest upon and enjoy.

When Sam again awoke, Jim alone was with him. He was much refreshed, and asked whether they had not better return home.

'Whenever you are well enough, we will do so. Every thing is settled for—I have got your money and mine too.'

'Oh, have you? Well, I have not thought much about money, or any thing else; I have been in a kind of dream, I believe.'

'Don't you remember any thing that has happened, Sam?'

'Why, I remember seeing that little girl hanging on the rock:—oh Jim, how I *did* feel; and I remember running as fast as I could, and just as I put my hand on her to catch her, off she slipped. I remember *that*, Jim; and I don't believe I shall ever forget it: and I remember holding her up out of the water, and trying to call for help; and then, just as I was giving up and going down, I felt something take hold of me; and after that, all seems to be confused. I thought they told me she was saved; and I thought I saw her once looking at me; but I don't know—may be I only dreamt it.' And Sam looked very anxiously at Jim.

'No, it's no dream, Sam; for she has been here a good while by you, and when she saw how pale you looked, she cried.'

'Did she?'

'Yes, and they all cried. And you don't know what Mr. Morris says—he says if it hadn't been for you, she would have been drowned before any of them could possibly have reached her: and that you have saved her life.'

Sam could make no reply. The thought that he had saved a life, and the life of one so beautiful and so much beloved, was too full of happiness, and it overpowered him. The door now opened slowly, and Peter's shaggy head made its appearance. He had a bundle under his arm—Sam's clothes, which had been dried and ironed for him. Seeing Sam sitting up, he hobbled to the bedside, took both his crutches under one arm, and throwing the other around Sam, gave him a hug—well meant, no doubt, and expressive of his kind feelings; but which would have been much more in keeping had Peter been holding on to a main-top-gallant-mast in a gale of wind.

Sam was soon arrayed in his old but clean garments. While he was dressing, Peter stood with his crutches properly adjusted for moving, his jaws working very rapidly, and his head nodding approvingly at Sam.

'And now, come, my hearty, you're all rigged. The ladies want to see you in t'other room; come.'

'Oh, no, no, no; I can't do that; I can't go, no how.'

'I tell you what it is, you're a good fellow of your age as ever handled an oar; but you are too dumbfounded perverse in your own ways. Here is you been a saving this child, riskin' your own life; and when they want jist to say to you, "God bless you," and kind o' relieve their own minds, you up and won't go.'

But Sam persisted; he would jump into the water again if that was necessary; but as to going into a fine parlor, and being looked at by fine ladies, it was not to be thought of. Peter was about to make some violent pleas against Sam's 'perverseness,' as he called it; when seeing the Major, he suddenly adjusted his crutches, stroked down his queue, and backed off to another part of the room.

We must now leave Sam to the care of these friends, and see what is going on beneath the humble roof of his parents; an eventful day it proved for him and for them.

Bill Tice had done the errand which Mr. Grizzle intrusted to him. A few days after, the old yellow gig of Mr. Richard Tucker was seen standing at Mr. Grizzle's door, while the two worthies were sitting together in a little back room, adjoining the store, with an old greasy account-book lying on the table beside them, and sundry papers in Mr. Tucker's handwriting open, and almost ready to be folded up and put into a dirty pocket-book belonging to said Mr. Tucker; which was also lying there, and waiting to inclose within its clasp an instrument fully charged with a power to torture, only surpassed by the wheel, which, in former days, twisted the joints of the wretched victims from their strong fastenings.

'A larger bill, Mr. Dick, than I thought I could muster up; and now you make the most of it.'

'Trust me for that; all I want to know is what my principal requires— that's all.'

And Mr. Tucker knit his bushy brows, and went on tying up, with a dirty blue string, the papers which had been lying on the table.

After securing them in this manner, he opened his pocket-book, and deposited them in it; and then, in the same careful manner, thrust the whole into an inside pocket of his threadbare coat. Mr. Tucker was about to do a very dirty job, and he was a man well fitted for the duty. He had a heart, doubtless, that beat and threw the vital current about his frame, just as other men have; and he had bones, and sinews, and flesh, and these could suffer pain as other flesh and blood; but to say that Mr. Tucker had a heart as others have, that would beat in sympathy with his fellow in distress, or that he could be made to feel shame, or pain, or sorrow, or regard, in that secret fountain where springs so much that sweetens or embitters life, would be wrong—wrong to him, because it would be saying that of him which was not true—wrong to the mass of mankind, who *have* feelings that can be touched. Mr. Tucker's appearance was in keeping with his character— little leaden-colored eyes, sunk deep in his head, over which scowled dark shaggy brows; a pale, cadaverous countenance, with no expression that one could lay hold of in an hour of distress, on which to found a hope that any compassion might be felt, or any mercy shown. A fit minister was he of that stern and barbarous code which legalised the torturing of the *poor* man—which allowed the tearing him away from the charities of home, and entombing him in the charnel-house of vice, debauchery, and filth.

Some feelings of compunction seemed yet to be lingering in the breast of Mr. Grizzle; for as Mr. Richard put his hat on his head, and buttoned up his coat, and fumbled about in the act of departing, he stammered out—

'It's right, you know; I ought to have my own. Folks cannot expect me to wait always for 'em—pay-day must come.'

'*Right!* to be sure it's right; and as you say he's running against you, and setting up his boy and others to hurt your trade—why, muzzle him, I say—who wouldn't?'

'I suppose it wouldn't be much use taking the timber and stuff that he is building that boat with?—there is nothing else to take.'

'No use in that; he hasn't done much to it but put the ribs together—it's of no value as it is. No—shut him up; that's the way—that will stop boat and all.'

'Well, well; you know the law, Dick, let it work. I shall have to find him in bread and water—that won't cost much.'

The day was drawing to a close, and the shades of evening were deepened by a heavy cloud which was rising in the west, and into which the sun was sinking. A muttering of distant thunder hastened the departure of Mr. Tucker. He sprang into his crazy old gig, and drove off at a quick pace to his deed of mischief.

Oakum had worked diligently on his boat all day, and continued his labor till a later hour than usual, in expectation that the little skiff would be along, and Sam would accompany him home. He had felt much uneasiness for the safety of the boys, and was very desirous of witnessing their return. Darkness was coming on, and a storm threatening; so taking a long look across the water, and meeting no signs of the boat, with rather a sad heart he walked towards his home. Their evening meal was eaten in silence, while, as long as the light permitted any view of distant objects, the eyes of the parents were directed across the water. They felt, as they had never before, how dependent they were upon their boy for his smile and his voice to cheer their hearts.

Scarcely had they finished their supper, when the yellow gig of Mr. Tucker drove up. Oakum and his wife cast their eyes at the gig, and then at each other. Instantly she perceived that trouble was at hand; for her husband grew very pale, and even faltered in his step as he walked to the door to admit their visitor. Mr. Tucker did not use much formality in his official visits, and entered without knocking.

'Mr. Oakum, I believe.'

'At your service, sir.'

'Here is an account, sir, I believe against you, lately put into my hands'—at the same time opening his pocket-book, and taking out one of the papers which he had so carefully put there but a short time since, in the little back room of Mr. Grizzle's store. Mr. Oakum took the paper, and asking Mr. Tucker to be seated, availed himself of the same privilege—for, to tell the truth, he was completely unnerved. He knew well what office Mr. Tucker held: he also knew something of the man; and a strange weakness came over him, so that when he unfolded the paper, and held it up to the light of the window, his hands trembled so violently, it was impossible for him to make out the sum that was charged against him.

'This is from Mr. Grizzle, I suppose, Mr. Tucker?'

'It is, sir.'

'I don't know that I can make out exactly what the amount is; but I suppose it is right. I owe Mr. Grizzle something, but I thought it wasn't much.'

'Much or little, sir, you've got it there; it is something over thirty dollars.'

'Thirty dollars! Ain't there some mistake, Mr. Tucker?' and Mr. Oakum looked at his wife in amazement. She, poor thing, stood like a statue, not comprehending the matter, but fearing it was something dreadful.

'I guess there is no mistake, sir. Mr. Grizzle took it from his book, and he ain't apt to make mistakes; but that is between you and him—it is no concern of mine.'

'Oh, no, sir; you are not to blame. I know I owe Mr. Grizzle, and I have thought of it a great deal, and am trying to get a little something ahead to give him; he shall have all I honestly owe him just as soon as my hands can earn it. I will call and see Mr. Grizzle to-morrow, and take him a little.'

Mr. Tucker now arose from his seat, put his hat on his head, and stepping up to Mr. Oakum—

'All *that* is well enough, sir; but it don't pay the bill. If you cannot settle it at once, you will please go along with me'—at the same time putting his hand on his shoulder.

'I have a warrant to take you, unless you can give me the money, or goods in the place of it. Shall I read the warrant?'

'There is no occasion for that, sir. I have not got the money, if it was to save my life; and goods I have none, only what you see here.'

'Well, sir, if you go peaceably, it is well enough; if not, I must read the warrant, for I have no time to lose—it is getting dark.'

Mr. Oakum arose, but his limbs could scarcely sustain him; big drops of sweat stood on his pale forehead, and a deadly sickness was at his heart.

'Oakum, Oakum! tell me what it is. What does this man want?'

'I don't see, Mr. Tucker, what good it is going to do Mr. Grizzle to shut me up in jail. I can't do no work there. And what are my wife and children to do? must they starve?'

'Jail! jail! Ah, sir; you ain't going to put my husband in jail! What hurt has he done you, or any body else?'

And she flew to her husband, and putting her arms around his neck, wept as though her heart had broken. But Mr. Tucker was not to be balked in the discharge of his official duties by the tears of either man or woman— some harsh things he said, which aroused the humbled spirits of this suffering husband and wife. Mrs. Oakum hushed her grief for the time, in order to quiet the distressed children, who were clinging to their father, and screaming in their agony when they learned whither he was going. Mr. Oakum, however, made no resistance to the imperious demands of the officer; but quieting the feelings of his family as far as he could, entered the gig with Mr. Tucker, and was driven rapidly away amid the darkness of the gathering storm.

As soon as Mrs. Oakum was enabled to collect her thoughts, apprehensions on Sam's account again oppressed her. She took her seat by the window, and looked in every direction; but the darkness had increased so rapidly, that objects could be discerned at only a short distance from the house. Occasionally the vivid lightning would, for an instant, throw its bright glare across the water, making the prospect distinctly visible. On one occasion, she thought she saw a small white sail; and every succeeding flash she watched, until her eyes were nearly blinded by the dazzling light, but nothing more of it could she discern. A startling peal of thunder proclaimed that the storm was at hand, and the rain began to patter in large drops, and then to pour its floods upon them. Just at that moment the door opened; and Sam, with his cheerful smile and pleasant words, was in the midst of them. They all flew to caress him; but missing his father, and seeing the marks of distress in his mother's countenance—

'Where is father?' he cried, 'is anything wrong—do tell me quick, mother.'

'Ah, Sam! what shall we do?'

All Sam's bright hopes were dashed at once; he durst ask no further. The day had been one of severe toil and imminent danger; but he had been richly rewarded in the approbation of those he esteemed so highly; he had been caressed by those whose rank in life was among the first in the land; and he had then about him a jewel of no inconsiderable value, given to him by Mrs. Morris as a token of her high approbation of his manly conduct, and of the obligation she should ever feel for the rescue of her child. All this had raised his spirits; and full of the fond anticipation of making his parents glad with the tidings of the day, he had landed with a happy heart, and hurried to his home. But now, alas! his father has yielded to the tempter, never, perhaps, to be restored, and all his proud dreams are gone.

'You need not tell me about it, mother. But I must go and try to find him; he may be somewhere on the road, unable to help himself, and exposed to this storm.'

His mother looked earnestly at him, as though not clearly comprehending what he meant; but it soon became evident to her.

'Oh! it is not that, Sam. Your father has been hard at work all day, and we were only worrying a little about you, as he felt so anxious ever since the storm we had in the morning—if it hadn't been for that, we should have been as happy as could be—when, all at once, that good-for-nothing creature Richard Tucker came in, and said he was sent by Grizzle; and in spite of all we could say or do, he has took him off to the jail.'

And she broke out again in a passionate flood of tears. Poor Sam was in a sad strait; but his heart was not so heavy as when under the impression that his father had fallen again into his evil habits. He resolved, however, immediately what course to pursue.

'I am going out, mother. Perhaps I can get him clear; if not, I shall stay with him till morning. I cannot leave my father alone in that dreadful place to-night.'

'Oh, Sam! what are you talking about? You cannot go out in such a storm, and then to stay all night in that awful jail.'

'I don't care for the storm, mother; and the jail won't be worse for me than it will be for him.'

'Well, Sam, I don't know what to say, my poor head is so bewildered. If it wasn't for these little ones, I would go with you.'

Sam immediately went to his chest, and taking out all his little store of money, put it with that which he had brought home that day—in all it amounted to three dollars. He then took the jewel which had been presented to him—a handsome broach, in the form of a harp, and set with stones, worth no small sum in money; but to Sam more valuable than hoards of gold, and which no money would have purchased from him—and placed it in the bag with his little treasure, then threw on an old garment, to protect himself in some measure from the rain, and telling his mother 'to keep up a good heart,' left the house. He took the road leading to Mr. Grizzle's store, and forgetting the fatigue of the day, hurried along as fast as the storm would permit. Mr. Grizzle was sitting at his counter, resting his feet on an old rickety bench, and humming a tune by way of company, for the usual visitors of the evening were not in.

Sam took off his hat as he entered, and walking up to Mr. Grizzle looked him full in the face, but was too much out of breath to speak.

The old man stopped his tune, and looked quite smilingly at Sam.

'Well, my lad, how do you do this evening? All well at home?'

'Here, Mr. Grizzle, is all the money we have; it is not much—but I thought may be you would take it; and here is something that is worth a good deal—you may keep it until we bring you the rest of the money. We can only get a little at a time, but you shall have it all as fast as we can raise it.'

'*Money*, boy! Who has said any thing to you about money? I haven't— have I?'

'Why, sir, I suppose you sent Mr. Tucker to our house?'

'Mr. Tucker! He has been to see you, has he? Well, he is a pretty hard customer. Why not give him the money?'

'But he has taken my father to jail, sir; and says he must have the whole of the money—and this is all we have got,' holding up to Mr. Grizzle his little handful of change. 'Here is three dollars, sir, and I will soon get you some more, and you may keep *this* until I bring it,' taking up also his brooch.

'What, gold, ha! You must be pretty well off at your house—pretty well off.'

'*Do*, Mr. Grizzle, take this, and let my father go. We will pay you every cent he owes, just as fast as we can; I promise you, sir, upon my honor.'

'Oh, you had better go to Mr. Tucker's, he will take the money, I guess— and that thing too; may be he can find an owner for it. It don't look as if it had been living among poor folks.'

Sam's heart was beginning to sink; he perceived that Mr. Grizzle was only mocking him. But he did not quite understand what he meant by 'finding an owner for it.'

'I am the owner of this, Mr. Grizzle.'

'Are you? you look a good deal like it.' And he cast his eye down at Sam, surveying him from head to foot. This was more than he could bear; his heart beat quick, his face reddened; he could not then have asked a favour of that old withered wretch, had it been to save himself or his family from certain ruin. He put his money and jewel back again into his pocket, picked up his hat from the bench on which he had laid it, and turning his back on the store and its owner, hurried away, wishing that he might never see either again.

The building used for the graceless evil-doers and penniless paupers of this vicinity was not a very sightly object, and its appearance was in keeping with its hideous character. It was a square, two-storied building, without any paint; the clapboards and roof were gray and mossy; storms and sunshine had played upon it for fifty years; and it was none the better for its age. In the upper story could be seen one room, with a small window at the end, with iron bars crossing sufficiently near together to keep a prisoner from getting through, if he was somewhat corpulent; but most rogues and poor men, that were not very stout, could, if so disposed, have found a way out with a little hard squeezing. But whether any did ever get out in that way I never learned—perhaps the sight of the iron was enough. The other apartments of the house had windows open as one could desire; glass may once have formed some obstruction, to the birds at least; but it had disappeared 'long time ago,' and in that place thereof, shingles, old hats, old clothes—any thing that would keep out the rain and the cold for the time being, was substituted. It was inhabited by a family, which, for want of all those qualities and qualifications that would have fitted them for any other situation, were content to abide here. Old Adam Tice had never been able to comprehend the difference between mine and thine. He was not particularly bad in any other way; but it was generally thought that his boys would, in time, carry out his principles a little beyond their parent; and his son Bill, whom we have been introduced to at Mr. Grizzle's, had, on more than one occasion, enjoyed the occupancy of the room with the grated window.

As there was but one apartment in this building suited for close confinement, it sometimes occurred that an unfortunate debtor, who had no friend to bail him out, so as to allow him the privilege, if such he should esteem it, of ranging the lot on which the house was built, and taking up his abode with Mr. Tice, must share the grated room with some vile character whose deeds against humanity had brought him there; and such was the case now. Two notorious vagabonds, guilty of flagrant crimes, the very offscouring of the earth, were there; and nightly they filled the old jail with noise and riot, as though fiends were holding their orgies. It made even old Tice shudder, as their horrid oaths rang through the building in the darkness of the night; and he almost regretted that he had procured the liquor which had thus given them the inspiration of demons.

I shall not attempt to describe the feelings of poor Mr. Oakum when he heard the key turned upon him, and found himself in such company. Some straw was placed for him at one end of the room, out of the reach of his fellow-prisoners, who were chained. He tottered towards it, and was glad to cast himself down upon it. Sorrow will sometimes lull her suffering children to sleep: oblivion, like a handmaid of charity, steals upon them and shuts up the senses. Helpless, and almost hopeless, his mind could no longer bear the thoughts that haunted it, but settled down into unconsciousness. Occasionally some dreadful oath would rouse him, or the deep rolling thunder, but only for a moment; when thoughts of home, and wife, and children, would with lightning speed flash upon his mind, and then, overpowered with his sad condition, he would again sink into unconsciousness.

At length he started from his bed of straw, awakened by the spring of the heavy bolt that was suddenly drawn back. He cast his eager glance upon the door; a light glimmered through a small square aperture at the top—the latch was raised—his senses he feared were leaving him; for there stood Sam, his dear, good child. Mr. Tice threw the light of his lamp upon that corner of the room, and Sam walked directly to his father.

'Oh, my dear boy, is that you? is it you, Sam?'

'I thought I would come and stay with you to-night, father.'

'Oh, Sam, I do not mind this for my own sake; I deserve it: my own foolishness has brought this on to me.'

'Don't talk so, father; you haven't done wrong. I will get you out, yet, and it will all be better than ever.'

His father could make no reply; his heart was melted, and thoughts different from any he had ever indulged before began to agitate him. God had not forsaken him; this child was an angel of mercy, sent to cheer his gloom and give hope to his heart. New and strange feelings towards his God arose from within—how good, how forbearing, how full of compassion. New feelings in regard to himself oppressed him. A great sinner, both towards God and the dear ones God had given him, could he be pardoned? He remembered the thief upon the cross; and his whole heart arose in one strong impulse—'Lord, help me! save me!' It was a simple prayer—it was only breathed—but it was heard in heaven. And swift as angels fly, sweet peace came down and stole into his bosom, and there, amid that gloom and in that dire abode, whispered of pardon, and hope, and a Friend above.

But where did Sam obtain that strong assurance that all would yet be well—*better* than ever? It was no fiction invented to soothe his father's troubled mind. Sam really felt and truly believed it would be so. Ever since that dark hour upon the rock by the water-side, when his companions came to him with their plan of enterprise, had *resolution*, strong as his love of life, nerved his heart. He had since then tasted the rich fruits of honest labor; and his eyes were enlightened, and his hope and courage made strong. His parents and sisters had already been made happy by his exertions, and his way was enlarging before him. The present hour was one of severe trial, but his courage was not shaken by it, and he believed most firmly that it would be with them 'better than it had ever been.'

It was a beautiful morning when Sam left the jail, and hurried on his way to carry what comfort he could to his home. He would have avoided every human being if he could, but just as he was about to pass the road which ran down to the blacksmith's shop, Mr. Cutter's two boys saw him, and being social fellows, ran up, and began, in their free-and-easy boy's style, to question him about what he was doing there that time of day, and where he had been, and so on. Sam's heart was about as full as it could hold. They were wild boys, but of a kind nature, and felt a right good-will towards Sam. They perceived that he was in trouble, for the tears stood in his eyes when they spoke to him.

'Now, Sam, what's the matter? tell me who's been hurting you. I'll give it to him—who is it? See if I don't.' And Bill Cutter doubled up his fists, and put himself in a posture to go right at it. Sam Cutter was a little softer in his composition than his brother; and while Bill was putting himself into a great rage with somebody or other, he did not care who, Sam put his hand on the shoulder of his companion:

'Tell me, Sam, what's the matter.' The storm, which had been so long pent up, broke forth; this made both boys more solicitous to find out the cause of his trouble, until Sam was compelled to tell the whole.

No sooner had they heard the story, than, seizing Sam, each by an arm, they fairly forced him along.

'Come along, right in, Sam Oakum, and tell father all about it.'

And on he had to go, straight through the old shop, into a little back yard, and then into a little old house. The table was in the middle of the floor, on which lay the remains of the breakfast which had just been eaten.

Mrs. Cutter was stooping over the fire, and doing something with a kettle which hung there; and as they entered, she turned her very large eyes upon the boys. I say large, because they were naturally very expansive, and because she wore on the bridge of her nose, right before them, a pair of nose spectacles; they were large, too, in contrast with the other features of her countenance, for while these were very round and full, everything else in sight was very long and sharp; her nose was long, and her chin was long, and her hands and arms were long; and other limbs long too, for when she let go the kettle and raised herself up, she appeared all length—of breadth there was nothing to mention, except the eyes.

'What upon airth is the matter? what are you doin' with that boy? See, Cutter, they've been a hurtin' on him—he's a cryin' now—oh the massys! Let him go, you good-for-*nothins* you, let him *go*.'

'No, we ain't been hurting him, neither—what do you think, father? they've been putting Sam Oakum's father in the old cage, they have.'

Mr. Cutter was sitting yet at the table; *he* and his good woman were the reverse of each other, in more ways than one. He was, as we have seen, very large and full-bodied. Standing and walking and going about, seemed to be, each of them, her natural situation; while with him, standing was not to be thought of if there was any chance for a seat; and when once at the table he seemed willing there to stay, until Mrs. Cutter had cleared plates, dishes, and the table itself from before him. As the boys entered he pushed himself round, and looked in quiet amazement at them.

'Who is *they*? who's put him in jail?'

'Old Grizzle, father; only think. If I ain't a mind to kill the old varmint; I'll burn his house down.'

'*Whist, hush, hold your tongue*, you scoundrel; how dare you talk so?'

And the old man, in his energy to do something to show his displeasure at such threats, caught hold of the pitcher, which yet stood on the table before him, and thinking not of its contents, elevated it above his head in a threatening manner at his lawless son. Cider he liked well enough in its proper place; but a shower of it on his bald head, and in his eyes, and so on, was another thing. It took him by surprise—he let the pitcher go, and put his hands to the afflicted parts.

Crockery is brittle stuff; it could not stand every thing, any more than Mrs. Cutter's temper could. To see the look of horror she cast upon the dripping head of her husband, and then at the broken pieces of her pitcher, the very last thing in the house 'her mother gin' her,' as she often said; with her long arms and bony fingers stretched out in the air, was rather frightful: The moment the old man could recover himself sufficiently to realize what he had done, and what he had to expect, he exclaimed, very significantly,

'Oh dear!' and rose up as hastily as he could, designing to retreat to his shop, his usual refuge from a storm.

'*Oh dear!* you may well say so—of *all things*. Well, Cutter, now you see what you've done. I've told you it would be so; the very last thing my mother gin' me—slam it right down on the harth—isn't that purty? you've been breakin' and breakin' all your life; and now you've broke the pitcher.'

He said not a word in reply, but taking hold of Sam Oakum pulled him along towards the shop. Finding that her husband was fast retreating from the sound of her voice, she turned the battery upon her two boys, who were eyeing the broken crockery with no very equivocal looks,

'And *you*, you villains! comin' and settin' your father crazy with your lies—*out* of the house with you, this instant.' And she made a push for the broomstick. They understood her kind intentions right well, having had large experience in that way, and did not wait for any further instructions; but made after their father with all speed.

Once in the shop, the old man felt safe. He had kept fast hold of Sam, and sitting down on his usual block, held him off at arms-length with one hand, while with the other, and the aid of an old handkerchief, he wiped down his bald head, and round, good-natured countenance.

'Oh dear! it was unlucky about that pitcher, I shall never hear the last on it. Tell me now, Sam, what is all this? It ain't true—is it? that old varmint ain't put your father in jail, has he? Don't cry now, but just tell me the whole on it.'

Sam told his story as well as he could, but it was hard work. He could command his feelings very well, when only thinking about it; but when compelled to speak his father's name, his lip trembled, and the words came out with great difficulty. Mr. Cutter had a very tender heart of his own, and Sam's story and appearance worked upon him more and more; so that he kept the old handkerchief wiping away long after the cider shower had dried off.

'And why didn't you come to me, and tell me about it? Ain't I known your father from a boy, and your mother too—bless her good soul; and do you think I would have let such doings as these gone on? That old varmint— is that the way he is goin' to serve folks? Send 'em to jail, to lay there with them dreadful rapscallions? Oh dear!—jist to think on it! And you was comin' here to tell me about it this morning; wasn't you, Sam?'

'No, sir, I was going home.'

'Going *home*? Why, where have you been?'

'I've been with father all night.'

'*You?* He didn't put you there *too*, did he? the old sinner!'

'Oh no, sir, but I went there to stay with him. I thought father would feel so bad.'

'You blessed child! Oh dear, what are we comin' to? And you ain't had no breakfast. Here, boys, go in and ask your mother to give this poor child a little something.'

'Oh no, sir, I thank you; I can't stay; for mother will feel bad if I don't go home; and I ain't hungry a bit.'

'Yes, you are hungry—you know you are—only you feel so bad, you can't eat. But I tell you, don't feel bad; you mustn't. Your father *shan't* stay there in that hole; I tell you he *shan't*! He shall see that he's got some friends. We ain't all dead and buried yet, I hope.'

'Oh, Mr. Cutter!' and Sam, as he said this, caught hold of him with both his hands; 'if you can do any thing to help to get my father out of that dreadful place, I will thank you all my life for it, and I will pay you every cent of the money, just as fast as I can earn it.' And he looked so earnestly into Mr. Cutter's face, and his bright black eyes sparkled with such an intensity of feeling, that the old man's heart must have been made of much *sterner* stuff than it was, not to have felt the appeal.

'There, go home—go home, Sam; don't say no more.' And he fairly pushed Sam away from him; and then he kept the old handkerchief going for some time, not saying a word to either of his boys, who stood looking after Sam, as he went away, and pitying him from their hearts.

'Now, boys, go and catch the old mare, and hitch her to the cart; and one of you must drive me to Billy Bloodgood's. Billy must help about this business, if I can only make him hear any thing; but it's like raising the dead.'

The boys went off with a good will, and soon had the old nag tackled to the cart, her harness being of a very simple kind, and easily adjusted.

Mr. Cutter had a way of his own about almost every thing, and it extended even to his manner of riding. Too bulky to climb very high places, he chose, generally, the lowest seat he could find; and the tail of the cart being more easily attained than any other part, and moreover, being easily resigned in case of accident, whenever Mr. Cutter rode, *that* was his place. He would sit pretty well in on the body, with his legs dangling behind, and one hand on each of the side-boards. To an observer, it appeared to be a very uneasy situation; for the mare had a peculiar gait, something between a rack and a pace, which not only imparted a quick up-and-down motion to the stern of the vehicle, but a lateral one likewise; so that from the time she started until she stopped, Mr. Cutter was not only carried onward, but every which way: there was no quiet for his body. He never complained of it, however, nor seemed to realize any thing out of the way.

Billy Bloodgood was just going out of his gate when Mr. Cutter drove up. Knowing that it would be useless trying to hold a parley with him out there, he told his son to drive close to the door; and taking Mr. Bloodgood by the arm, pulled him along, determined not to let him go, as he was well acquainted with his peculiarities. So, holding on with one hand to the side of the doorway, and with the other to his friend, he entered into Mrs. Bloodgood's sanctum—her kitchen, parlor, and bedroom. Puffing and blowing, he seized the first chair he could find, and bestowed himself upon it.

'Now, woman, do you make this husband of your's sit down, for I want to talk to him; and he'll be running off if you don't see to him.'

'Why, what's the matter, Uncle Sam? you're all in a heat, and out o' breath. Ain't nothing happened to home, has there?'

'Happened? Yes, there has something happened—there's always something or other happening in this world; but that ain't neither here nor there. I can get along with that. The wind will have its blow out, and then it will stop, and so must a woman's tongue. But I tell you, make that man of your's sit down, and do you come and listen to me, and then try to git it into his head, for it's beyond me to do it.'

Mrs. Bloodgood did as she was bidden; for she had great respect for Uncle Sam Cutter. She placed a seat close beside him for her husband, and another for herself, immediately before him.

'Do you know that our neighbor Oakum is in jail?'

'In jail! Oh dear, how you *do* talk!'

'It is true—I tell you so.'

'Then it's Grizzle—I know it is. First, he's 'ticed him to drink, and then he's come upon him. Ain't it so, Uncle Sam?'

'Yes; but hear me. Oakum ain't the man he was—don't you know that? He's a clean changed man. He's to work now every day, and brings home all his earnings every night to his family, and stays to home, and acts like a man; and his wife looks like a new critter, and things all round his house look so you wouldn't hardly know it. And now, jist as they are beginning to be a little like folks, and have things right end up, that old varmint takes the law on him, and puts him in the old cage, among them rapscallions there, jist as if he was a thief or a murderer.'

'Oh dear! jist to think on it.'

I've Been Thinking | 81

'And there's that blessed child of his been through all the rain and thunder and lightning, and went and stayed there all night, because he couldn't bear to leave his father alone—jist think of that; and that poor woman, all stark alone with them little children—jist think of that. Don't it make your heart ache?'

'Oh dear, dear! what are we comin' to?—jist think of it.'

Mrs. Bloodgood had her own peculiar ways, and was not always very particular what she said or did, when overcome by the little vexations of life; but she had a feeling heart, and would cry as hard as she would scold, if there was any thing calculated in an especial manner to bring tears; and now they were chasing each other down her cheeks faster than she could wipe them away.

'I don't wonder you cry about it. I tell you what: when that little fellow took hold on me this morning, and begged me to help his father, and looked up at me so pitiful, and said that he would thank me all his life, and pay every cent of the debt as fast as he could earn it—why I tell you, Sally, I cried like a child. And now, I tell you what it is; we mustn't leave that man lying there like a thief. I can't eat, nor sleep—I can't do it, Sally. I haven't got but little; but Billy must help—it's thirty dollars. I know it's a great deal for poor folks to raise, but it must be done, somehow—mustn't it, Sally?'

Mr. Bloodgood had been a silent spectator of the scene—he could not be said to be a listener. He saw that Mr. Cutter was very much engaged, and that his wife was quite to the other extremity of her feelings; but what was to pay he did not know. He kept looking first at one, and then at the other, for some explanation, taking large pinches of snuff all the time from a horn box which he held in his hand.

'Any body *dead*?'

Mrs. Bloodgood put her nose close to his ear, and hallooed—'No!'

Mr. Cutter pushed his chair back a little—the unearthly noise startled him.

'Why! do you have to holler at that rate? I should think you'd split your throat, or your nose, or something or other. I never heard such a noise.'

'Oh dear! I tell you, Uncle Sam, he gits wus and wus. I do candidly believe it's the snuff; he stops every thing up with it. His head ain't got no more sound to it than the harth stone.'

'Well, I don't know but it's the best thing he can do, if he's got to have sich noises as them made in it. I should want to stop every thing up too; and how upon airth you are ever going to tell him what I want, I don't see. Let me get a little ways off afore you begin; my head sings now like a dozen teakettles.'

With that the old man pushed his chair off against the opposite wall, while Mrs. Bloodgood undertook the task of explaining matters to her husband, and she accomplished it in much less time than could have been expected. Being nowise friendly to Mr. Grizzle, she handled his name in a very free way; and as her husband confided in her management, when she was through with the story, he looked at her very significantly—

'Shall I do it, Sally?'

'Yes, yes; do it—quick.'

So he looked at Mr. Cutter, smiled, and nodded, and then left the room.

'Well, well; all things was made for some use. I often wondered what your nose was made for, but I see now. But it will be the death of you, yet; you'll split something or other one of these days.'

'Why, no, Uncle Sam, you see I'm used to it; but it does make me weak at the stomach like, it takes sich a power of wind to keep it up any time so; a body can holler pretty loud two or three words, and not mind it. But I s'pose it's my lot, and I must be content with it.'

Mr. Bloodgood soon returned, making signs to Uncle Sam to draw up to the table. We must leave them to arrange matters, and carry out their kind designs as best they may be able.

How beautifully the water sparkled with the bright rays of the morning sun, and how clean the shore looked, and how fresh every thing appeared, as Sam drew near to his home; but how very sad his heart was, none but such as have suffered like him can well imagine. But sad as were his feelings, it did not hinder his attending to all the duties which devolved upon him. The net was examined, and the fish for the morning's meal brought up. The pigs were fed, and the boat looked after, and all things done as usual. It was a solitary meal, *that breakfast*, and soon ended. But the best fish were frying by the fire, and on the griddle was a fine thick bread-cake cooking, and a little basket was brought and placed on the table, and a clean cloth lay beside the basket; and Sam had his hat in his hand, and was leaning against the fireplace, watching his mother, as she went about the little room getting things together.

'May be he'd like a little pickle, mother. You know he eats it sometimes with his breakfast.' And the mother made no reply; but wiping away the tears that started as reference was made to him, she went directly to the cupboard and brought the pot of pickles; and then the fish was taken from the fire, and placed on a plate and put into the basket; and the cake was taken from the griddle, and broken in two and laid on the fish; and the pickle, and a little salt and pepper, and a knife and fork; and then the clean cloth was put over the whole, and Sam, taking the basket, walked straight out of the house, and his mother threw herself into the chair, and wept aloud.

As Sam ascended the little rise of ground behind their dwelling, he looked across to the house of his friends, Jim and Ned, to see if they were out—as he then felt a sight of them would be good. There they were, working away in their garden. Presently one of them stops and looks round, walks to the fence, jumps over, and is running toward Sam, with Jowler after him.

'There comes Ned. What shall I say to him?'

'Sam, how are you? ain't this a beautiful morning? What have you got in your basket? where are you going?'

'Oh, I am going a short distance.'

'If you are not going too far, I'll go with you. I'm tired of hoeing. Jim has had me up ever since daybreak, and I mean to rest a few minutes. But what is the matter, Sam? What makes you look so? You ain't well, are you?'

Sam did look pale, for he was alarmed at Ned's offer to accompany him.

'Oh, I think you had better not go with me: it is something of a walk, and as you have been at work so long, you will be tired.'

'No; I shan't be tired. But now, Sam Oakum, tell me what's the matter,' at the same time taking hold of him. 'There is something the matter, I know—you always tell me every thing.'

'I know I do, Ned; but somehow I do not like to tell you this. Haven't you heard any thing.'

'*Heard* any thing? No. Do you think we should not have been down to see you, if we had known that any thing was the matter? But *do* tell me, Sam.'

'Father is in jail.'

'That's Grizzle.'

'Yes.'

Ned stooped and caught up a good-sized stone, and aiming it at another still larger, sent it with such force that it was shivered into small fragments. He then looked at Sam a moment, with his hands in his pockets. He dared not speak, for his heart was aching so hard. It would have been a great relief to have cried; but Ned never cried—he could do any thing but that. He felt so much like it now though, as he kept his eyes on Sam, who looked so sad and pale, that all at once he turned short round, and walked away towards home; and Sam went on his way toward the jail.

The two miserable beings who had filled the old jail with their ravings through most of the night, were now asleep; and as Sam was admitted again into the miserable room, he cast his eye upon them as they lay in all their loathsomeness. Never before had he seen human nature in such an appalling form—their garments filthy, and torn into shreds; their hair, long and matted, lay over their faces and among the straw which formed their bed; their faces bloated, bruised, and bloody. He shrunk back involuntarily. He cast his eye to the further end of the room, and it met the smile of his father. He hurried past these dreadful objects, and placed his basket beside his pale and sorrow-stricken parent. Sam started, when he saw how *very* pale he looked, and how great a change his countenance had undergone since he last saw the daylight shine upon it. He took off the cloth which covered the basket, and upon that he placed the good breakfast his mother had prepared; and then he saw his father put his hands together, and that his eyes were closed, and his lips moved. He had never known him to do so before. Could it be that he was praying for a blessing, ere he tasted this token of love from earthly dear ones and heaven's bounteous King? Oh, Sam! how little can you realize the ordeal that parent has passed since the last setting sun. But the agony that racked his spirit has purified it also; and it has turned, 'trembling, hoping,' to its God. When years have passed, and you shall stand by his dying bed, and walk in the church-yard where rises the little mound of earth over the resting-place of his body, you will think of this night, and you will bless God for his goodness to you and your's.

'It is very good, Sam; and it is very kind in you all to think of me so.'

'Oh, father, don't say so; it makes me feel so bad.'

'To think how much trouble I have been to my family.'

Sam could stand it no longer, but wept aloud.

'I don't wish to make you feel bad, Sam; but all your kind feelings, and all your mother's kind feelings, make me think how wrong I have acted, and wonder how anybody can care for me.'

'But they do care for you—everybody cares for you. Uncle Sam Cutter says you shan't stay here—*that* you shan't.'

'Did he say so? Well, I thank him for his kind feelings; and I hope, if the Lord please, I may get my liberty soon, that I may be able to work and earn an honest living, and pay my debts. But, Sam, this place ain't so bad, gloomy as it looks. A bad life and a guilty conscience are harder things to get along with than this jail. I have spent worse hours, looking at you and your mother, and the little ones, with a fire burning in my bosom, than I spent here last night. I never knew before that there could be such things.'

'What things, father?'

'Why, Sam, that there could be such peace within, when all about me was so horrible. But I believe God has done it—and all for my good. He does everything for good.'

Sam was utterly confounded at hearing such words from his father; but he rejoiced to hear them. He sat as long as he thought consistent with duties at home, and was preparing to return, when their attention was arrested by a bustle below stairs, and a loud puffing and blowing of some one ascending to the room.

'What steps you've got here, Mr. Tice!—so high, I can hardly get my old carcass up. Oh, dear, dear, dear; what a world this is!'

The heavy bolt was drawn; and as the door, creaking on its hinges, slowly opened, the portly form of Mr. Samuel Cutter appeared, filling the open space, and looking with a wild stare into and around the room.

'You can go clean in, Mr. Cutter, an you like to; and I'll shut the door, and you may stay as long as you like.'

'You will, hey? No, no, Mr. Tice, thank you, I'll do well enough here;' at the same time putting his hand out, and holding fast to the door. 'None of your shutting up; it's bad enough to look at, without your turning the old lock on a body. *Of all sights!*—are these men dead?'

'Oh it ain't nothin', Mr. Cutter; only they've been a little lively last night, and they're a sleepin' it out, I guess, this mornin'.'

'You don't call them human critters, laying there in that shape, Mr. Tice, do you?'

'Yes, they *be*, only their hair is got tangled a little. I should a'most think they'd been a fightin', by their looks—they *do* look bad, that's a fact.'

More noises were now heard below, and there was the trampling of horses at the door, and soon a lively treading up the stairs.

'What does this mean, Mr. Tice? the jail door open, and people going in and out. Are the prisoners gone?' And Mr. Richard Tucker bustled up into the room. He was followed by Billy Bloodgood, and Uncle Sam Cutter's two boys. Mr. Richard seeing the doorway barricaded by a pretty large body, made no apology for hastily pushing through, and fairly taking the old gentleman quite into the room. He was about to shut the door when his arm was seized, and held by a grip as effectual as though an iron vice had embraced it.

'Stop, stop, man; none of your shutting up, with my carcass in such a den as this. And besides, you came here now to let folks out; so the sooner you set about it, the better.'

Mr. Richard was full of wrath, but he knew whom he had to deal with; and seeing likewise that Billy Bloodgood was looking at him very earnestly, and pointing towards Mr. Oakum at the other end of the room, he had no alternative; so called aloud in a very quick manner,

'Mr. Oakum, you are at liberty, you are released; you can go.'

Sam jumped up, and caught hold of his father:

'Oh, father! come, come, father, quick!' And he fairly pulled his father along; who, amazed at the suddenness of his delivery, and weak with the agitation his mind had endured, almost staggered as he followed Sam to the door.

'Come along, man, come along; don't stay a minute longer.' And old Mr. Cutter hobbled out, partly leaning on Mr. Oakum, and partly pulling him down the stairs, and out of doors.

To describe all Mr. Oakum's feelings, when he found himself at liberty, and learned that a full settlement of his account had been made, and that it had dwindled down, under the scrutinizing eye of Billy Bloodgood, to the sum of twenty dollars, and that he could pay this amount back at his own convenience; or to describe the joy which danced in the heart of Sam when he saw his father once out of that place, and Uncle Sam Cutter shaking him with both hands; and Mr. Bloodgood nodding his head, and smiling, and running round—it would be vain to attempt.

It was a bright spot in Sam's life, and it was a good day for more hearts than one; for it was the means of winning into the little circle of working boys the two sons of old Mr. Cutter: they became diligent from that day forward, and were constant in aiding their father, either in the garden, the shop, or the field.

CHAPTER VII

The establishment of Mr. Cross, up in the barrens, had not much to boast of as to its architecture or location. It consisted of a long, low building, formed of logs, but covered with boards, and the roof shingled. Attached to it were several buildings, constructed entirely of logs, but well shingled roofs were over the whole of them, and they were otherwise finished, so as to impress the beholder with the idea that the owner was in very different circumstances from those who occupied such buildings for many miles circuit. In front of this main house ran a piazza, its full length; while upon a tall pine tree, nearly opposite the centre of the premises, hung a rude sign, with the owner's name, D. Cross, in large letters on the bottom. The inside of the building presented a mongrel appearance of store and tavern; a little of both, and not much of either. There was a counter, and small scales upon it; with decanters, and a few dirty tumblers at one end. Barrels were standing in different parts of the room. There were one or two plain board tables, and a few benches, besides two chairs with backs, and several without. Three large casks were placed together against one side of the wall, and the faucets in them clearly told for what purpose they were used. Behind the counter ran some long shelves, upon which lay jumbled together a little iron ware, a little crockery, and very limited assortment of dry goods.

The location was not an unpleasant one for those who admire the seclusion of a forest; for lofty pines towered on all sides of it, except to the north, where a clearing having been made, probably when the house was erected, a thick growth of scrub pines had come forward, and presented the appearance of a swamp.

There was, however, somewhat of a clear space immediately around the building, formed by the meeting of three or four roads, running off into different directions, and pointing out this spot to be, as it really was, the centre of attraction and influence to all that region.

The owner of this domain, Mr. David Cross, had become, from causes which have been explained in a previous chapter, a person of some consideration; he owned quite a number of acres of heavily timbered land, connectively with his house; and by various means had managed to bring the whole population, at least for some miles circuit, into a state of dependence upon himself. He was not gifted by nature with a very commanding form, being rather under than over the medium height. This deficiency, however, he did all he could to remedy, by holding himself very erect; and as he was a little inclined to be fleshy, it sometimes even appeared that he leaned backwards in his efforts to make the most of himself.

The only member of Mr. Cross's family in any wise related to him, was his son David; a young man of some activity in the way of business. But having been tutored entirely by his father, it may be supposed he had not the most correct notions in matters of morality; although, as yet, no very flagrant charges had been laid up against him in the minds of those who dealt there; for the very good reason, that the elder Mr. Cross chose to keep things in his own hand, and bear all responsibility. As to the mother of David, little was known respecting her—it was supposed she had died when her child was an infant, for he had no remembrance of her.

David was not unpopular with the inhabitants of the barrens. Being of a lively turn, and of careless, open manners, they felt a freedom in his presence, which was quite in contrast with the servile subjection they ever had to realize when dealing with his father.

As the tavern of Mr. Cross was the only place where the laborers he employed could find a lodging place during the season of the year when their services were required—the distance from their own homes being often too great to allow of return until the close of the week—it was seldom that the place was without sojourners; and too many of them had but a scanty allowance for their families, after their six days' toil.

It was a very warm day among the pines; no breeze abroad, and the air from the heated sand almost suffocating. Mr. Cross was behind his counter, busily employed in stirring the toddy stick, and waiting upon those who were calling for their favourite mixture; some were leaning over the counter, some resting on the benches, and not a few were lying at full length upon the piazza, and in the shade of the pine, scanty as it was, which served for the sign-post of the tavern, when the rumbling of a carriage was heard, and the unusual sound attracted the notice of all present. Those who were prostrate, arose at once, and looked forth through the different openings; and those who were in the act of drinking, suspended operations, and held their glasses on the counter, casting glances of inquiry at Mr. Cross and at each other.

'It's Dave, I suppose,' said Mr. Cross; 'although I didn't think he'd be along this hour yet.'

'That aint Dave,' replied one of the men; 'for it comes very slow, and sounds heavy: I can tell Dave's buggy a mile off, by its rattle.'

Mr. Cross, apparently satisfied that there was truth in the remark, walked slowly from behind the counter, and approaching the door, those who were standing there hastily made way, and left the post of observation to him alone; they collecting in groups on the outside. Convinced that it was not his son's carriage that approached, the little man stood with his hands in his pockets, his person straightened up, and his eye intently fixed on the road upon which the heavy vehicle was rumbling, and glimpses of which could be seen through occasional small openings in the pines.

Soon the cleared space before the tavern was gained, and every eye turned instinctively towards Cross, as though asking an explanation from his countenance. The ruddy, or rather purple hue which it usually bore, immediately assumed a higher color; his hands were withdrawn from their resting-places, his head uncovered, and bustling through the crowd which surrounded his door, he was bowing, and smiling, and doing his best to play the agreeable, the moment the superb vehicle drew up before his sign-post.

The travellers were indeed persons of no small consideration, if an opinion could be formed from their equipage. The carriage was large and airy, hanging low and gracefully upon long sweeping springs; of a dark olive color, which contrasted finely with the light drab linings of the inside. The horses were two noble blacks, caparisoned in brass mounted harness, and driven by a negro somewhat advanced in life, and perched upon a heavy luxurious cushion. He was neatly dressed, in the fashion of days that were passing away, and was very much absorbed in the management of his team; which, although covered with lather and dust, were evidently full of mettle, and not at all fagged by their travel. Within sat a gentleman and lady, youthful in appearance, with two children; the eldest not over six years of age.

Mr. Cross did not wait for the footman to alight, but advancing to the door.

'Mr. Rutherford, your servant, sir,' opened it, and threw down the steps, before the gentleman had time to inform him that he was not intending to leave the carriage.

'Your lady will surely want to rest a little; our accommodations, indeed, are not much to boast of, but poor as they are, we shall be proud to have you use them.'

The lady bowed to Mr. Cross, acknowledging that she felt obliged for his offer.

'You must excuse us at present, Mr. Cross; we have some miles farther to ride, and if you will show the footman where to procure a little water for our horses, I will be much obliged to you.'

'Certainly, certainly; here, men, water, water; don't you hear? some water for these horses.' There was a great rush among those standing near to accomplish the request; but whether to obey Mr. Cross, or to oblige the traveller, may be questioned; for they had heard his name, and therefore knew that a man of more importance than Mr. Cross was present.

But as there were reasons why the last-named gentleman should, if possible, have an interview with his visitor, he felt that an effort must be made to obtain one.

'If Mr. Rutherford could favor me by stepping aside, but for a moment, it will not detain—'

'It would be scarcely worth while, Mr. Cross. I presume I know what you wish to converse about; and I am not just now prepared to give you an answer.'

'Ay—well, sir—I won't presume to dictate, sir; only you know we usually make our contracts about this time, so that we may make some calculations for hands, etc.'

'That's true, sir; but to be plain, Mr. Cross, I am not sure that I shall not make some other arrangement, at least, so far as my interest goes in these barrens. I do not feel satisfied with our present plan—we pay great wages, you must be aware.'

'Stand back, men, stand back; don't you know civility enough not to be crowding the gentleman?' Mr. Cross had his own reasons for not wishing too many listeners; for some ideas might possibly be conveyed to them not consonant with his interest.

'Our people are rough, as you see, madam,' addressing the lady, 'and you'll pardon their ill manners.'

'No pardon at all necessary, Mr. Cross; these good people are not the least in our way.' This the lady said in a voice sufficiently loud to be heard by all present; and then, with a pleasant smile cast upon the group, she asked,

'Will one of you be kind enough to bring me a glass of water for my little girl?'

Not one, but several glasses were, in an instant almost, at the carriage door. The lady took them all; and as they were returned to the brawny hands held out to receive them, dropped a piece of silver in each.

'God bless you, lady!' responded at once each of the lucky attendants, and a smile of pleasure lighted up all the dark countenances of the half savage-looking beings, who were gazing in wonder at the equipage and its inmates.

Mr. Cross was compelled to be a silent spectator of this little scene; but the dark scowl which passed across his features told plainly that it was not quite agreeable to him.

'Am I in the direct road to Widow Brown's?' inquired Mr. Rutherford, casting a glance at the little man, and then around upon those present, as though it was a matter of no consequence from whom he received the answer. It came readily from many of the bystanders; the voice of Mr. Cross being lost in their louder exclamations; even if he answered at all, which is doubtful.

'Yes, sir—yes, sir; its about six miles from here; but you must turn to the right hand when you get to the edge of the great swamp.'

'Thank you, thank you all; and here is a trifle for you, my friend,' singling out the one who had procured the water for the horses, and tossing him a silver dollar.

'God bless you, sir—you're a gentleman.'

'Good day, Mr. Cross.' He bowed respectfully to the host, and to all the admiring group, and the heavy carriage rolled on its way.

Mr. Cross walked back into his stronghold with a very dissatisfied air, while the men gathered outside in little knots, discussing the strangeness of the whole scene, and wondering what ailed the old man, 'he seemed so out of sorts.' Scarcely had the carriage disappeared, when a rattling was heard, and the rapid and heavy stamping of horses' feet, and David Cross tore up to the door, among the groups of foresters, scattering them to either side, with as little consideration as though they had been so many sheep. Curses deep arose in their hearts, but came not forth at their lips.

'Here, Jo, you put Bony in the stable, and rub him down—won't you?'

'Yes, sir,' was the ready answer. But the man addressed shook his head so significantly, and jerked the horse so rudely, as he turned him round, that if Mr. David, Junior, could have seen it, he would have understood that his exploit in driving was not much relished by others, if very agreeable to himself.

The elder Mr. Cross immediately led his son into a private room adjoining the store, and with much anxiety in his countenance waited for the result of the errand upon which he had been sent.

'Foster says, he has closed the bargain with old Ross; he is to give you a quit-claim deed for all his right and title to the property in the barrens, for the sum you named.'

'That's good—did he say anything further?'

'He said something about my telling you that he was on the look out; that he would hunt like a cat for a mouse; but the old fool was afraid to tell me what he meant.'

'Michael Foster is no fool; but, I suppose, he thinks it best to be mum. Yet do you know Rutherford has been here?'

'No: has he?'

'Yes; and he refuses to make any contract this year; and I could see, by his management with the men, what he's at: but he'll miss it. He'll have to stoop his head yet, high as he holds it now.'

David made no reply; but, whistling a lively tune, walked away, and mingled with the men, who were again gathering around the counter.

The travellers experienced no difficulty in finding their way, and soon drew up before the humble residence of the widow.

'It looks better, my dear Mary, than I expected,' said Mr. Rutherford, as he alighted from the carriage. He was about to enter the dwelling, when Mrs. Brown appeared at the door. She was neatly dressed for one living in so poor a place—that is, her plain dark calico was put on with care, and she wore shoes and stockings—articles not often seen in the barrens. She wore no cap, for her light brown hair was not at all changed by age, and her countenance was as fresh and fair, almost, as at twenty-one. She seemed surprised for an instant—

'Have you forgotten me, Aunt Mary?'

'This ain't Mr. George Rutherford?'

'Yes, it is—once your little Georgie.'

'Oh, dear! how glad I am to see you;' and the tears started to her eyes. 'And that is Mrs. Rutherford, and these are your dear little children. How they *do* look *just* as you used to look.'

'We are all well acquainted with you, Mrs. Brown; for my husband is continually talking about you.'

'Oh, dear! I never thought to see any of you again; for I did not suppose you would ever get so far out of the world as to come here. I cannot ask you to go into my poor house; but there are some seats under the trees, where your lady might sit down, and—'

'Oh, Mrs. Brown, you don't think that your Georgie, as you used to call him, has got a wife who would not go into a house many times worse than yours, to see one he thinks so much of; so, with your leave, we will all go in, for we have come on purpose to see you.'

'I am very happy, if he has got a lady who knows his worth.'

'Take care, Mrs. Brown, what you say; I am afraid you did a little towards spoiling him when a boy: he is not out of danger yet.'

The family now passed into the cottage, while the widow and old Cæsar had a few kind salutations to make, 'ere she followed and took her seat among them.

Many were the questions asked about the old homestead, for twelve years had passed by since she was last there. Deaths, births, marriages, changes of circumstances, and relations, how they had accumulated during that period! and how often the tears would start, and the lip tremble, as the recital went on! Her own story was but a short one; for many things she was obliged to pass over, or touch lightly upon.

'But where is the little girl you had with you, when last at my father's? she must be almost grown up now.'

'Oh, no; she is but a little girl still; she is only sixteen now; but she is very obedient and kind-hearted.'

'Just like her mother.'

'Oh, I don't know as to that, ma'am; but she is an obedient child, and a great comfort to me—and the best of all is, I hope she is a Christian.'

'That is good,' exclaimed Mr. and Mrs. Rutherford, at the same time.

'Ah—then you both love good things yourselves; don't you?'

'We hope we do.'

'The Lord be praised for his mercies. It seems to me always a great thing for the rich to be pious—they can do so much good.'

'Yes, if they have a heart to do good. Is your daughter at home, Mrs. Brown?'

'No, ma'am; but she will be here soon. She has gone to visit a neighbour a little south of us, among the farmers. We have but a poor neighbourhood around us; and you know young people want some one of their own age to be with and talk to.'

'Why is it, Mrs. Brown, that the people in the barrens are so poor, and apparently so degraded?—they get work enough, and are well paid for it.

My husband is very anxious about the matter, and wishes to remedy it if he can.'

'Oh, well, ma'am; I don't know that I have got the right idea of things; but it has appeared to me these many years that there must be wrong management. Our men work hard, but are only able barely to live, as you see; and for so many people to be all poor together, is a great evil.'

'Do you think, Mrs. Brown, that they get their pay?'

'I think they do, ma'am, in a certain way. Mr. Cross settles with them every month, and keeps things square; but you know, ma'am, when a man gets so much power into his hands as Mr. Cross has, he may be tempted to do wrong because no one can bring him to account for it. The men are obliged to take the wages he sees fit to allow them, as there is no one in this region to give them employment.'

'And charges them what he pleases for the goods they must purchase?'

'It is pretty much so, ma'am. They must have the necessaries of life you know, ma'am; and although they purchase only such things as their families absolutely need, yet it is so managed, that they are brought a little in debt at each settlement. Some think that he charges almost double what the goods cost him; but, situated as they are, no one dares complain, and so they go on from year to year.'

'This is slavery I think, Mary, with a vengeance,' said Mr. Rutherford, looking at his wife.

'It is just as we expected, my dear.'

'Well, I hope, Mr. Rutherford, that I have not done injustice to Mr. Cross. He has been good to me and mine. Perhaps, after all, the people think hard of him without sufficient cause.'

'You have only confirmed my suspicions of the state of things here. You know that I own a large part of these barrens; and, therefore, it is my duty to look into matters, and not suffer evils to exist, if I can remedy them.'

Mr. Rutherford then proceeded to touch upon matters more immediately relating to the widow's personal interests, and which, in fact, had been one of the objects of his visit. It was in reference to her removal from this region, so destitute of privileges, to her former home, beneath his own roof, where her children could be usefully employed, and herself made comfortable.

It was some time before she could make any reply to this generous offer.

'You must not hesitate, Mrs. Brown, to accept this offer; for I assure you, that I heartily join with my husband in it.'

'Oh, I thank you, ma'am; I believe you are sincere, and are acting from the kindest motives, and perhaps you will think it strange that I should hesitate a moment about accepting it.'

Just then, the conversation was interrupted by the entrance of Hettie. Her appearance surprised Mr. and Mrs. Rutherford—the fine glow on her cheek, the raven blackness of her hair and eyes, the pleasant smile that immediately lighted up her countenance, the simple curtsey that she dropped, all so pretty and so natural—they had not expected to meet so lovely a flower in such a waste; and the widow must not be blamed if she indulged some little pride as she presented her to their friend. Hettie was her bright star; hope always rose when she appeared. An increasing interest was excited in the minds of Mr. and Mrs. Rutherford, and the subject of her removal again introduced.

'You cannot tell,' replied the widow, 'how much I feel the kindness of your offer; and were only the interest of myself and Hettie to be consulted, I should not long hesitate. But, oh! Mrs. Rutherford, you cannot yet tell how a mother feels towards a wayward son. William is not just what I could wish he was, but he still clings to me. I know he will not be willing to leave these parts, unpromising as they are: for me to separate from him, and allow him to go without restraint in the midst of so many temptations, would be like giving him up to ruin; and I cannot but hope he will one day be different from what he now is; the Lord, you know, has many ways to bring back the wanderer.'

Her friends could urge no further the whole of their request, but ventured to say—

'Will you not, Mrs. Brown, let us have Hettie? We will do for her as well as we can.'

This proposal was one that she felt it her duty to accept, however trying to be separated from one she loved so dearly.

After a short consultation with her daughter it was decided that she should accompany them. Wishing to give them an opportunity to make some little preparation, Mr. Rutherford concluded to drive into the open country, which lay a little to the south of the widow's cottage—the scene where our story commenced.

It was with an united exclamation that they first met the view which opened to them, as they emerged from the pines.

'Ah, how beautiful!'

It was, indeed, a striking contrast to the region through which they had been travelling.

The country was little varied by hill and dale, and in no wise improved by the hand of man: for the houses which could be seen were but unsightly buildings, and all the enclosures of the rudest kind; yet common-place as was the face of the land, in connection with the extensive water view, there was much to justify the exclamation—it was a panorama delightful to those who had been so long riding amid the dark monotony of a pine-forest.

On either side of the strip of country which lay immediately before them, and around the whole view in front, was water: first a clear river stealing down on the right, and then another on the left, each hastening to mingle their waters in the beautiful bay, ere they rolled to the ocean; in the distance, a long line of land stretching towards the east, as far as the eye could reach, encircling an immense bay, and losing itself where sky, and earth, and water are mingled in one; while beautifully breaking the wild expanse of water, a strip of land ran out into the bay, over whose crest could be seen, in the distance, the white sail winging its way to the broad ocean.

Even old Cæsar felt the animating influence of the scenery; and urging on his horses by a cheering word, the carriage rolled along as fast as was becoming such a stately concern.

'Whoa-a, whoa-up—whoa there.'

'Oh, Cæsar! what's the matter?'

There was, at the same time, a fearful leaning to one side.

'Nuttin', missus; only de wheel cum off.'

It was, to be sure, nothing else; but that of itself was sufficient to prevent any farther progress for the time being. Cæsar and his master were soon down; the horses detached from the carriage, and the wheel picked up and brought to its place.

''Tis all right, Massa George, only de linch-pin is gone; may be me find um.'

And very diligent was the search for the lost pin, but to no purpose; the prospect, indeed, was not the most agreeable; for a long road must be retraced ere home could be reached.

A young man from an adjoining field, seeing their dilemma, hastened to offer his aid. Very soon rails were procured, and by means of them the heavy coach was raised, and the recusant wheel replaced; and then the young man who showed much readiness to assist, as well as ingenuity, procuring a bit of hard wood, began whittling it into the shape of a pin.

'Mister, what a' yo goin' to do wid dat 'tick?'

'I'm making a pin for you, daddy.'

'My golly! you no t'ink dat hold dem big wheel on. No blacksmith nowhere here?'

'Yes; there is one not far off; but you want something to keep your wheel on until you can get the carriage there.'

'Why me no bring him here when he makes de pin?'

'Why, you see, daddy, he will want the measure of the hole to make it by; and the old man does not like to walk very much, as he is fat and clumsy. It will be as much as we can do to get him to make the pin at all; he don't like to work such hot weather.'

'Ay, ay. Well, den; you right, bubby.'

With that Cæsar prepared to attach the horses to the carriage, while the family walked on towards the little low building with a high chimney, which was pointed out to them.

As the carriage drove up, a very fleshy person was seen waddling towards the door, and putting one arm out on each side, supported himself in the doorway. He looked at the coach, and the horses, and the driver, alternately, in great astonishment. He saw the old black smile, but took no notice of it; and fixed his eye at length on the long sweeping braces, as though wondering where such powerful springs were made.

'Massa Cutter forget me.' The old man cast his eye up.

'Massa Cutter no 'member Cæsar?'

'Cæsar—Cæsar—what, not Cæsar Rutherford? No—yes—so it is— why, you old rascal, how do you do? Give us your fist. I thought, when you showed your teeth at me, that I'd seen you before. But you grow old, man—your head is all getting white.'

'Ha, ha, ha; Massa Cutter growin' old, too, and big! My! what a sight! Good livin' I 'tink here, Massa Cutter.'

'Good living—there's no living at all—it's too hot to live; nothing but salamanders could stand it. But what's brought you here?'

'Oh, you see, Massa Cutter, me lose de linch-pin; so dis young gemman tell me de blacksmith close by; but I no 'spect to see Massa Cutter—ha, ha, ha!'

'And you want me to make a new one, do you?'

'If you please.'

'Here, Bill Andrews, since you have been so helpful to these folks, and helped them here, you may just come and help me; so take hold of them 'tarnal old bellows, and blow for your life.'

'That I will, Uncle Sam.'

The old man, although reluctant to move about much, made expeditious work with his hammer; the pin was soon made and fitted to its place, and the carriage ready for another start. Before this, however, Mr. Rutherford had reached the shop, having left Mrs. Rutherford and the children to enjoy a fine shade at a little distance. As Mr. Cutter had been acquainted with his father, it afforded the former an opportunity of making many inquiries about events long transpired, some of which, being connected with Mr. Cutter's removal to his present house, occasioned, on his part, very long and heavy sighs, and serious shakes of the head. At length he could hold in no longer.

'Oh, dear, oh, dear! it makes me feel bad all over to hear you talk about them places and things;—to think what an old fool I've been to come to such a place as this.'

'It does not look like a very thriving place, Mr. Cutter.'

'Thriving! there's nothing thrives here but rum and deviltry. *Thriving!*—I tell you what, the *old 'un* thrives here, no one else, and a great haul he'll have—he's fixing for it. No schools, no meetin'-houses, and no nothing that's good;—the men most all drunk and lazy, and the boys going to the d——l, if I must say so, asking your pardon, as fast as they can.'

'This is a poor account of your place, Mr. Cutter. What do you suppose has caused such a state of things?'

'It is beyond me to say, sir; there seems to be a kind of curse on the place; and it is my candid opinion, if something ain't done here soon—some preaching, or something else of that sort—we're a gone case;—even a dumb Quaker would be better than nothing. He might walk round in his square coat, and frighten the old 'un a little.'

Mr. Rutherford could not restrain a smile at the earnestness of the old man, and the singularity of his idea.

'From your description, Mr. Cutter, you are not much better off here than our people in the barrens.'

'Not much to boast on, I tell you, sir. Only they can't raise nothing, and must depend upon old Cross for work to buy their bread with, and he charges them just what he pleases; and if they should grumble, or ask for their money to spend elsewhere, he would turn them off entirely, and then they might live on huckle berries and pine knots.'

'They are badly off, I believe, sir; but I hope to be able to make some change in things there. The people are, no doubt, imposed upon, and I shall not allow it to be so if I can help it.'

'Bless your young heart for saying so; but you must look out for Cross; he's a precious villain—I *tell* you.'

'I believe he is no better than he should be; but I shall try to manage it, so as not to injure the poor folks, at any rate.'

'Well, I'm glad on it, for there are some clever people among them. There's the widow Brown; why you must know her? she used to live in your father's family.'

'Oh, yes, I know her well, Mr. Cutter; and part of my errand down was to see her. Her daughter, I hope, will go home with me to live.'

'What! Hettie! Hettie ain't going away—and yet she ought to go out of such a hole as this. She is too pretty and too good to be round here. What's the matter, Bill? Where's the use of keeping the old bellows creaking, when there's no iron in the fire?'

'Oh, I didn't think. You are done, ain't you?'

'Yes, I hope so. I've pounded myself all in a heat. But what makes you look so pale, man?'

'Oh, nothing; I ain't pale, am I?'

'Yes, you are pale—go sit down, man.'

'No; I thank you, Uncle Sam. I believe I will go home now, if I can be of no more use to the gentleman.'

Mr. Rutherford, seeing him about to depart, stepped up, and cordially thanked him for his kind and efficient services; and taking out his purse, was about to remunerate him handsomely for his trouble.

'Oh, no, sir, nothing; I thank you.'

'But it has taken your time, and you have been of great service to me; allow me to make you some compensation—thanks from a stranger are not worth much.'

'They are worth a good deal to *me*, sir, since I have found out who you are.'

'Why, what do you know of me?'

'My father removed from your place, sir; and I have often heard him speak of your folks, how kind they were to him; perhaps you may remember him, Zechariah Andrews?'

'Remember him? certainly I do; and are you his son? Well, this is strange indeed:' at the same time taking Bill's hand and giving it a hearty shake. Many inquiries were made and answered; and the interview closed by an invitation on the part of Mr. Rutherford, that whenever he might need a friend he would call upon him.

'And now, Mr. Cutter, good by,' giving the old man his hand; 'I hope you may live to see things look brighter than they now do.

'I hope so, sir; but I tell you there is but little chance of it. The old fellow has danced here so long, it will be hard getting him off the ground—preachin' might do it. But I want to say one thing to you—look out for Cross; he ain't too good in my opinion for any thing—he's a dangerous man, depend on it. But I won't keep you waiting. God bless you, and keep you out of harm's way.'

CHAPTER VIII

I suppose my readers are about tired with following our heroes on their little voyages; but as this is to be the last they will make in the old skiff, and as it is connected with some interesting circumstances regarding our friend Sam, we must go with them once again.

It was but a short period after the scene of trial through which Sam and his family were called to pass. A pleasant sail they had made to the fort that morning; their stock of goods had been disposed of, their empty baskets stowed away, and they were just on the point of casting off for their return, when Peter appeared, coming through the gate of the castle. As soon as he passed the sentinel, he hobbled along towards them as fast as crutches would let him.

'Hulloa; 'vast, there, my hearties.'

The boys readily stopped, and waited his approach.

'Here, you Sam, jist come here, follow me.'

Sam was utterly at a loss as to what was to pay now; but as Peter turned short about, and was making his way back again, as though he expected of course his summons to be obeyed, Sam had no alternative but to jump ashore and hasten after him, and he had much ado to get up with the old man before he entered the gate. Peter hobbled along through the hall at the entrance, then turned to the right, and, by a narrow door, entered a dark passage, saying nothing all the while, only turning his head back occasionally to see that Sam was following; then up a broad stairs, into a long gallery studded with doors. Into one of these Peter entered, and, waiting until Sam passed in, shut it.

'Now, my hearty, see what I've got for you. Take off them old duds o' your'n, jist as fast as you can.' Sam being somewhat in amaze, was looking at the queer little room, with the hammock hung up at one side of it, wondering how Peter ever contrived to stow himself away in it; in the meantime Peter was busy untying a large bundle, and taking out sundry articles.

'Here, you sonny, jist put these on, and see how they'll fit;' holding up at the same time a pair of blue broadcloth pantaloons. 'But what are you about? why don't you doff your jacket and trousers? You ain't a goin to put these on over, are you?'

'Oh, no, sir: but you don't mean to have me put on such fine things as these?'

'And why not? didn't my lady git 'em 'spressly for you? and didn't she take me along with her, purpose to pick out a true sailor's rig? So off with the old riggin', it's stood long enough.'

'Did *she* get them? Oh, she is very good. I am sure I don't deserve—'

'*Don't deserve!* Yes, you do *deserve*; so down with your dumbfounded perverseness, for once, and do as you are bid.'

Sam was indeed confounded, but he could not do otherwise than put them on. A better fit could not have been, and the suit was complete throughout. Blue roundabout, and trousers to match, of good broadcloth, finer than anything Sam had ever felt of before. Suspenders of blue and white, all finely figured; blue check shirt, with a large flowing collar, around the edge of which and down the bosom ran an ornament of white. Vest there was none, as Peter said 'it was of no mortal use.'

Never was a father prouder of a son, than was Peter, when the whole rig was on. He turned Sam round to all points of the compass; examined him, as he said, ''fore and aft.' The shoes were the only articles Peter did not fancy.

'Pumps is the only things fit to go on a sailor's foot, but my lady reasoned me out of it. They're good taut under-strappers, no doubt, and they'll do you a deal of service; but they spoil the looks, and there ain't no shuffle in 'em. But howsomever, perhaps as you're along shore now, they'll do you a good turn. But, do you hear? never put your foot on a ship's deck in such clumpers as them.'

'Oh dear! how good they are to me.'

'Good? to be sure they're good. But mind, my hearty, *there's One above'* — and Peter pointed his finger upward, as he said this—'who has made the wind shift round for you so fair and square; mind *that*, and don't think it's all luck that's made such big folks kind to you. You're but a youngster now, and can't be 'spected to understand how all these things are brought about; but an old sailor like me, that has sailed in all weathers, has seen things that will make a man feel that there is *One* at the helm can steer for him when he can't do nothing for himself.'

Sam looked at the old man with fixed attention, and drank in every word, his eyes sparkling with the deep emotion they aroused within him.

He thought Peter no longer a poor maimed sailor, but some being from a better world, who had put on for a time a rough and forbidding garb.

'And now, my hearty, see here.' And Peter began to pull out sundry other articles of dress.

'That there rig you've got on ain't for storms, nor everyday sarvice; a man wants something tight and tidy for Sundays, and sich like—but here's your real stuff to brave all weathers in. This will stand you for rough and tumble and all sorts of work. These trousers is the regular duck; jist feel 'em, Sam. They're stiff like, I know, but you'll soon make 'em limber; and this here jacket is the jinivine blue nanking; there's no tear about it that I'll warrant you.'

Sam had given up in amazement at the multitude of good things showered upon him. He knew not whether to laugh or cry—he did a little of both—it was so good, so far above any thing he had been thinking of; the feeling which came over him, and which we all, in our youthful days, have experienced when clad in a new suit, was so *very new* to him, that he was oppressed by it; and as Peter held up the duck trousers and the blue nankeen coat, he proceeded to unrobe himself, thinking he was required to try them on too.

'Now, what is the lad about?—Hands off; let alone. Ain't you going right down to show my lady what a spanking fit it is? So we'll jist bundle these up with the old duds, and you'll take 'em along—you hear? and let 'em lay in the boat till you git home.'

Sam would have made some objections, if he dared; but Peter took things in his own hands, and seemed to feel that, for once, at least, he must be minded: so rolling the whole together, and tying them in a very knowing manner,

'Now come along, my hearty,' he stumped it out of the room, and through the gallery, and down the stairs, and laying the bundle in the hall, crossed to the apartment where Sam had formerly been introduced to the presence of Mrs. Morris; and before he had time to reflect or make opposition, Peter was knocking at the door.

A very pleasant smile and exclamation of delight, on the part of Mrs. Morris, greeted Sam as he entered.

'Why, Peter!—who would have thought they could have fitted so well; and how very apropos they look. A sailor boy, he is now—is he not, Peter?'

'All but the shoes, please you, madam.' And Peter, not having his hat on, touched his queue.

'Oh, well; I think master Sam will be much pleased with the shoes, especially as he is on shore now. But let him come here—give me the neckerchief, Susie.'

Susie walked to the table, and brought the little parcel and placed it in her mother's hand.

'Here is a present from Susie; she has hemmed it herself, and I suppose ought to honor you by tying it on; but as she is a little bashful about it, I must do it for her.'

Sam was too much confounded to make any opposition; but his flushed countenance told how he felt.

'I suppose I cannot put it on after true sailor fashion, but I believe it must have a single tie, and hang loose, in this style. Will that do, Peter?'

'That's the thing, madam.'

'What shall I ever do for you, ma'am, you are so good to me?'

'Oh, perhaps you will do a great deal for us yet; and you know, my dear boy, that we are under obligations to you we cannot soon get rid of.'

'I am sure, ma'am'—and Sam looked intently at Mrs. Morris, his whole countenance beaming with honest emotion—'I don't know what I have done that you should say so. If you mean my trying to save Miss Susan, why I am sure, ma'am, if I had not done it, I wouldn't be fit to live. I would do it again, if I knew I should die for it; I am sure I would, and so would any one.'

Mrs. Morris could not repress the starting tear, nor could she make an immediate reply. Sam's whole demeanor took her by surprise—she did not expect such a burst of genuine gallantry.

'God bless you, my good fellow! you have a noble heart, and will make a proud station for yourself, yet; but keep in mind, that *the path to honor lies through difficulties and dangers.*'

As she said this, her hand was smoothing down the dark curls which lay, in all their natural carelessness, around Sam's fine forehead.

'But, Peter, only think! we have forgotten the hat—what a pity!'

Peter made no reply, otherwise than by handling his queue, and rolling his quid from one side of his mouth to the other.

'How could you let me forget it, Peter?'

'Oh, ma'am, don't think of it; you have given me too many things already.'

'Please, my lady, he'll do well enough, for all that. If my lady has no further orders, I must go.'

'Nothing further, Peter.'

Sam made the best bow he could, both to Mrs. Morris and to Susie; and Susie ventured, for the first time, as Sam made his obeisance to her, to say, very gently indeed, 'Good by.' It was not much beyond a whisper, but Sam heard it. Whenever the scene in that room came up before him—and it kept presenting itself very often—he loved to dwell on that part of it. Susie would be before him with her pretty smile, and those words, so soft, 'Good by,' would ring and ring in his ears.

To say that Jim was astonished at the change in Sam's appearance, as he came from the fort and took his station in the boat, would describe but a very little of what Jim really did feel. He was amazed—he was pleased—no, he was delighted. He loved Sam like a brother; and when he heard from Sam's own lips what had been done for him,

'They are the best people, Sam, I ever knew. But what will they say at home? I wonder what Ned will do? You must take care, or he will pull you down in the dirt. Clothes *do* make some difference, don't they?'

'Stop, my hearties.'

The boys looked back.

'Just come ashore here,' beckoning to Sam. 'You see my lady forgot about the hat, but, thinks I, there's a chance for me now; so I stops in slyly, and rummaging the old wallet, found enough stowage there to get this little shiner: so try it on, sonny, try it on.'

'But you shouldn't do so: I am—'

'No you ain't; so try it on.' And suiting the action to the word, he displaced Sam's little old tarred hat, and mounted a new one, all glistening with its bright polish.

'That's the rig, now; it don't sit quite ship-shape as it ought, but it will work to the head, and it will keep the rain out, I'll warrant *that*. But I can't stop here, for the Major's boots must be cleaned; so a good passage to you, my hearties.'

With that he bore away for the fort in quick time, paying no kind of heed to all Sam said about thanks.

'I tell you, Sam Oakum, I should not know you if I met you in the road. Nobody will know you; Ned won't know you, see if he does.'

'I don't hardly know myself, Jim, I feel so queer.'

The wonder which Sam's appearance excited on their return was full as great as Jim had anticipated. On reaching the shore, Ned and Jowler stood ready to receive them. Ned stepped up to Jim, who had jumped ashore, and was carrying the little stone anchor out as far as the rope would reach, and whispered,

'Who's that? Where's Sam?' Then Sam walked deliberately from the stern, and jumped ashore. Jowler set up a bark at him, and Ned fixed his eye upon him in some doubt until Sam smiled. He then commenced a retrograde movement, increasing the distance between him and Sam, and going round and round him, eyeing him from head to foot; while Jowler kept by his side, barking as he followed Ned round the circle. Ned knew *Sam*; he was *sure* he did, and so did *Jowler*, as soon as Sam spoke to him, and began to sneeze and wriggle himself about, and to manifest great shame that he had made such a mistake. Ned was too much surprised this time; it sobered him. He knew it was *Sam*, his old playmate; but *such* a change! How had it come about? He felt a kind of diffidence in approaching him; he almost wished for the old patched clothes and the little flat hat; but that feeling was only momentary, a flash through the mind. The neat trim of the clothes, the improved appearance of Sam's whole exterior, really delighted him; and instead of flying off into some extravagances, he took Sam's hand, and shaking it with all his might,

'Did Major Morris give you this suit, Sam?'

'No, it was the lady.'

'She *is* a lady. I should think you would love her, Sam, very much. Ain't they nice, though, Jim? Just look at this shirt collar and the bosom, and this handkerchief round his neck, and the hat and shoes. Oh, Sam, I am so glad you need not wear the old clothes any more;—*do*, won't you come and let mother see you and Ellen, just to see what they will say.'

'But he will want to go home, first, Ned, and show himself there.'

'I will come up this evening, right after supper.'

And again they separated for their different homes, and Sam hastened, with his bundle under his arm, hardly able to keep from a run, he was so anxious to see how they would feel.

They were at supper as Sam entered. His mother dropped her knife and fork and jumped up from the table; her hands were raised, and her whole countenance expressive of the most pleasant surprise.

'Why, Sam! where *did* you get these from? Oh, how nice! do father, look at him.'

Mr. Oakum had pushed his chair, and a smile passed over his weather-beaten countenance as he looked at Sam; and his heart blessed God for him. He was pleased, indeed, and almost proud to perceive what a fine-looking boy he was, but he knew his worth as few could know it. He could not speak, but he felt of the clothes and smiled, and then wiped the tears that would come in spite of every effort to keep them back. He felt that there was something more than good luck in all this. Sam was already reaping the fruits of the promise, 'Thy days shall be long in the land which the Lord thy God giveth thee.'

CHAPTER IX

How swiftly pass the beautiful months of summer; its flowers and its fruits come and go in succession, and must be enjoyed in their season, or not at all.

To our boys it seemed to have flown more rapidly than ever; the constant occupation of every day and almost every working hour, caused the days and weeks to pass away imperceptibly and pleasantly.

And now, the long wished-for period has arrived, when the great contract with Major Morris is to be fulfilled. The boat is ready, and will carry quite a load. The farmers are busy digging, and each is anxious to deliver his quota as soon as possible. It was well for Jim that he stipulated in the bargain to receive them only as he wanted them. Jim's thinking habits were of great service to him.

A new hand must be obtained to assist in navigating their little vessel; her size, the quantity of freight, and the season of the year, all demanded it. Sam Oakum felt that this devolved upon him, but Jim insisted upon it that they would unitedly pay for the extra help.

'I shall not allow that, Jim, no how. You give me now one-third of all we make, and you do all the business. So you see I am going this very night to speak to Sam Cutter; he will be a good fellow to row with me, and you can steer, and I shall pay Sam out of my own money.'

He was as good as his word, and found Sam Cutter ready enough to go with him; so a bargain was soon made, and as Mr. Cutter's potatoes were the first engaged, twenty-five bushels of the lot were carted early in the morning, and put on board. Jim was there ready to receive them, and as soon as delivered, counted out the money.

'There, William, is six dollars and twenty-five cents. It is all in quarters, but it is just as good. Give that to your father, and when I take the next load I will pay for that in the same way. Twenty-five bushels, at twenty-five cents a bushel, make just six dollars and twenty-five cents, don't it?'

Jim said this because William Cutter seemed to be in a maze, as though not exactly comprehending the matter.

'Oh yes, it's all right, no doubt; but I say, Jim Montjoy, where did you get all this money from? I tell you what, I mean to work, see if I don't, if it brings in money at this rate.'

'Why, we have had some pretty hard pulls for it, have we not, Sam?—or rather you have.'

'Yes, we both have, but no matter for that; it makes the money all the sweeter. You see now, William, how this thing works—your brother and yourself have been busily engaged all summer, cultivating your potatoes and other things; now you have dug them and received your money, that pays you for your work; we now carry them off to a distance, where they are wanted more than they are here, and sell them for enough to pay us for our risk, and labor, and expense of freight. If you had not labored and raised them, we should not have them to carry away, and make a profit on; on the other hand, if we could not find a market for them abroad, you would not have received half the value for them you now get; so you see how your plough and hoe, and our boat, help one another.'

'And your *head*, you ought to have added, Jim; for my boat and his potatoes would not have been worth much, without that head of yours.'

William Cutter was no great philosopher, and perhaps did not clearly comprehend the drift of Jim's argument; but he felt the silver pieces in his hand, and realized that it was a larger sum than had ever been there before; and he was satisfied, that in some way it had been obtained by the enterprise and labor of Jim and Sam and as he walked along towards home he said to himself a great many times,

'If working will do it, I'll work, see if I don't; there will be more potatoes and beans to sell another year, see if there ain't.'

The new boat proved her value on her first trip; she was not a fast sailer, but she rode the waves well, and would bear a stiff breeze. How rejoiced was Sam, as he sat at the helm, to witness the beautiful manner in which she would meet the swell, and bound over it like a bird of the water.

Old Peter had also much to say in her praise.

'He did not 'spect to see such a ship-shape craft; she ain't made to run fast, but she'll bear the wind, and she'll ride the waves, and that's what you want, my hearties. But what's her name?'

'Oh! we have not given her a name yet, we haven't thought about that!'

'Never thought about that? but you must think about it; what is a boat without a name? but I s'pose it ain't worth while to do no such thing on this craft o' your'n, seeing she is launched, and in sailing trim; but I tell you what, if you ain't given her a name, I'll do it; you must call her Susie, do you hear?'

'Would you?'

'Yes would I; and where can you get a prettier name, or one that will bring you better luck than that?'

'Well, if you say so; it's a pretty name, ain't it, Jim?'

Old Peter was determined to see that his favorite name was fastened to the boat; and in a manner that could not have been expected from him, printed it, in very legible characters, on the inside of her stern.

'Now, good luck to her! and don't you, boy, ever leave her while there's a plank to stand on; hear that?'

'Yes, sir; I shall not leave her for a trifle.'

The potatoes and beans proved very satisfactory to Major Morris. Jim received his money for each load, and was thus enabled to carry out his plan of paying for them. No sooner was a quantity brought down to him, measured and put into the boat, than he was ready with the pay; it was counted out to them in good silver money. Many wondered where it came from, and made up their minds that Mr. Montjoy had left his family quite a property, for all that was said about his dying poor.

No time was lost by Jim in completing the contract; every day that would answer was seized upon to carry a load. He neither counted profits, nor indulged in the least recreation, until the whole matter was settled.

A full month passed, using their utmost diligence, before they took on board the last load, and had the satisfaction of delivering it safely, and receiving from Major Morris, not only the full balance due, but an expression of his perfect satisfaction with the whole affair. One hundred dollars Jim and Ned could now call their own, for although Ned said that it ought to belong to Jim, he would hear of no such thing; Ned, he said, had worked as hard as either of them, and sometimes harder.

'Well, Jim, what would all the working have amounted to without those thoughts of yours? and only to think how I laughed at you.'

'We won't mind that now, Ned; but if you won't laugh, I will tell you what I have been thinking about again.'

'Do tell, Jim? I will never ridicule any of your thoughts after this.'

It happened that the boys were sitting on their favorite rock, enjoying the calm decline of one of autumn's loveliest days.

'Come, Jim, I promise you I won't laugh.'

'Why, to tell you the truth, Ned, I have been thinking whether there was no way that we might be supplied with such things as we need from a store, without going to Grizzle's; I am tired of it, for my part.'

'There is no use of thinking about that, Jim, or talking about it either; we have had that over long enough; we cannot help ourselves, and there's the end of it.'

'I don't know that; I think we might help ourselves.'

'How, Jim? Come, let me hear.'

'Do you remember, Ned, I once told you about a boat I saw at the fort, which had come from a distance with stores for the garrison? there were large square chests of tea, just as they came from China, and barrels of molasses and sugar, and casks of rice, and a great variety of things, enough to have completely filled Mr. Grizzle's store.'

'Yes; I remember you told us about it, when you came home. But what of it, Jim? What good will they do us?'

'I do not expect that those particular articles will benefit us, especially, but I have thought a great deal about the matter since then; and now, what I was going to propose is, to put your money with mine, and let me lay it out in tea, and molasses, and sugar and some other things.'

'Why, Jim, now you *are* crazy. Why, when should we ever eat up a hundred dollars' worth of such things?'

'But you are too fast, Ned; you don't wait to hear what I have to say. I intended, when we had procured these things, to let the neighbors know of it, and when they wanted, we could sell to them for a small profit. I know many would prefer buying of us rather than of Grizzle.'

'Why, Jim!' and Ned jumped down from the rock, and placing himself immediately before his brother, looked up at him with great earnestness.

'You mean that we should set up a little store—don't you, Jim?'

'Yes, it would be something like that.'

'And then, perhaps, after a while we should have a great many things, and a great many people would come to buy of us; I know they would, for they all like you so much.'

'I don't know about that, Ned; but I think we could sell things cheaper than they have been accustomed to buy them, and, if so, they will surely come; and if we can take such little things from them as we have sold at the fort, and give them a fair price—'

'Oh, Jim, only think of it—hurra, hurra!'

'Do, Ned, stop; you will frighten all the folks.'

'What is to pay now, Ned?'

'Oh, Sam, is that you? hurra, Sam.'

'What ails him, Jim?'

'Oh, he has got into one of his tantrums again.'

'I tell you what, Sam Oakum, you don't know what Jim has been thinking about this time; it beats his *old* thinking, I tell you.'

'Why, what is it, Ned? Come, tell.'

'Oh, Sam, Jim is going to set up a store, and do all manner of things.'

Jim and Sam could stand no more; so they broke out into a hearty fit of laughter. Sam, supposing it to be a joke, took no farther notice of the matter.

'You make me laugh, Ned, whether I will or no; but I don't feel much like laughing just now.'

'Why, what's the matter, Sam?' said both boys at once.

'There has nothing happened to me; but I have just been talking with Bill Andrews—he feels pretty bad. Bill is in trouble.'

'There, Jim; I told you so. Don't you remember the day your boat was put into the water, Sam? I saw then that something was the matter with Bill.'

'I hope he has not taken to any of his old ways.'

'Oh, no, Jim; I don't think Bill will ever take to them again. But you know Bill's mother?'

'She has not turned him away, has she?'

'No, Ned, not exactly; but I am afraid he will go away.'

'Oh, Sam! don't say so, for Bill is such a clever fellow.'

'I know he is'—and Sam's eyes began to glisten, and his lip to tremble— 'he is a real clever fellow; and to think how well he has behaved, and how different he is from what he once was. I should not think his mother could do so.'

'Has she been scolding him, Sam?'

'Pretty much so, Ned. You know how Bill used to let things go—almost any how—he says he did. Bill is sorry for all that; he is very sorry—I know he is. But I tell you what I believe, boys, that when we have done wrong, even if we are sorry for it, and try to do better, something or other comes up after a while to make us smart for it; perhaps we did not feel sorry enough, or may be it is to make us sorry all our lives; I suppose we ought to be. Well, as I was saying, Bill used to be much at Grizzle's, and Grizzle let him run in debt as much as he pleased.'

'I tell you what, Sam Oakum, I would not go in debt for any thing. I had rather live on raw clams and sea-weed.'

'So would I, Ned. But, as I was saying, Grizzle knew well enough that Bill's mother had land. He knew he should get his pay.'

'But don't you remember, Sam, when you and I went there last summer to engage potatoes, Bill said he only owed Grizzle a trifle?'

'I know he did, Jim, and so he thought, but Bill has been careless. He has taken potatoes there every year, as he thought, enough to square his account; but he never saw how it was, nor had any settlement made, and it has run on until lately; and when Bill asked him, for the first time, for his account—what do you think? Grizzle up's with a bill of more than eighty dollars.'

'Eighty dollars!'

'Yes, Jim, eighty dollars and upwards. Bill said when he saw it, he felt as if he should drop down.'

'Did he pay any of it? I would not have paid one cent of it until it had been pretty well examined. You remember your father's account?'

'Bill says he was confounded by it, and so afraid that his mother should hear any thing about it—for you know she is such a queer woman—that he paid Grizzle all the money that he received from you—thirty dollars.'

'Oh, what a pity!'

'Well, you see, Jim, Bill was so afraid his mother would know it he said it would make her about crazy.'

'Yes; but for all that, he ought to have told his mother.'

'I suppose he ought; but she soon knew it. For what did Grizzle do, but send Dick Tucker there; and he has taken the cattle, and other things, to pay the bill.'

'Oh, Sam, I am sorry for Bill. I wonder what his mother did say?'

'Bill says she called him every thing she could think of; and then she cried and hallooed so loud, that he had to go for the Widow Brown to come and pacify her. But he says he can stay at home no longer; so he is going across the barrens to see a Mr. Rutherford, who promised to be a friend to him; and he says he never means to come back, until he gets money enough to pay that account; and he is coming here to bid you good bye.'

'Sam Oakum, this is too bad. I have been thinking how Bill might be a great help to us, and himself too.'

'It is no use; he is done for—his cattle are gone, and so there is an end of it. But don't say any thing to Bill about this, nor let him see that you feel bad towards him.'

'We don't feel bad towards him. Why, Sam Oakum, we like Bill Andrews almost as well as we do you; but there he comes.'

Bill never appeared to better advantage than he did that evening: his countenance was naturally one of those bright and playful ones, over which there could always be seen some streaks of sunshine. He had really been through a severe trial; and had not his principles been well established, he might have been driven by desperation to his old habits; but his resolution against those evil ways was strong. And although Hettie had been for some time absent, yet her advice was before him, lifting his mind to better things, and creating a true disgust for what was low and corrupting. His look was sad, but not cast down. He gave his hand to the boys, and shook theirs with great cordiality. His eye indeed glistened, and his lip quivered; but these were only tokens of the pain it gave him to part from friends whom he loved so well. Few words were spoken. Ned had an abhorrence for tears. He therefore turned suddenly away, and began throwing stones very violently at some invisible object. Jim and Sam were not made of such stern material; and I do not suppose it ought to be set down against them, that, as soon as Bill's back was fairly turned, and on his way, they had between them quite a time of it.

On the morrow, just as the sun was beginning to pour forth a flood of glorious light, Bill shut the little gate that led from his mother's door-yard, and turning round as he did so, gave a smile through the tears which were flowing to his mother and sister, who stood wringing their hands and weeping aloud, on the little stoop that projected from their front door. He smiled, to let them see that he had no unkindness in his heart; and his tears were witness that he was on no errand of pleasure. Yet he lingered not, but, brushing away the tears, and putting his bundle closer under his arm, walked with a firm step straight on his way. The sky was clear and blue, except where the beautiful sun-light was expanding in the east, and imparting a rich golden tint. The earth was whitened with the autumnal frost, and crisped under his footsteps, and the thick leaves rustled as he brushed along and disturbed their repose. His course was directed towards the Widow Brown's, where he must stop and say 'Good-bye,' and perhaps get a message to Hettie, whom he expected to meet before the day was over.

He walked briskly on; the sun had not yet penetrated the thick pines, and the cold air of the night still floated undisturbed as he entered the barrens. A lively fire was crackling on the widow's hearth, and at a plain, but clean-looking table, sat Mrs. Brown and her son. Coarse but wholesome was the fare spread out upon it; and both arose as William entered, urging him to sit down and partake with them; having had but a little appetite when he left his home, the keen air and the walk had prepared him to enjoy refreshment. Their meal ended, a little parcel taken for Hettie, a warm shake of the hand, and God's blessing implored upon him, and he was off.

This going to seek one's fortune is no trifling matter; the battle of life, where each is striving for his own particular benefit, and cares not who sinks so long as he himself securely floats, demands all the vital strength; and little else must claim our care or notice, save the great struggle.

Bill was yet a stranger to life, only as it glided along in the quiet seclusion, and that seclusion not the best adapted to bring forth man's noblest efforts; beyond a bare support, and perhaps sometimes a thought of sharing his humble portion with her who had been a sort of guardian angel to him, his wishes had not hitherto aspired. No wonder, then, if trifles had a power to disturb him, which, to those immersed in scenes of busy life, would be but as an insect's buzz—a gentle brush, and it is gone. William Brown had left the cottage with him, and pleasant had been their chat together for a few miles; when about to separate, he merely said,

'Well, I wish you good luck; and if you see Hettie, please say to her that Dave Cross will be along by Rutherford's next week, and that he will stop and bring any word home that she wishes to send; but I guess, between you and me, it is only an excuse to have a chat with Hettie.'

Immediately after parting, Bill crossed the old bridge by the mill, and went on his way; but something had disturbed the inner man, for, as he ascended the hill, he paused where two roads met, one leading to Mr. Rutherford's, the other to the nearest town. A large stone lay at the point where they met: he threw his little bundle down, with an air that might mean, perhaps it did,

'I don't care what becomes of you or me either;' and then took a seat on the stone, leaned his chin on the head of his hickory staff, and looked at the grass and the stones and the old fence, and occasionally at a stray bird, as though there was something wrong about them. He waited a good long hour, in thinking, and hesitating, and vexing himself, and then trying to make the best of it; and finally picked up his bundle and started off, not in the direction of the town, but straight towards Mr. Rutherford's. It was late in the afternoon before he accomplished his journey, and found himself entering the gate which opened into the extensive grounds surrounding, as it was commonly called, the Rutherford House. He had never seen any thing like it before, and a more pleasant or home-looking place was seldom to be met with. There was a beautiful green lawn, with a long broad gravel road extending to the house; and there were large trees, spreading their long and drooping branches, scattered thickly over the lawn and lining the road, and the house was nestled beneath the shelter of some of the very largest and most graceful of the trees. It made no pretensions to architectural beauty, but it was large and well built; and the multitude of outhouses, and extensive range of barns and sheds, all in good order, spoke of room for man and beast, and of comfort too. Bill thought nothing of all this, his heart was full of misgivings as to how he should be received; to him it was all fine, too fine for the like of him; and he looked at some of the outbuildings, as he passed along, to see if there was any place he could feel at home in, for the night.

George Rutherford, the inheritor of this lovely spot, had of earthly goods a bounteous store; but he had, also, what many an inheritor of earthly substance does not possess, a noble heart, large in its embrace of his fellow-man in all conditions, ever going out in its kindly feelings towards some object of benevolence; humble in every thought connected with himself, and with devoted zeal seeking to aid, to comfort, and to gratify the most menial of his dependents, and the most degraded and sorrow-stricken of his neighbours, far or near. Although rich blessings crowned his days, and sweet was the cup of life he quaffed, he felt most truly that no desert of his had earned them. Gifts of mercy he called them all; abounding gifts—too good, but as the tokens of Infinite Benevolence to the most unworthy.

He wanted, with all this, something of that shrewdness so essential to the getting or preserving property; this world so teems with those who covet all their eyes behold, who ask no counsel from the law of heaven or the code of earthly justice, so long as forms of law will screen them in their sly grasping after acres and goods, that a man needs, with all the piety of a saint, something of the serpent's cunning. It is not enough that he covets no man's silver or gold, that he wrongs no man of his due, that he extends his hand to the helpless, that he be ever ready to lift to his own level those who are struggling below him: he must take care for himself. Riches are fleeting substances, with wings ever ready for flight; he who enjoys the blessings they can bring, must give all diligence to 'see well to his flocks and herds; for riches are not for ever'; nor do they descend to many generations. Mr. Rutherford had already experienced some trials in this way; his confidence had been too strong, his sensibility for others' feelings too acute, and there was great danger that he might yet be a heavy sufferer, because he did not learn wisdom, as he might, from some of the trials he had already passed through.

Whatever doubts may have disturbed Bill's mind as he was walking up the broad avenue, they were all dissipated the moment he was recognized by Mr. Rutherford. He grasped his hand with the cordiality of a friend, took him at once into the house, and into the presence of his lovely wife.

'You remember, my dear, the young man who so kindly assisted us at the time of the accident to our carriage.'

'Indeed I do,' said Mrs. Rutherford, rising and bidding him a hearty welcome.

Bill was put at once at ease; he never before could have supposed, that persons who lived so very differently from what he had been accustomed to, could be so affable; they seemed to him to feel and act as if he was as good as any of them; asked him as many questions as old Sam Cutter would have done, and seemed as pleased with all the little news he communicated, as though he had been a city resident, loaded with tidings from the gay and stirring world. The little children, too, in all their sprightliness and beauty— those speaking images of the parent's heart—came fondling round him; his plain rough garments were unheeded by them, and he was soon as familiar with the little prattlers as though they had been the children of his nearest neighbor.

But where was Hettie? Bill wondered much why she was not among the first to come and greet him. He did not ask; he heard her name spoken by the little ones, and his heart would beat and his breath grow short, and once he thought he heard her light step in the passage; and then sad thoughts would come and sink his spirits, so buoyant from his kind reception. But Bill had yet to learn some lessons in the school of life.

Mr. Rutherford soon invited him to walk abroad, thus affording an opportunity to unburthen his mind, for he evidently had come for some express object. With much patience Mr. R. listened to his whole story, making no reply whatever until the budget was empty, nor, indeed, until some time after. Poor William thought that he had come to little purpose, and was anything than a welcome visitor. Mr. Rutherford, however, was only thinking in what way he could best serve the young man. He might indeed have taken him into his own family, and given him such employment as he had been accustomed to; but he thought he could perceive talents fitting him for a different sphere of life.

'How would you like to go to the city, and try your hand in a store?'

'I don't care where I go, sir, nor what the employment; if I can only have a chance to take care of myself honestly.'

'It will be very different from anything you have been accustomed to; the work may not be any harder, but it will be very constant, and without much chance for relaxation, merchants think that business is a substitute for everything else.'

But William was not to be daunted by any prospect of toil; and Mr. Rutherford, after telling him all he knew of the routine of business, proposed to give him a letter to a friend of his in an extensive business.

'He will do all that can be done to procure you a situation, and then you must do the rest yourself; but remember, William, that the most strict attention to everything you are called to do, an unflinching integrity, and a determined perseverance, will be requisite to gain success; and unless you have made up your mind to exert every energy, you had better return and engage yourself with whatever you can best at home.'

William's fine countenance was animated with an expression that told how his heart was touched.

'So far, sir, as any exertions, day or night, to make myself useful and acceptable will do it, I fear not; and I hope my friends will never have to regret any efforts in my favor. A sense of gratitude, if nothing else, I trust will keep me watchful over myself.'

'Well, William, I will write this evening; I hope you will succeed, and I think you will.'

As they entered the house on their return, Hettie was just coming into the hall. Her appearance seemed to be accidental; perhaps it was. She blushed deeply, smiled a very little, and gave her hand to William in rather a timid manner. He was prepared to accost her warmly, but the peculiarity of her address chilled him; he felt a restraint he could not overcome, and his greeting was much like her own. She asked after her mother's health, thanked him for his trouble in bringing the little parcel for her, and then withdrew, leaving him to follow Mr. Rutherford, who was waiting at the parlor door to receive him.

William was tired enough that night to have slept soundly, but his thoughts would not be quiet; so he hailed the dawn with delight, and was ready immediately after breakfast to go on his way. Mr. Rutherford took him into a small room adjoining the parlor, and handing him the letter,

'There, William, I hope you will find this sufficient, and here is a trifle for you in case of need; if ever you become a rich man, you can return it:

let me hear from you how you succeed.' So saying, he placed a little roll of bills in his hand, and bidding him God-speed, at once opened the door, apparently wishing to avoid the shower of thanks which he saw beaming from the eye of the young man.

'Oh, sir, I never shall forget your kindness, and I hope I may yet prove it to you.'

Mr. Rutherford made no reply; he was not indifferent to gratitude, but he did not care to be thanked personally. It was reward enough for him that he had made a fellow creature happy, and done what he could to give a helping hand to one just venturing on the deep waters. Long may that heart enjoy such draughts of pure happiness; and when, in years to come, you meet reverse of fortune, if such shall be thy fate, these stores, laid by in heaven's chancery, will be a refuge at your utmost need; and little deeds of love like this, long, long forgotten, will come like heavenly messengers, and with interest accumulated beyond the miser's compound gain. In the dark hour when clouds, blacker than the tempest's murky robe, shroud all the prospects of your earthly comfort, when hope of all deliverance that man may bring has gone, and your sickened heart turns away from earth, then shall you know that good deeds are not lost, even here below; and what your generous heart, inspired from above, devised to aid, to comfort, and to bless your fellows, has been a hidden treasure reserved against the time of deepest need.

William went joyfully on his way, he had unrolled his little treasure, and counted fifty dollars. How his heart blessed the noble man; what a spring of love and hope burst forth from it, sending a quickening influence through all his frame; how elastic his step; what a cheerful light sparkles from his eye. The prospect before him is no longer dark.

Immediately after passing the house, the road wound gradually around the premises; on one side skirted by a clump of woods, and on the other by a heavy stone wall, surmounted by shrubbery, so thick that nothing could be seen through it. Suddenly a little gate opened, and Hettie came down the steps, her face wearing that sweet smile with which she had in days past always met him.

'I was afraid, William, that you would be past before I could get here, and I felt as if I must see you, just to say, good-by.'

William was taken by surprise; he seized her offered hand, and grasped it warmly, but he could not speak.

'I have wanted to see you very much, William, and to have a long talk with you about many things; but I suppose you must be going, and I must be back to my work. But, William, do you think you will like it in the city? You know things are so different from what you have been used to.'

He was intending to be very stiff in all his bearing towards Hettie, but he made awkward work of it. There was she, looking up into his face with all her wonted interest, and how could he meet those eyes, and not return their look of pure and kindly feeling? So he gave it up: all his bad intentions flew off like mist, and his eye glanced as kindly as hers, and his voice softened into the old tones of friendship.

'I know, Hettie, that they will be different; but I think I shall soon get used to them, and then I feel like taking care of myself, and who knows but I may get along as well as some others who go there, and come back with plenty of money in my pocket? I think, then, that some of my friends will not be ashamed to speak to me, or to acknowledge old friendships.' And as William said this, he looked at Hettie with so much meaning, that she could not mistake its reference to her.

'If you think, William, that your prosperity will make a difference in the feelings of your friends towards you, or, at least, of some of them, you are mistaken. You may succeed as you anticipate, or you may not; you may return wealthy or poor, as you now are; if you only bring back as true and kind a heart, William, you will find some to welcome you, who will rejoice more in that, than in any great change in your circumstances.'

And Hettie cast such a meaning in her look, too, as she fixed her eye full upon him, that he could not mistake its reference either. He saw the tears glistening in her mild eyes, and he could have done all manner of things to himself for speaking as he did.

'Forgive me, Hettie, forgive me, if I have said any thing to trouble you; I know that you, at least, will not be affected by my condition, if my character is only good.'

'I cannot say any thing more about the future, William, than that I am very sure I shall ever feel a deep interest in your welfare, and my ardent prayer shall be, that you may be kept from the many evils which I am told lurk around one going into the city, as you do, a stranger to its temptations.'

'I know, Hettie, they say that I shall run a great risk in many ways, and I feel that I need something to keep my mind fastened on that will help me to avoid the evil, whatever it may be, and that will strengthen me in doing right. You have been such a helper to me, Hettie; you know from what a dreadful state you once delivered me; you have great power over me. I am now going from you; will you not let me carry along with me that promise which I have often asked? If you would only say that it *might* be one of these days, I should go away happy; the hope would be like your presence with me.'

Hettie cast down her eyes as William continued talking; she heard him quietly through, and then replied, in a voice that trembled indeed, but the words were well chosen, and came from her heart.

'That promise, William, I cannot make now any more than I could have done before this; you and I are to be separated for many years perhaps; great changes may take place in that time; you will see many things very unlike what you have been accustomed to; your views about persons and things may change with your circumstances, I shall think of you as a dear friend, as a brother, if you wish it; I will pray for you when I do for myself, and as earnestly, William; but farther than this, you must not ask me.'

William ceased, for he knew Hettie well enough to be certain that she would yield nothing more. He parted from her as a brother might leave a sister, dearly loved; he saw the deep color mantling in her cheek, and the tear that artlessly rolled over it; he could not say the parting word. She stepped back through the little gate, and as it closed, he went on his way to seek that fortune, which, at times, played before his fancy in all the witching forms of earthly prosperity. How often will this parting scene haunt his waking and sleeping dreams, through the long years that will intervene ere a sight of one so dear to him now will bless his eyes again; and how often will he admire the firmness and prudence of this earthly friend of his heart!

CHAPTER X

Sam Oakum had not forgotten the promise he had given old Mr. Cutter in the hour of his deep trouble; nor had he forgotten the kindness which prompted the old man to fly to the rescue of his parent. Every cent was precious in Sam's eyes, as sacred to repay that offering of mercy; he would no sooner have squandered it than he would have stolen; week after week, on every return from a trip, he would slip up to his little chest, and deposit there the earnings of the day. The additions were small, for he was obliged, occasionally, to expend some part of what he earned for little comforts that his mother needed; his father being rarely able to procure money for his labor. Small, however, as were the additions, the store increased. He had already carried to Mr. Cutter five dollars, and received his hearty blessing, and such a squeeze of his hand as Sam did not forget for the rest of the day.

Jim had squared up with him the moment he had received the last payment; and as Sam looked at the heap of money which Jim said was his share of their enterprise, he was too happy to say any thing. He looked up at Jim, whose calm clear eye turned from the money to Sam, and then back again to the money, as much as to say—

'It's your's, Sam, honestly come by;—it's all right, why don't you take it?'

Ned, who was standing by also, and watching Sam, understood better than Jim what the matter was.

'Why don't you hurra, Sam, and let it out, and not keep choking up so? I know how you feel;—shall I go it for you? Hurra, hurra, hurra!'

'Ned, what does ail you? what is the use of making such a noise?'

'Oh, nothing; only you see I want to help Sam out with some of his feelings; he is too full to hold.'

Sam had to smile, and that started a tear or two, and then he tried to say something about gratitude to the boys; but Jim stopped him short.

'Now, Sam, you must not feel so; you have earned that heap of money just as much as we have ours, and we ought to thank you; for how should we ever have got along without you and your boat.'

'Oh,' said Sam, as he began to gather up his money, and looking archly at Jim, 'you would have thought out some other way, I know.'

Jim had to smile a little; and Ned, throwing his arms on Sam's shoulders, and leaning over him, as he picked up the pieces of money.

'Sam Oakum, I am as glad to see you put that money in your pocket as I should be to put it into my own; and so is Jim, I know.'

Sam believed every word that Ned had spoken, and after making a plan to meet together that evening, he went on his way. His pockets were heavy, but his heart was light; and as he passed the rock which had ever been memorable to him since the hour when he sat there in his despondency, and the boys came to him with this plan of enterprise, he could not but say to himself,

'What a grand thing it has been that Jim Montjoy had those thoughts.'

Mr. and Mrs. Oakum were just about to sit down at their humble board as Sam entered.

'Here, father; see what the boat has done.'

'What is it, Sam?' said his mother, looking earnestly at him, her hands raised, and her countenance expressing great anxiety. Sam made no reply, but commenced unlading his pockets, and piling the money in little heaps on the table.

'It is father's; it has all come of the boat. If father had not built that boat, we never could have got all this; and now he can pay Billy Bloodgood the fifteen dollars, and then we shall not owe a single cent to any one; there is the whole of it—twenty-five dollars—don't it look nice, mother?'

Mrs. Oakum let her hands drop as soon as she understood the matter; but it was only to take up her apron—they had work to do with that. While the father, overcome with the sight of such abundance, and the noble spirit of his boy, could only say, in a very trembling voice,

'God bless you, Sam.'

That was a happy meal, though plain and coarse. A spring of living joy was bubbling in each heart, and sparkling forth in pure and blessed thoughts towards God and man.

Sam would gladly have had his father carry the money which was to repay Mr. Bloodgood, and never been known as the procurer of it. But to this the kind parent would not consent. He felt, and truly too, that it would be a mark upon his son's early life, not soon obliterated: and he was willing to have himself forgotten, if the dear boy might but be strengthened in the path of honor and virtue.

The next morning Sam was up with the early dawn, and busy with his daily routine, that he might be ready to go on his pleasing errand. Breakfast over, he dressed himself in his best blue suit, and with the money in his pocket and his parent's blessing, started off, his heart as full of happiness as it could well be. Thoughts of the dark scene which he had passed through, when kind friends, like angels of mercy, came to his aid, he could not repress, nor did he wish to; the darker *then*, the brighter *now*. How his heart beat with pleasure as he walked briskly on, and drew near to the humble abode of Billy Bloodgood—rough, to be sure, was the exterior, and the peculiar habits of its owner too visible in the strange confusion around the premises; but Sam thought only of his kind heart and ready hand in an hour of need.

Things had not yet been put to rights at neighbor Bloodgood's, and as Sam entered the house, there was not only a confused state of pots and kettles, and relics of the early meal, but the good woman herself was all wrong somehow; she was in quite an undress, and moved about amid the domestic articles surrounding her, with that quick, jerky air, which generally denotes an unsettled state of the inner man or woman.

Sam wondered why things did not break, they rang against each other so sharply. If he was somewhat surprised at this, he was much more so at sight of a stranger, seated near the door, but a little behind it, which circumstances prevented him from noticing before. He was a stranger, not only to Sam, but he must have been to all those parts, for he was like nothing seen in that region for many miles' circuit; his air and contour was that of a gentleman. Sam had already seen enough of the world to know that. He was quite a youth, probably not over nineteen years of age; his countenance manly, and rather stern at the first glance; but Sam thought, from a particular twist of the corner of his mouth, that he was more amused than vexed with the state of things around him. His form was slender, and his complexion pale, like one who had never yet been exposed to the wear and tear of life; his light brown hair was thrown carelessly back from his forehead, and displayed to great advantage that index of the mind.

He arose almost immediately upon Sam's entering, and with his hat in hand, bowed to the mistress of the house, who cast but a sideling glance at him, and then stooped down to rattle some of the dishes, without, apparently, any other motive than to let him see that she was too busy to attend to *him*.

'You think then, madam, there would be no use in my waiting to see your husband?'

'No; I don't think there's no earthly use in seeing *him*. I tell'd you, again and again, we ain't got no young ones to send—and that's the long and short on it.'

'Good morning, madam.'

The young man spoke kindly and courteously, and then left the house, walking with an erect carriage towards the highway.

'Good morning, Aunt Sally.'

Mrs. Bloodgood, then, lifting herself up, and putting a hand on each hip, looked with a very stern and fixed gaze through the open door, until the stranger had fairly got out of hearing; and then, without answering Sam's salutation, began to rattle away in her usual style, when by any cause somewhat excited.

'*Him* set up for a schoolmaster, with his fine clothes on, and his bran new hat, and his bowin' and scrapin', and his *madam*, and all that kind of palaver; he ain't nothin' but a chicken himself. No, no: I've seen enough on 'em in my day; there ain't no good comes on 'em; they put more mischief in the heads of the young 'uns than they've got naturally, and that's enough we all know.'

'What's the matter, Aunt Sally?'

'I tell you what, Sam Oakum, I don't want none of them Yankees round me. I don't see why the critters can't stay in their own country, and do some honest thing there for a livin', and not come trampussing away down here with their larnin', that don't do no airthly good, but make the young 'uns lazy, and wanting to be gentlemen like themselves; and what old Molly Brown sent the critter here for, I don't see.'

'Does he want to set up a school, aunt Sally?' said Sam, looking at her with a very anxious countenance.

'He *did* want to; but I guess he's got enough on it; and I'm so glad he's took himself off 'fore Bloodgood come in, for he's just fool enough to be clean took with him; and he's got his head set about havin' a schoolmaster, and I don't want none of the varmints round.' But looking at Sam very closely, and coming up to him, and feeling his coat and his trousers, and then holding him off at arm's length.

'*Do tell!* where upon airth, Sam, did you get this? How smart you *do* look. This has been gi'n to you, I know, by them great folks over the water there?'

'Yes.'

'Well, ain't that clever on 'em, Sam? but you're desarvin' of it, and I'm glad on it. It does a body's heart good to see your mother's child look so smart and tidy. I didn't hardly know you when you come in, and that plaguy man put me into such a pucker, I didn't hardly know what I was about.'

Sam had become very impatient to be off; he had anticipated a great deal of joy from his errand, in the proud satisfaction of paying a just debt; but he thought not of that now. He had learned enough to know what the stranger's business was, and he could not endure the thought of his leaving the place in such a manner; so taking out his money, and handing it to Mrs. Bloodgood,

'There, Aunt Sally, is the money which Mr. Bloodgood, so kindly helped my father to, when he was in trouble; won't you please tell him that we all thank him very much, and hope we shall never forget how good he has been to us?'

'You dear, blessed child!' Aunt Sally could say no more, for she saw the tears in Sam's eyes, and her own heart was very peculiar—it was soon set on fire.

'You will tell him, won't you, Aunt Sally? and that father says, if he will only let him know any time that he can do any thing for him, or for you, day or night, he will gladly do it; and mother says so too; for you don't know how happy it made us all, when you lent this money, and how very happy we are now, to be able to give it back to you.'

Aunt Sally sat down, and taking up her apron with both hands, cried as hard as she had scolded but a few moments before. Sam laid the money on the table beside her, and wishing her good morning, made speed towards the highway. He saw the young man at a distance, walking rapidly, and bending his course away from the place, on the direct road to the barrens; his only chance to overtake him was by a cross cut over the fields, and through a little clump of wood, around which the road to the barrens passed. And while Sam is hurrying across the lots, I must introduce the young stranger a little more particularly to my reader.

Henry Tracy was indeed descended from New England parents, but was not, as good Mrs. Bloodgood supposed, a real Yankee; for his father had emigrated from the state of Maine when quite a youth, and his mother from another of the goodly sisterhood, when a child. They had settled in one of the middle States, and Henry's birthplace was one of our largest cities; great pains had been taken with his education; his mind was uncommonly well stored for one of his age, and his manners distinguished by a gentlemanly grace; but, above all this, his heart had been nurtured by the tender care of a mother, whose love for the truth, whose meek and blameless life, and whose heavenly-minded temper, gave a power to the pure and holy thoughts which she was ever breathing into the ear of her son; they stole into his heart like the dew upon the tender plant.

He was now an orphan, and cast upon the world, with the choice of depending upon the charity of friends to assist him in completing his education, or using what education he had already received as a means of support, and of further progress; he wisely chose the latter. Having a slight acquaintance with Mr. Rutherford, he had, on calling to visit the family, been directed to this region, and the "Widow Brown, to whom Mr. Rutherford advised him to apply, could think of no one more likely to take an interest in a school than Billy Bloodgood. His reception there, and the general appearance of things, had discouraged him from any further attempt, and he was hastening back to seek a spot more congenial to his own feelings, and where there might be at least some desire for instruction.

Sam had to be expeditious, and was barely able to accomplish his object by running across one entire lot, and through the clump of woods. Breathless with his haste, he was unable to communicate his wishes, or to apologize to the young man for coming upon him in so abrupt a manner, who looked with much surprise at him for an explanation.

'I hope you will excuse me, sir, for stopping you; I met you, just now, at Mr. Bloodgood's. I did not know what your business was, sir. But do come back, we want you very much.'

'Want me! What do they know about *me*?'

'Oh, I mean, Sir, they want a teacher.'

'Mrs. Bloodgood says that no one here wishes a teacher, that the people think they are better off without any instruction.'

'But they do not all feel so, sir; do come back with me, and I will take you to a man that will tell you all about it.'

Sam's appearance pleased Mr. Tracy, and the earnestness of his entreaty induced him to consent to return and see what new feature the place might present.

They were not long in reaching the spot to which Sam wished to conduct him, a very unlikely place in appearance to give encouragement to literature, being no other than the workshop of old Sam Cutter. The old man was in his usual seat, holding, or rather leaning upon the handle of his large hammer, and from his short breathing and flushed face, showing signs of his having just been wielding it. Running round the shop, with a tongs in one hand and a hammer in the other, was Billy Bloodgood, helping himself, with some directions and aid on Mr. Cutter's part, in repairing an old farming tool. He paid, as usual, no attention to the new-comers, except a slight nod of his head, and a pleasant smile to Sam.

As Sam entered and motioned to Mr. Tracy to come in, Mr. Cutter passed his broad hand across the top of his head, smoothing down his bald forehead, at the same time saying.

'Your sarvant, sir.'

Mr. Tracy bowed to him politely, taking off his hat with as much respect as if in the presence of one of the great ones of the earth.

Sam Oakum lost no time in communicating to Mr. Cutter the object of the visitor, and the circumstances under which he had met with him and brought him back.

'Right, Sam, right; but of all things, to think of Sally Bloodgood treating the gentleman in that sort. But that's the way with them; they're a match for the old one, any time; all but your mother, Sam, she ain't like the rest on 'em.' And then turning to the young man,

'Sorry, sir, you've had such an indifferent reception, but what can't be cured must be endured. Billy there knows that; but you see it don't matter to him whether she scolds or coaxes; he can't hear nothin' no more than the iron he's poundin' on.'

'Is that Mr. Bloodgood? Mrs. Brown advised me to call upon him; but his good wife gave me such an account of things, that, but for this young gentleman, I should have made no further effort.'

'Ay, ay, Sam knew well enough, the young rogue, who to come to; but dear me, you look like a lad that has seen fair weather and easy work; do you know what kind of a place you've come to?'

'Only what I have seen of it this morning, sir; and Mrs. Brown said that she thought a teacher was much needed.'

'Ay, that she might well say, much needed; that is, if you can teach them any better manners than they've got now: they're a hard case, my dear young man, most gone to the evil one altogether.'

Mr. Tracy smiled. 'I hope not quite so bad as that, sir.'

'Not much short on it, I tell you; but things look a little better than they have, and I ain't sure but a considerable lot on 'em might be got together;

that is, the boys, I mean but—' and the old man regarded his young visitor with a very inquisitive countenance—'you don't look as if you could live on clam shells and oyster shells, and eels, and sich like; I'm afear'd you ain't used to them.'

'Oh, yes, sir, I can eat what the rest of you do.'

'Well, my young friend, you can't judge always from the looks, what kind of fare a man has; but howsomever, if you can get along with such things as I've tell'd you of, why you won't starve, for you see we've got plenty on 'em; and as to the boys, do you, Sam Oakum, up and tell the gentleman what you know about it, and not stand stretching your mouth and grinnin' at me.'

Sam soon numbered quite a company of boys, and girls too, that he knew would be very glad of a chance for schooling, and many more that would no doubt come if the gentleman 'would only make a beginning, and open a school.'

As Henry Tracy had perhaps full as much desire to do good, as to receive compensation for his labors, seeing the strong desire manifested by Sam, and hearing him tell how very anxious some of his companions were to learn something, he made up his mind to try the experiment.

Sam was almost beside himself for joy; it was the only one thing now wanting in his cup of happiness. His deficiency in every kind of knowledge acquired from books, was felt by him daily as a sore evil. 'If he could only read and write, and calculate like Jim Montjoy,' was for ever coming into his mind, a wish unalloyed by envy or any other evil feeling towards Jim, but filling his heart with sadness. Old Sam Cutter was no less rejoiced, for his boys were but little in advance of Sam Oakum, and now that they had taken such a favourable turn in their course of conduct, the old man felt that a school would be a crowning mercy. Some little difficulty presented itself as to where the teacher should take up his abode; there were good reasons why Mr. Cutter could not offer a residence under his own roof; the house was but small, *too small*, he found for himself, sometimes, and he durst not venture upon an addition.

Sam Oakum would have rejoiced could his home have afforded accommodations such as he might ask a stranger to partake of, and a person of Mr. Tracy's appearance. Mrs. Montjoy's was the only place that Sam could think of where any thing like comfort could be had.

'I know—I know all that, Sam; Mrs. Montjoy is a nice woman, and the house, though small, is tidy-like, and the boys are good fellows, a credit to the place; but you see, Sam, we must 'be wise as sarpants' about this business. You know how the folks feel, full of their jealousies and nonsense; and if the teacher should go there, they would say that he felt himself above folks, that he was too good for the like of them, and all that, and you see,' looking at Mr. Tracy, 'we've got to take folks as they are, and make the best on 'em.' And then turning his eye towards Sam, 'The Widow Andrews' is the place. Bill, you know, is gone; sorry for that, but he's gone, and no help for it; the old woman is queer, but where is one on 'em that ain't, sometimes? Yet she is pretty good in the main, and she'll be proud to do her best; and if the gentleman won't be frightened at a little squall once in a while, he'll git along pretty comfortable there: now, don't you think so, Sam?'

Sam thought just as Mr. Cutter did; and as Mr. Tracy was not particular as to accommodations, provided they were cleanly, and he could have a room to himself, it was accordingly decided that he should accompany Sam there, and see what could be done. There was nothing very inviting in the appearance of things, to one who had been accustomed to a very different style of living: the house was a one-story building, placed very flat on the ground; both the roof and the sides were covered with shingles. Moss had accumulated so as to contend with the shingles for the precedence, and if the latter did the most good, the former was the most distinctly to be seen. But it was situated in the midst of a green grass plot, and the grass was short and velvety to the tread, and a few old cedar trees surrounded it, which tended to screen its imperfections, and make it pass for full as much as it deserved. A fence ran before it, much dilapidated, sufficient, however, to keep out the larger animals, where the green short grass grew up to the window.

The widow was evidently flattered by the proposal, only she feared 'the gentleman might find their living very different from what he had been used to.'

Mr. Tracy was satisfied, from the appearance of things within doors, that neatness was one trait which the widow certainly had, whatever others he might discover on further acquaintance. She showed him her best room, and which she was perfectly willing to yield up to his use. It was large enough, with an agreeable view of the surrounding country, and Henry thought, when he should get his books around him, he could make himself at home.

Mr. Cutter would have been glad to introduce the young man to Billy Bloodgood, but he dared not undertake the task, and suffered Billy to hammer away, and took no notice of the inquisitive glances which his good neighbor kept casting towards him. As soon, however, as the visitor had departed, still holding the hammer and tongs, he made up to Mr. Cutter, and putting his head close to his ear, hallooed in a voice almost sufficient to have made the sound reach his own tympanum.

'Who's that?'

'I ain't deaf; you needn't holler at that rate into a man.'

'Who did you say? I didn't hear you.'

'Dear me, what *shall* I do? I'm all out of breath a talkin' to that youngster.'

'Don't hear.'

Uncle Sam made a desperate effort, opened his mouth, drew in a long breath, put his hand up to form a trumpet, and applying the machinery as near as possible to Billy's head, called out,

'He's a teacher.'

'A preacher?' and Billy nodded and smiled; 'that's *good* going to stay here?'

'Bless my soul, what *shall* I do? I shan't try agin', no how.'

'Sally'll be glad to hear that; where is he from?'

Uncle Sam looked first one way and then the other, as though meditating an escape; but he hated to move, and in fact he knew there would be little use in trying it, for Billy would be after him so he finally cast an imploring eye up to his neighbor, who stooping down and looking very inquiringly into his face.

'O dear, dear! I ain't got no breath to do it.'

Billy shook his head.

'Don't hear.'

'No, nor you won't if the sound has got to come out of me; it can't be done.'

'Don't hear what you say; speak a little louder.'

'I don't know.' Old Sam made noise enough this time, and if it could have been concentrated might have gone to the place, but Billy had heard something, so he nodded his head.

'From below? what place? anywhere near by?'

'Dear, dear, he'll be the death of me!' Uncle Sam was indeed in a bad case; he had at no time any breath to spare, and to be called upon to expend it, first in working with the big hammer, and then in blowing trumpets, was a little more than his good-nature could stand. He was very red in the face, breathed short and heavy, and with his old straw hat flapping violently to catch fresh supplies of air, looked wildly about for some loophole whereby to creep out from this dilemma. Just at that moment, and as Billy was again upon the point of asking for more light on the obscurity of the last sound that reached him, the shop door was darkened by the entrance of no less a personage than Sally Bloodgood herself. She came in so rapidly, that she was nigh being foul of Uncle Sam; as it was, she only impeded the motion of the old hat. She was not at all in a visiting dress, having come, as she said, 'just as she was,' to see her neighbor, Mrs. Cutter, for a minute. 'But do, la, Uncle Sam, what ails you? your face is as red as a turkey's comb. You seem to be all blowed out. It's Bloodgood, I know it is. He's been asking you questions, I know he has. You hadn't ought to try to talk to him, Uncle Sam; it's enough to kill you.'

'I believe you,' turning his eyes up at her very expressively; 'you're right there, Sally.'

Billy Bloodgood now engrossed his wife's attention, by telling her the great news, 'that there was a preacher come, a nice-looking young man.'

Mrs. Bloodgood looked at Mr. Cutter for an explanation.

'Do *tell*, Uncle Sam, was he a very youngerly man, very fine and delicate like?'

Mr. Cutter nodded assent.

'La, me, I wonder if it's the same one that called to see Bloodgood, this mornin'. A preacher?—who upon airth would have thought it? he never said nothin' about preach'n'.'

Mrs. Bloodgood had her own reasons for being so surprised; and as Uncle Sam Cutter saw clearly that her thoughts were very much troubled about the matter, he came to the conclusion to let her enjoy her mistake:

'It will teach her, may be, to be a little more careful of her tongue.'

But, as Billy Bloodgood was the principal man to whom Mr. Cutter looked for aid in sustaining and encouraging the young man, the fact that he wished to teach a young school among them, must be communicated to him. Utterly hopeless of any power in himself to do the thing, he, without any ceremony, took hold of the loose covering which hung about the person of the lady, and fairly forcing her down upon a rough seat, near himself,

'Now you see, woman, I give it clean up; I shan't never try no more to drive a word into Billy's head. I can't do it—it will kill me.'

''Tis hard work, Uncle Sam, ain't it? it takes such a power of wind. But you see somebody's got to make him hear, and I 'spose it's my lot; and what a body's got to do, you know, Uncle Sam, why, they must submit to it: but it takes my breath clean away sometimes, and makes me so faint and gone, that I can't hardly hold myself together.' And the good woman, pressing her hands very hard against her sides, exhibited to Uncle Sam the desperate efforts she had to make, at times, to keep things in their place.

Billy stood close by, with one hand on Uncle Sam's shoulder, looking very complacently at his wife, and nodding every once in a while, as though he understood perfectly what she was saying.

'Fine-looking young man; smart, I guess.' And then stooping over, and looking into Mr. Cutter's face, 'You didn't tell me what place he came from.'

'Where is it, Uncle Sam? jist tell me, and I'll make him hear, I'll warrant.'

'Why, Sally, I don't know where he's come from. No doubt Heaven has sent him from somewhere or another, and I don't much care, I am so glad to see any thing in a decent shape come to do a little good among us: he may have dropped right down, for all I know.'

'Do, la, Uncle Sam, how you talk; you're enough to frighten a body. But I must tell Bloodgood somethin' or another.' So, raising herself a little, putting one hand on each knee, and placing her prominent member close to her husband's ear, who was still bending down and looking earnestly at Mr. Cutter, she was about to give one of her blasts, when she was suddenly arrested by the powerful hand of the latter.

'Stop, Sally, stop!—not now: none of your hollering here, I can't stand it. Wait till you git home, and then you can tell Billy all about it.'

Billy, finding that there was a sudden interruption to all correspondence for some cause he could not well define, and being accustomed to such events, put a stop to his inquiries for the present.

How vast a change of feeling is sometimes effected by the passing away of sunlight, with the bustle of its busy hours and the silent shades of evening!

Henry Tracy had made a busy day of it; he had met with unexpected success in engaging scholars, and had procured a room in a building, once used as a court-house, in which to hold his school. Gratified with his prospects, he sat down to the clean supper table with the Widow Andrews and her daughter, with feelings much more buoyant than could have been expected in one so young, for the first time a sojourner among strangers. He delighted them by the ease and pleasantness of his manners, so that when he retired, which he did soon after supper, the Widow Andrews looked at her daughter, and lifting her hands in expression of her admiration—

'Who could ever ha' thought of it? Why, it's jist as easy talkin' to him as to Uncle Sam Cutter.'

'Oh, mother! its as easy agin'.'

The moon was in all her splendor, and her pale rays fell trembling through the foliage of the cottage. Taking a seat by the window, Henry looked out upon the beautiful night, and his heart filled with emotions to which he had hitherto been a stranger.

Home, that idea so satisfying to the soul, that spot to which our wishes fly when in sickness or sorrow, was nought to him now but the resting-place of his past joys and trials—a beautiful vision that had left an impress on his heart, which time could not obliterate; although, like a vision, it had passed away, his bosom heaved with the swelling thoughts that rolled like ocean waves heavier and mightier in upon him. He drew from his breast a golden locket and unclasping it, held the miniature it enclosed beneath the rays of the moon; his lips trembled, as the sacred name of *'mother'* broke from them. 'Yes, I will ever think of thee, thy sweet love has made my home a paradise, and thy pure piety and gentle counsels have won me to the path of peace. My Saviour's image hast thou ever borne before me, until my heart has learned to love Him as my best and dearest friend. Oh, may my life be such as thy last dying prayer entreated it might be; and may I be led by the Holy Spirit in the way that leads to where thou art.'

CHAPTER XI

It was a very bright to-morrow in Ned's imagination, as he lay down to rest; for then he was to accompany Jim and Sam, and was to see the fort, and old Peter and Major Morris, and perhaps little Susie too; and the new plan of Jim's was the object of their errand. If the day in Ned's imagination was brighter than the one which actually dawned upon them, it must have been a beauty indeed. The sky, the water, and the land opened in loveliness; the bright blue above was reflected from the glassy water, and the golden beams, that poured in full glory from the east, were thrown back by the fading forest in all variety of colors. This was to Ned a holiday indeed, and his active spirit enjoyed it to the full; faithfully had he toiled through the long summer days, nor even thought of relaxation. Now, the summer labors over, sweet was the rest, and exhilarating the prospect of new scenes and faces, which, with that morning's dawn, came playing before his view.

Major Morris was not a little pleased, as he listened to Jim's simple exposition of the plan he had in view; his generous heart rejoiced to know that what he had already done to aid and stimulate these youths, had turned to so good account.

'And you say that you have laid by one hundred dollars from your trading with me this summer, and so you begin to despise your old business? You wish to find some easier way to make a hundred dollars? Ay, ay—like all the rest of us.'

'Oh, no, sir—no, sir; we do not think of giving up our garden; we expect to work at that the same as ever.'

And then Jim explained how he intended to manage, which convinced Major Morris that the scheme was not only well laid, but included much closer attention to their work than heretofore. He looked at the boys with deep interest; the smile, which had played round his lips while speaking to them, passed away, and his keen black eye turned from one to the other, as though scrutinizing their very spirits. Sam's honest eye, as black as the one which was fixed on him, twinkled and turned aside, as the Major, after surveying the brothers, rested his gaze on him. What he saw in Sam, or what strange visions passed before him, wherein poor Sam acted a conspicuous part, may one day be revealed. A sigh at last broke the spell; he turned towards Jim.

'Your plan, my good fellow, is one which meets my approbation, and any thing I can do to assist you in it, I will do with pleasure; but you know from past dealing with me, that my efforts will be merely directed so as to enable you to help yourselves.'

'You are very kind, sir. I thought your judgment would be safe for us to follow, and that perhaps you could give me some directions as to purchases, and therefore I have taken this liberty.'

'Your plan of setting up a small store is a good one; on many accounts: but you must bear in mind that great attention will be required, both in purchasing and selling. You will be in danger of losing some of your profits by waste in retailing; you will also be in danger of losing goods and profits too, by selling to those who will never pay you; and you will run some risk in the transportation of your goods, or of your money, so far by water, although this latter risk can be guarded against. What I would say to you then is, that this business, although small at first, will require the most strict attention in all its details; and I would also say another thing, if I did not fully believe that all of you have been trained to those correct principles, without which no man can or ought to rise to honor or prosperity.

'I can assist you by introducing you to a house in the city, where you will be well dealt with; and as our boat sails to-morrow morning, you had better remain here, and I will accompany you.'

Ned was ready for a caper; he looked at Sam, and rubbed his hands together very fast. Sam shook his head, as much as to say, 'Be quiet, Ned.'

Jim blushed, looked at the boys, and then up at Major Morris.

'I thank you, sir, for your kind offer; but having no idea of being able to do any thing so soon, have left my money at home.'

'So much the better, then there will be the less risk; I will arrange for the payment of your goods in the city, the same as if you had your money with you, and when we return, you can settle with me here.'

Jim was not very clear about this matter; but confiding in Major Morris, assented to remain, thanking him again for his kind interest.

During this conversation, Peter stood back at some distance, leaning on his crutches, and chewing a tremendous quid of tobacco with great diligence, and occasionally smoothing down the end of his queue. Ned, while listening to the Major, kept an eye on Peter, scanning him from head to foot. No sooner had the Major withdrawn, than Peter hobbled towards the boys, who were standing on the steps by their boat, and making preparations to return; he threw his crutches down, and taking a seat on the stone coping close beside the boat, listened attentively to Jim, who was giving directions to Sam and Ned about some small matters at home, and about their coming for him on his return to the fort.

'I suppose,' said Jim, looking at Peter, 'that I shall be back here by about three o'clock to-morrow afternoon.'

'Bless your soul! what kind of a kalkelation have you run foul of now? you are out of your reck'nin' by a whole day at the least. Why you see, my hearty, you won't start from here 'afore say nine o'clock to-morrow mornin'; with the wind aft, or a little quaterin', say she goes eight knots an hour, which is good sailin' for sich kind of craft, it will take you all of four hours and no balks to git to the landin'; so you see' (giving his head a bob, and a corresponding motion to his queue) 'you can't be there 'afore one o'clock, no how' (another bob); 'well then, if the wind is fair to carry you there, you don't think it is goin' to chop round jist when you're ready to come back, and blow astern all the way home, do you?'—looking at Jim again.—'No, no; the wind and weather don't care for nobody; we've got to take 'em, jist as it happens, and make the most on 'em. So you see, you may jist knock overboard all your figurin'; it won't do you no good; you've got to stay one night in the city, at any rate, for the boat never starts till the next mornin'; and if you've good luck, may be about three o'clock you'll be in, and may be not.'

Jim was rather puzzled to make out from Peter's reckoning when to tell the boys to come for him; but Peter, seeing him in doubt, gave his own directions.

'Here you, Sam, jist harkee; there won't be no need of your bein' here afore day a'ter to-morrow; then you see, you can jist hoist sail, and come along easy; no hurry; you be here by three o'clock, plenty time enough. Now you see, don't make no kalkelations about goin' home that night, 'kase— you hear me now?—sposin' the wind should take 'em right dead ahead, they can't get in no how afore six o'clock, and may be not then, and there's no tellin' when.'

Jim found it a more serious matter, this going to the city, than he had anticipated. Peter's experience soon convinced him of that; as he could give no more certain directions to Sam than he had already received, he must let him go with what he had.

The sail was hoisted; Peter had untied the rope, giving at the same time a sharp good-natured lecture to Sam, for making his boat fast in such an unsailor-like manner. Sam took it all in good part, for, in truth, he had not done the thing; it was some of Ned's handiwork. Jim stood on the stairs, giving Ned all sorts of directions and injunctions.

'Yes, yes, Jim; I'll see to it, never you fear.'

Off goes the little craft.

'Good-by, Sam; good-by, Ned. Take care of yourselves.'

'Good-by, Jim.'

'Good-by, my hearties; haul in that bow-line, and don't let it drag in that fashion; and haul your peak taut; you'll have a stiff breeze, but she'll bear it. Good luck to you.'

Gently the boat turned off, and took the swelling breeze. The boys looked back, to give a parting nod.

'Oh, Sam, who is that? ain't she a beauty though!—is that Susie? See, Sam, she is shaking her hand to you.'

Sam made no reply; he touched his hat lightly, as he had seen Peter do to the Major.

'I tell you what, Sam, I don't wonder you jumped into the water; I would have jumped, too, if I had been here.'

'I wouldn't be looking round so, Ned.'

'Mustn't I? Well, I'll look ahead then. I thought sister Eller was pretty—but—but—may be it's the dress though.'

Sam was in no talking mood; he kept his eye steadily fixed on the sail, which was swelled finely out, and making their boat skim along towards home to his heart's content; and as Ned received only monosyllables in reply to his many questions, he soon tired of putting them.

Large cities have their evils, and they are not few. Hither the idle and the vicious throng, for here are dens to hide them from the public gaze, and companions to uphold them in their evil courses, and finery enough to glut their polluted appetite; but with the evils, are many things that tend to bless society. Here the good man finds many kindred spirits, too, and like coals to burning coals, they kindle in each other a warmer glow, and spread around them, in a wide and fervent circle, a cheering, healthful influence. Here busy industry plies her daily, nightly task, and meets with large reward, and hangs out her trophies to the gaze of the vast multitude, urging them on to diligence: here wealth erects her glittering palace; and here the darkest den of poverty is found. Here emulation and sympathy have each objects of heart-thrilling interest, sufficient to awaken all the energies of the jostling throng. Deeds of charity, which make us proud of our species, are here originated and carried into execution: and here, too, deeds of horror are enacted, that make us feel how like the very fiends of hell sometimes is man.

Excitement, in all its various forms, keeps up a constant whirl; all feel the influence for good or ill, and onward all are pressing. The mind of man is tasked, until its energies, too strongly, constantly impelled, give way, and then the victim droops, and plods along, and sickens at the strife, and longs to be at rest.

When the first view of the city broke upon the gazing eye of our hero, he scarcely knew what to make of it. The tall spires running up against the distant sky; the crowded masts that, like a wintry forest, lined the shores; the mighty mass of buildings, heaps on heaps, spreading for miles on either side; the boats of various size and shape crossing and recrossing, and sweeping by them with the arrow's speed; and as they neared the land, the busy throng of people hurrying to and fro; the confused and deafening noise, the smoke and dust, the huge hulks, old ocean-travellers, that lay fast corded to the strong stout piles; the long projecting piers, around whose dark-green slippery base the turbid waters swelled, and beat, and broke— all, all were new to Jim; and in mute wonder he looked and thought, until their little vessel glided into her resting-place, between two vast walls of docks.

"Well, James, what do you think of the city?" said Major Morris, coming up to where he sat at the bow of the boat, and putting his hand kindly on his shoulder.

"I hardly know, sir; but it seems a very busy place." 'Yes, busy you may well say, every one is in a hurry here, and we must be so, too, as we are rather late to-day, and I fear my friend will have left his store.'

Jim hastened to accompany the Major, who, already on the wharf, was mingling with the crowd; it took him, however, some little time to learn how to make haste in a city, and not before he had received a few stout thumps against some other hurrying mortals, and a few harsh curses as an awkward country booby. But Jim heeded them not, for the Major walked fast, and to lose sight of him would be a dilemma indeed, amidst such a Babel. He twisted this way and that, sometimes running close to the wall, at others jumping off from the side-walk among the carts, and then quickly back again, over bales of cotton tumbling from the doors; around hogsheads of molasses, barrels of flour, puncheons of rum, bars of iron, old anchors, coils of cable, droves of little, ragged, dirty children, huddling about empty sugar hogsheads. Verily Jim had a time of it; he was not naturally one of the hurrying sort. To get around and through all these obstacles, and to keep his eye on the Major, at the same time, required more activity than he had been accustomed to use.

After travelling in this way, as Jim fancied, a long distance, he rejoiced to see the Major make a halt, and enter a large store, the passage-way of which was blocked up with piles of tea-chests, casks, bales, boxes, and men. Jim squeezed along behind the Major, who, opening a glass door, entered a small neat room, where every thing was in perfect contrast with the confusion without: a large double desk occupied a considerable portion of the apartment; it was situated between the two front windows, and covered with fine green cloth; every thing upon it lay in order; each little paper seemed to be there by design. The windows were clean, and the glasses on the shelf shone brightly, and the floor was covered with white sand, and dust and cobwebs appeared to have no license there. At the desk two young men were busily employed with immense folios, working away in silence, occasionally passing a word with each other in a very low voice, and that only in reference to the work before them. A spell seemed to be upon Jim as soon as he entered that room; he had never felt so before, not even when first introduced into the parlor of Mrs. Morris; every thing wore the appearance of so much exactness, every thing was done and said in such a calm, thoughtful way, it was so still and orderly, it seemed to Jim that matters of great moment alone occupied each mind.

Mr. Thomas was a large dealer; hundreds of thousands passed through his hands every year, and his extensive business was managed by him with perfect ease, because he had grown into it; unlike too many of modern times, who, aiming to catch the golden shower, involve themselves in a complication of difficulties, purchase without judgment, and sell at random, only anxious that their books shall show, at the end of the year, a large balance in their favor, whether realized or not.

He had begun in a small way, and gradually increased his business with his means; never suffering himself to be allured by a tempting speculation, nor to engage in any undertaking beyond what he could well manage, he neither worried himself nor his friends. It was a busy place, though, that store of his; from early dawn until late at night, there was one continued round of active duty; but extensive as his sales were, he despised not the most insignificant of his customers, bestowing equal attention to him who wished to spend his hundred dollars, as to those who yearly drew from his vast storehouse their tens of thousands. An upright, manly course he had ever pursued; he was an honest dealer as well as a wealthy merchant.

Major Morris knew well the man into whose hands he committed our young merchant; and it required but a few words in private to interest Mr. Thomas in his welfare, almost as much as he had himself been. The story of the youth immediately took with him, and Jim's modest and intelligent look added force to what the Major had related concerning him; and then, when

Major Morris left the office to attend to business of his own elsewhere, he made Jim take a seat beside him, and with the familiarity of a friend, drew from his own lips a rehearsal of all he had done, and what he wished to do; inquiring into all the particulars respecting the place where he lived. Jim had but a plain and simple story to tell; but before he had finished, the heart of the merchant was so engaged in his plan, that he thought of him not as a customer, out of whom he might honestly make a small gain, but as one whom it would give him great pleasure to direct and aid. What a priceless jewel is integrity of heart! and happy is the youth who, trained to virtue, goes forth into the busy paths of life to act his part. A mild but steady light illuminates his track; his very countenance is radiant, and his plain, simple speech, which tells the meaning of his heart, wins every honest ear, and wakes a chord respondent in each noble soul; he needs no varnished tale, no flattering words, no cringing bows; a better passport to the confidence of all he carries with him, in his own honest purpose.

With much patience Mr. Thomas made out a list of such articles as he thought would be the most saleable, and gave immediate directions to have them carefully put up. He then opened to Master Jim such a method of managing business, that he felt almost in a hurry—a thing Jim was not often guilty of,—to start off and get to work. Jim was not given to vanity; he had never felt that he had any thing to be proud of, but when he saw the cart loaded with the different articles intended for him, neatly marked with his name and place of residence, and when he received his bill made out in the most particular manner, and receipted by the clerk with a most significant flourish beneath the signer's name, and when Mr. Thomas cordially shook his hand, wishing him all success, and that he might have the pleasure of seeing him soon again, he was highly gratified, and would not just then have exchanged his place and prospects for any one he could think of.

Sam and Ned, although somewhat confused by Peter's directions, had reached the fort a short time before the arrival of Master Jim with his little cargo. It was a happy meeting between the brothers, for they had never before been separated for a single night. How Ned stared, when he saw the boxes, and bags, and barrels with Jim's name upon them! How he would have shouted, if he dared, but Sam was close by him.

'Keep still, Ned; you know it won't do here.'

'But only to think, Sam, what a grand thing it is—only think, to have a store, and people buying things, and all that; and you in a great vessel bringing goods to us—hurra, Sam!'

'Do, for goodness' sake, Ned, stop; what will they think?'

Sam was in great perplexity; he felt that their character was in danger; but Ned promised that he would keep in, at any rate until they were out of hearing. Jim was fortunately out of the way, having gone with Major Morris into the fort, to settle their business matters. Old Peter, however, was a witness of the scene, and Sam had great respect for Peter, and feared that he would be horrified at Ned's disregard of the rules of propriety; but the old man shut up one eye, and screwing his countenance into a grimace almost frightful, sat and shook his sides, and worked away at his queue, making no noise whatever. Spasm after spasm came over him and passed away; and whenever he looked at Ned, off he would go again, shaking and wriggling and pulling at his queue, but making no noise. At length, beckoning to Sam to come near, he whispered,

'He's full on it, I tell you;' and then another screwing of his face and a hearty shake—'he's a real boy, every inch on him. I only wish the Major had a heered him—how it come out, ha?' and then shake, shake, went the old man's sides. Sam, however, was greatly rejoiced that the Major was not there, and kept Ned very busy in stowing away the goods in their own boat, and did not feel quite at ease, until they had left the fort a good distance behind them.

There was business enough on hand now for all our boys. The little end building was entered upon in earnest, and soon converted into quite a respectable-looking store, except as to size; in that respect it had not much to boast of. Sam labored with as much interest as either of them; and as they were all too busy to converse much while the store was in preparation, it was not until the evening of the second day after their return, that they could get a chance for talking. As the weather was too cold now to meet under their favorite tree, it was concluded, for the future, to make the store their rendezvous.

'I tell you what, Sam, who would ever have thought of this six months ago? It is a regular store—ain't it? There are the shelves and the counter, and the barrels, and the canisters, and the scales, just as Grizzle has them, and a great deal nicer. But that little desk which Jim has fitted up so snug in the corner there behind the counter—that must be some city style. I never saw such a thing round here—did you?'

'No; but it looks well—don't it? and that green cloth on it. Jim means to have everything snug here—don't he?'

Ned did not reply, for Jim entered just then, and looking round with a smile, took his seat opposite to them.

'Now, Jim, tell us all about your trip, and what you saw, and how you managed, and where you bought the things, and all about it.'

'Oh, Ned; I cannot tell you half that I witnessed in that great city. You must go there yourself one of these days; it is a great place, and every one is busy, and all seem to be in a hurry to get along, as though they had something to do that must be done at once. It was as much as *I* could do to get through the streets; but the gentleman to whom Major Morris introduced me, treated me very kindly, and told me how we must manage: said he, "You will find that the people in your place have got very little money (which you know, boys, is true), and if they can only buy for money, you will be able to sell very little. Now you must do this: you must offer to take from them any thing they have for sale—butter, eggs, yarn, wood—no matter what, in payment for whatever they want to buy of you."'

'We should be in a fine fix then, Jim; what should we do with all the stuff—they would only take a small part at the fort, you know.'

'Just wait, Ned, and you shall hear. "All these things," said he, "are wanted in the city, and are as good here as money. As soon as you get a supply of this kind of produce, load up your vessel and bring it to me; I will either take it of you or dispose of it. You can get more for it here than it is worth with you, and so you can make a profit both ways."'

'Oh, Sam, did you ever hear the like?'

'But just wait awhile, Ned. He said also, "that as soon as the people here found that they could purchase goods of us cheaper than they had been accustomed to, and get a larger price for their produce than they had ever received, which you will be able to do by trading here, you will not only get all the business of the place, but they will be stimulated to raise a great deal more, and so every year you will find your trade increasing;" and he said, "before two years, you will require a large sloop to do your carrying business."'

'Just hear that, Sam—hurra!'

'Now, Ned, keep quiet; it is not accomplished yet; and things may not work just as Mr. Thomas thinks they will.'

'Oh, but I say, Jim, it will work—I know it will—hurra! Only to think of it—a large sloop in two years—hurra! Why don't you hurra, Sam? You will be captain of her—you know you will.'

'I could hurra, Ned, if it would do any good, for I feel as glad as you do; but it is not always best to make a noise about it.'

Sam had not forgotten the alarm he had received from Ned's shouting a few day's back.

'Well, I don't see what you and Jim are made of: where's the use of any thing good, if a body can't let it out a little?'

Jim soon got Ned back to real business, by asking him to read over the bill of goods, and call off the articles, while he and Sam examined them, and placed them away in readiness for use.

We must now leave our boys, for a time, to try their new experiment, in order that we may bring forward the other parts of our story.

CHAPTER XII

Henry Tracy found himself surrounded by not only a large number of scholars, but such as listened to him with the strictest attention, and applied themselves to their tasks with unusual diligence. It was, however, to him a sad sight, to behold so many of them, and some almost his own age, commencing the first principles of education. The labours which devolved upon him were arduous, but the more he found to do, the greater was the interest he took, and the more untiring his zeal for their benefit. He walked amid his little community with no lordly air; great indeed was the disparity between his attainments and those of his pupils, but he felt it not, or felt it only to humble himself before God, that so superior had been his advantages.

His power over them was unbounded. An influence had been gradually stealing over their minds, which caused them to listen to his instructions as though he was a messenger from heaven. It proceeded from the combined power of religion, intelligence, and refinement. He had, on opening his school, gathered them around him in solemn act of worship, and every day, morning and evening, he publicly commended himself and them to God, and poured out from his feeling heart such warm petitions for them all, that many a hard and careless youth would wipe away the starting tear, although he could not tell why that tear had come. And then through all the day he ministered to their intellectual wants, with so much kindness in his manner, and so efficiently too; he threw around him such a charm by his gentle, yet manly deportment, treating them with the same respect that he wished to be observed towards himself, that the most obdurate were soon softened. No harsh words ever escaped him, even when their improprieties affected him the most keenly; nothing but the expression of sorrow or surprise, brought out in that delicate manner, in tones low and touching, which seldom failed to start the blush on the cheek of the delinquent, and check at once whatever was wrong. Slowly, too, but most effectually, an influence was stealing ever the parents. It arose from the deep respect which they saw their children felt for their teacher: it flashed upon them as they met him in his daily walks; his lowliness, his pleasant smile, and his soft clear voice affected them, they knew not why; and wrapped itself around their hearts. There was no letting down of his own good manners, no seeming condescension to their ignorance; he conversed with them as his equals, and poured forth the thoughts which were uppermost in his mind, in as good language as he could command; and he ever left an impression of his mental power and moral worth that made them think and talk of him when he was gone, and wish that their children at least might be like him.

The error which good Mrs. Bloodgood had fallen into in regard to the calling of the young man, was soon cleared up, but not until she was, herself, won to him; and as she could not get rid of some troublesome remembrances of their first interview, she took the greater pains to trumpet abroad continually her good thoughts concerning him now.

'Of all the men that ever I sot my eyes on, he's the best; he's an angel on airth; he's clean too good for it, don't you think so, Aunt Sally Cutter?'

'Why I don't know, Sally,' and the old lady straightened herself up, and pushed her spectacles further on her nose; '*men* is *men*, and there ain't much angel about 'em, as ever I seed; but I 'spose he's as good as most on 'em; but they are all clean took with him, and what do you think?'—stretching her long arm out, and raising it over her head;—'Cutter has taken it into his head now, that, preacher or no preacher, he means to get him to hold some kind of a meetin' or other, and he's gone this very blessed day with the old mare to the Widow Andrews' to see him about it.'

'Do tell, Aunt Sally, it ain't true? has Uncle Sam gone, though? Well that's jist what Bloodgood's been talkin' on; he'll be so glad; but, poor soul, what good will it do him?'

It was indeed true; Uncle Sam Cutter had been long impressed with a sense of the need there was for some public religious services; he had in his youth been accustomed to mingle with those that kept 'holy day,'—he had gone to the house of God with the multitude, and he had never lost the savor of those solemn seasons; the remembrance came over him as he toiled in his shop, or sat by his door in the deep shades of evening; he mourned in secret that he had ever pitched his tent in Sodom. Oh! how he longed once again to hear the peal of the church-bell, calling the worshippers to the house of God; but he was now too old to remove to strange places, or do much towards obtaining such privileges as he felt were needed; and yet to think of leaving his family in such a moral waste, without some effort to remedy matters, he could not. He had listened attentively to all that his boys told at home about the teacher, and he thought what a pity it was that some of the older sinners also could not have the benefit of his prayers and instructions. 'We all need it bad enough,' he said to himself one day, as he sat on his old block by the shop door; 'bad enough, bad enough. Oh dear me! to think what a heathen set we are, goin' whip and cut to the Evil one, and nobody to say "Whoa!" to us, no more than if we were fat sheep goin' to the slaughter-house.' With that the old man began to fan himself very fast with his straw hat, his lips moving all the while, as was his habit whenever he thought hard. His train of ideas at last led to the conclusion that something must be done; so ordering up the mare, he was soon off for the Widow Andrews', resolved to lay before the young man such a picture of their condition as would not fail to move him, 'if,' said he, 'he has any bowels of mercy in him.'

The Widow Andrews was much surprised to see the old cart drive up to her door, for her good neighbour, though a very kind man, was an indifferent visitor. She did not wait for him to alight—a business never rapidly performed—but ran out to the little gate, and with an air of great wonderment looked up at the old man, as he sat dangling on the tail of his carryall.

'What's the matter, Uncle Sam? there ain't no bad news, I'm hoping. But do tell! what a pucker you're in; you are clean blowed, ain't you, Uncle Sam? Do git down and come in, and let your boy tie the horse, and rest you a bit, and take a little breath.'

The old man was somewhat put to it, for the old mare had not been exercised of late, and she had several additional gaits to try that day, and the road to the Widow's was none of the best.

'Is the teacher to home?'

'La me! what's to pay now, Uncle Sam? there ain't no turn up, I hope? But it's jist what I've been a fearin'; he's too good for 'em, I knew it, and I've told a good many on 'em so: he's jist an angel. Oh dear! if you've come to have him druv away, Uncle Sam, it will break my heart, and it will be the ruin of the place; and where will they ever git sich another?' And the old lady began to wring her hands, and to run upon her high notes at such a rate, that Uncle Sam began to be restless, and making a desperate effort to get some wind into his speaking apparatus, he let off at her in no very moderate terms.

'Do, woman, stop with your clatter; you'll frighten the mare, the next thing, and she has a'most killed me a'ready; there ain't no need o' your howling and caterwauling at that rate. Why, dear me! can't a body ax to see the teacher, but you must set up all that noise and squalling? I don't want to hurt a hair of his head; so jist put your hands down and git into the house, and I'll come in to rights.'

So telling Dick to stop yanking the beast, as it only made her worse, and to sit there and try to keep her quiet until he came out, he let himself down, and puffing and blowing, from his sudden and extra effort, he waddled through the little gate, and reaching the stoop, sat down on the low broad step.

'Do please come in, Uncle Sam, and take a chair.'

'You please tell me, first, if the teacher is to home.'

'Why, you see, Uncle Sam,' coming up and almost whispering in his ear, 'he ain't jist to home, but he'll be here in a minute; he's gone to take his evenin' walk down in the grove there. You see he goes out jist as reg'lar as can be, every livin' day, right after tea, straight down to the grove, and there he stays awhile, then back he comes agin; and Mary and I have been tryin' to make out what it is he's a doin' all alone by himself there. Mary says he's 'mantic like, as she calls it, but I don't believe it's no sich thing. Do, la, there he comes, now; jist see how still and quiet he walks along, that's the way he does every livin' day; so come in, Uncle Sam.'

Mr. Cutter, however, much preferred seeing the young man, alone, and chose to remain where he was. It was but a few minutes after the widow had retired, that Mr. Tracy entered the gate, and seeing Mr. Cutter, walked quickly up, gave him a cordial shake of the hand, which was as cordially returned, and rather more so than his fingers could have wished; and politely invited the old gentleman into his private room, as Mr. Cutter had intimated his desire to say a few words to him.

It took the old man some little time to recover himself after the operation of being ushered into a strange apartment, and getting himself fixed in a convenient seat. And after he had revived enough to begin to talk, a great many commonplace things had to be said before he could get at the subject of his errand. To that however, he was finally led by Mr. Tracy's remarking,

'That he began to be very much encouraged about his school, the boys were attentive to their studies, and to all the regulations of the school.'

'Yes, sir, I believe the boys is in a fair way now to learn decency and manners, and may be something else; but I've been a thinkin', sir, whether you couldn't do a little something or other for the rest on us here, who are too big and too old to go to school.'

Mr. Tracy was at a loss to imagine in what way his assistance could be required, but he ventured to reply,

'That any thing in his power, whereby he could be of service, consistent with his present duties, he would gladly do.'

'Glad to hear you say so, for seeing you've got the larnin', there ain't nothin' else in the way; and sure am I, if you knew half the need there was to have somethin' done, if it is ever so little, just by way of decency, if nothing more, you would be more willing than you say you are. You see, my young friend, the Evil one has got a hard grip on us, and nothin' but preachin' and prayin' will ever make him let go; and even that won't do some of us much good if we don't have it soon. You see I am an old man, it ain't long that I shall be hobbling about here. I can't put off the evil day, as you who are just beginnin'; there are a good many things that tell me that I am 'most to the bottom of the hill, so you must not wonder if I feel a little anxious to have things more in a righter shape than they are with me at present. And there are a good many in all, just about as far on the road as I am; and for folks to be livin' on the edge of the grave, and never hear a word about any thing good; oh, my dear sir! if there is any pity in you, you'll begin right off, and try to do somethin' for us.'

Henry Tracy was deeply affected by this address, for the old man spoke as if in earnest, and the tears that rolled freely told how much he felt.

'I cannot, perhaps, fully understand what you would have me to do, my dear sir. You know that I am not at all qualified to preach, and whom to direct you to I know not.'

'You can do all the preachin' that is needed, I ain't all afeared for that. All you have got to do is to give out in the school, that next Sabbath afternoon there will be a meetin' in the school-room, and all can come that's a mind to. There ain't no need of nothin' further, and God'll bless you for it.'

Mr. Tracy would have made very decided resistance, had he consulted his judgment alone; but his own feelings were too much in unison with the old man's; the want of public religious privileges he had begun to feel most deeply, on his own account, and for the multitude around him. He could not resist this appeal; with a humble yet resolute heart he replied,

'Well, Mr. Cutter, I will do as you say; and may God assist me, and grant His Spirit with us.'

'May the Lord bless your dear young heart!'

The old man could say no more, but with his heart overflowing with joy, he arose, pressed the hand of Mr. Tracy, and in silence hobbled out of the room and through the gate, and took his usual seat, waiting for his son to untie the beast and drive him home.

The tidings that their young teacher was to hold a meeting on the Sabbath day soon spread throughout the place; and when he proceeded to give public notice to his school, it was only a confirmation to the boys that the report was true.

It was a calm, lovely autumn day; and as Henry Tracy walked on his way by the path which he had chosen for his daily route to the school-house, his feelings were lulled into delicious repose; the rustling of the leaves, the stillness that reigned in field and wood, the waning tints of nature, the modest tones of the school-bell, calling all within its reach to the place of meeting; the little groups which could be seen in different roads, bending their steps thither; it seemed more like the Sabbath day than any he had spent here yet.

He had done what he could to prepare himself, and he had a strong consciousness of being in the path of duty; and he felt a composure in view of the undertaking which he could not have anticipated. A few persons were collected round the door; they immediately followed him as he entered: to his surprise a large congregation was waiting his appearance.

As he took his seat on a little platform that had been prepared for the occasion, and cast his eye over the assembly, like a flash of light his usually pale features were crimsoned with a deep blush, and then away it flew, and a deadly paleness that alarmed every beholder came in its place. A sympathy was excited in every bosom; his youth, his modesty, his grace of manner, his unostentatious effort to do them good, like a talisman spread its charm over all alike, and prepared them to receive whatever he should say, with the deepest attention. Henry was obliged to arouse himself, in order to overcome the oppressive weight that was becoming heavier every moment; he therefore proceeded at once to the business before him. He gave out a hymn, which he read with much propriety, and then inquired if there was any one present who could lead in singing; but as no one seemed ready to undertake, he commenced a familiar tune. An electric shock could not have surprised them more, than the melodious notes which rolled forth upon their delighted ears. Henry Tracey was gifted—for a gift surely it was, as no power of accomplishment could ever have imparted it—with one of those rich voices which might have entranced the multitude on a public stage, but its melodious tone had only rung beneath a parent's roof, and its sweetest, most touching notes, had only been drawn forth in praise. Quickened by the music, soon every voice that could follow joined fully in; but above them all, louder and sweeter as the hymn went on, floated those rich strains which Henry poured forth, as from a heart burning with intense devotion. Enraptured, solemnized, softened, the whole assembly, both speaker and hearer, were happily prepared for the remaining services.

The prayer which followed was short and well ordered. He addressed the Being before whom angels veil their faces, with that humility of expression, with that pouring out of the heart in natural tones for a sinner's necessities, which plainly showed he was making a petition for wants which

God alone could supply, and not framing forms of sentences to interest or please man.

The passage of Scripture which he had selected was the story of the Prodigal Son, a portion of that blessed volume peculiarly precious to himself; and one with which he had become most familiar, and into the touching scenes it delineated, he had entered with his whole heart.

In a very simple manner, he first explained the meaning of a parable, and the reason why our Saviour chose this method of instruction. Being well versed in ancient manners and customs, and the scenery of the eastern world, he delineated and filled up what was necessary to convey to the minds of uninformed persons, a perfect idea of the whole story. Every eye was riveted upon him, and his energies were strengthened, as he went along, by the deep interest which he saw was awakened among his hearers.

When he had gone through with the story, and brought the prodigal back to his father's arms, he then proceeded to show how clearly it illustrated the sinner's erring path away from God, the fascinations which drew him on, and the misery to which they lead. Here and there a tear would be seen to start, and occasionally a head would droop: it was evident that there were many before him whose real character he had touched. At length he reached the turning point, the resolve of the sinner in his extremity, that he will arise and return to his God. The heart of the speaker filled with deep emotion; his voice trembled, his language became more glowing, his words flowed rapidly; he forgot himself, and free from all embarrassment, poured out the full feelings of his soul. His excited audience sat wrapped in solemnity, and yielded up their hearts to the enchanting theme: like fire in the stubble, the flame flew from heart to heart; tears flowed freely, and when he ceased, there was stillness like the house of mourning, interrupted only by the stifled sob.

He sat down a few moments, and then informed them that the meeting was over. Some arose, but stopped and looked wistfully towards the desk, as though they might yet hear something more; others sat still and wept. Henry prepared to depart; he walked slowly through the benches, preceded by a few persons who were leaving the house.

As he approached the door, his hand was seized in a powerful grasp. He looked round, and recognized at once his warm-hearted friend, old Mr. Cutter. He sat on the end of one of the benches, and by his side was Billy Bloodgood. Billy looked at him and nodded and smiled, while he wiped away the tears that overflowed his twinkling eyes. Billy had not heard a word, but he had a very tender heart; he was rejoiced to be where God was worshipped, and when he saw all around him affected, he yielded to the impulse, and wept too. Uncle Sam *had* heard, and every word had gone deep into his heart. It was no sympathy of feeling with those around him, that caused the big tears to flow so freely; he thought of none but himself and his God: his sinful lost estate had been set before him: he knew it was his own, he felt it to be true. He listened to the voice of the speaker, telling him of the love of God, and inviting him to trust in it; he believed, and yielding to the call of mercy, had cast himself into the arms of his Saviour, and found peace. No wonder that he seized with such convulsive grasp the hand of the dear youth. Henry fixed his eyes upon the old man; he saw his emotion, he saw his lips quivering in a vain effort to speak. His own heart ached, and tears came to his relief. Mr. Cutter made a desperate effort, shaking the hand which he still held,

'God bless you! God bless you!'

Henry hurried away to his home.

Long was this day and this meeting remembered in the place. It was the commencement of a great moral change; the darkness which had so long brooded over it was rolled back, and the light that streams from Heaven's mercy came to bless their spirits. A train of rich and lasting benefits followed quick, and spread a charm over this long neglected and desolate spot, which, from a dreary wilderness, converted it into a garden of the Lord.

CHAPTER XIII

Six years in the early part of our life makes a mighty change in our personal appearance, the current of our feelings, and our course in life. Childhood and youth are ever anticipating the fancied joys of twenty-one, but that blissful period once past, and the goal reached, how much of innocent and heartfelt happiness is left behind! But time must on, and we must on with him, and meet each era of our being as best we may.

Six years have made a vast change in the face of things within our village. The little store, which Jim and Ned started in the wood-shed of their mother's house, has been transferred to a large and commodious building situated near the water, and contiguous to a wharf, where are snug moorings for the good sloop Fanny, now under the command of Sam Oakum. Along the shore, where the few fishermen's huts alone gave signs of life in former days, are now decent dwellings. Docks and building: the frames of vessels of various size are lying in their cradles; and the noise of the lively hammer can be heard through the long summer day. Young men, the former companions of our boys, are now engaged at their trades, or preparing to man the different vessels when ready for a voyage. Above the beach, and in the town more properly, as great a change is manifest; old houses are neatly repaired, and new lines of fences supply the places of the old, tattered inclosures; while here and there, on sites commanding the finest views of the beautiful water scenery, are mansions that bespeak the wealth and taste of their owners; and, to crown all, a neat church sends up its lofty spire from a knoll near the water's edge, the last object that holds the eye of the mariner as he leaves this his native home to breast the stormy ocean, and the first to bless it on his return, and bid him think of Him whose wonders he has seen on the deep.

All these results have not been accomplished alone by those whose youthful energies gave the first spring to life and activity in the place.

Things had, indeed, gone prosperously with them. Their trade, although small at first, rapidly increased; the opportunity they afforded the inhabitants to dispose of their productions advantageously, soon stimulated to increased cultivation. A display of goods from the city introduced a better and neater style of dress, and that led to more neatness in their dwellings, and every thing around them. The timber from the barrens became an article of great demand; and those comparatively valueless wilds bade fair to yield an immense revenue to their owners.

But in addition to all this, a few wealthy families from other parts, attracted by the pleasantness of the location, had come among them; and with these was the early patron of our boys—Major Morris and his lovely family. He had not retired from the service; for the sound of war was rumbling in the distance, and dark clouds were fast rising on our political horizon, and it was no time for a brave and good man to withdraw from his country's need. But he was tired of the unsettled manner of life to which he had been so long subjected, and resolved, so soon as a favorable opportunity should offer, to retire, and enjoy the sweets of home and domestic life. He had long admired the location, but perhaps might not have decided to make it his place of residence, but for an old friend of his—one whose life had been spent upon the ocean, and who could no more be easy without the sight and smell of salt-water than the fish who sport upon its sunny bosom—Commodore Trysail, a bluff, high-tempered, warm-hearted sailor. He had won high honors early in life, but for some cause, in an hour of excitement, had thrown up his commission. He had amassed a handsome fortune since then by engaging in the East India trade; and although never condescending to command even his own ship, he had made several voyages to Bengal, attending solely to business matters. He had now some fine vessels of his own, and having relinquished all idea of going abroad, had resolved to locate where he could enjoy what he had so long been accustomed to, without storms and billows. Having visited the place, in company with Major Morris, he was at once charmed, and they both decided to make it their home, and do what they could to build up things around them. No wonder, then, if six years has affected such an entire change in the aspect of things.

Mr. Grizzle was yet alive, and kept his old place, but his stock of goods had not been replenished for some years. The advantage of the new store were too many for him to compete with. Goods new and cheap, a generous price for all country produce, respectability of character, good manners, and perfect fairness in dealing, all these made the odds too much for Mr. Grizzle to contend against. He gave it up. One corner of his counter yet received a few visitors; for through the day could be frequently seen some old tottering wreck of humanity, with bald head, and long thin locks, stirring eagerly the ancient toddy-stick in a large flowered tumbler, and then, with trembling hand, raising the much-loved mixture to his longing lips, already quivering with age, and soon to be at rest in the grasp of death.

There had been, for some time past, a little mystery about a newly-erected house—and mysteries in small towns are always troublesome things. It was a neat and pleasant cottage, finished with much taste, and with every convenience for a small family. It had been placed on a very pretty location, not far from the hut where Sam Oakum and his parents lived, just on the rising ground which overlooked their humble place of abode, and commanded a full view of the whole panorama of bay and land and ocean, that stretched before the eye to the distant horizon. The question could not be solved all the while it was building, for whom this pleasant habitation was intended. Curiosity was on tiptoe; it formed the subject for many a long gossip over cup of tea, and so awakened the imagination of our good ladies, that all sorts of stories were circulated in reference to it.

'Can any body tell me?' said Aunt Sally Bloodgood—as she sat pouring out tea to a select party of her own, with a tea-pot in one hand and a water-pot in the other, dressed in her new calico gown of the freshest pattern, and no more looking like Aunt Sally when we first saw her, than nothing at all. Casting her eye round, as she put the two pots down, upon the inquisitive countenances of her neighbors—'Can any body tell me whose that house is a building *for?*' and after looking round from one to the other, her eye finally settled upon her good friend Mrs. Cutter, as though she expected, if any body knew, she must.

'You needn't look at me, Sally; I knows nothing about it,' leaning her long body over the table, and shaking her thin visage very significantly. 'Cutter, you know, don't go about much, and when he does hear any thing, he keeps it all to himself; a body has to ding their life out to get any thing out of him. We have fixed our old house, so that it is kind of snug like, so it ain't for us, no how; and who is a-goin' there, the massy only knows.'

'They say,' said a very comfortable-looking personage, with very round cheeks, and ample proportions—'they say, Mrs. Andrews, that your William is a-building that 'are place for himself; and that he's a coming back and goin' to be married to Hettie Brown, and they are to live there.'

'Now did I *ever!*' and the Widow Andrews turned up her eyes towards the ceiling—a common way with her—put her two hands together, and rested them on the tea-table. 'I don't see what people mean; I ain't heered no sich thing—have you, Mary?' appealing to her daughter, who sat beside her, and began to move about in her chair, and to smooth down the very stiff collar that encircled her neck. 'I don't see what people talk so for; I believe they do a-purpose;' and the widow began to slide up on her high notes, which at once aroused the energies of her daughter Mary.

'Oh, *do* Mother! don't mind if they do talk; it don't hurt any body; it don't make it so, you know;—does it, Mrs. Bloodgood?'

'Do la, no; and if it did, where's the harm?'

'Well,' said the fat lady, 'I guess you will all see: for every body knows the two young folks is dead in love, and they say he's made a power of money; only some say he won't have Hettie after all, jist because she's been out to service.'

Mrs. Bloodgood now saw that the harmony of her party was like to be destroyed, for the Widow Andrews was beginning to fan herself, and breathe short; so like a skilful commander, she brought all her forces to bear, in order to turn the attitude of affairs.

'Now, Aunt Peggy!' addressing the fat woman, 'do, la—I wouldn't talk so. Folks say a great many things they don't know any thing about. 'William is a brave boy; and if he's got ahead in the world, I'm glad on it; but who he will marry, or when he will marry, I guess there ain't any body that knows. Don't you say so, Mrs. Andrews? But, do, la! Here I've been a talking, and your tea is clean out; let me give you another cup; and, Aunt Peggy, won't you hand round that plate of cake? and won't you all help yourselves? and them baked pears, they are fresh and nice; I did them up this very morning—but may be some of you would like the preserves? Sally Cutter, you just hand the Widow Andrews that saucer of preserves.'

The tea, and the cake, and the preserves, now demanded general and particular notice; and between eating and drinking, and praising the good things, and asking for receipts, a very delightful state of confusion and loud talking about all manner of things, showed how successful was Aunt Sally's effort to maintain the peace.

Nor was Aunt Sally Bloodgood's the only tea-circle that was disturbed by this unaccountable affair. It was a great marvel, and the poor builder actually lost the good-will of more than one of the tea-drinking old ladies; but he did not seem to mind it, for he went on in a quiet way to finish the thing. And when he had done that, he locked the door, put the key in his pocket, shut the little gate, and went to work at another job.

CHAPTER XIV

Mary Oakum was in personal appearance a lovely young creature, and an equally lovely spirit breathed forth in every word, sparkled from every look, and shone forth embodied in her whole conduct. She had the same black hair, the same flashing, deep-set hazel eye, the same laughing mouth—she was a beautiful miniature of Sam, only replacing his nut-brown complexion with a pure red and white. Mary was now seventeen, not tall of her age, but gracefully formed, and very feminine.

Susan, the youngest sister, was in a different style; for her hair was light, and her eyes blue, and her complexion, though fair, without color. Although two years younger, she was nearly as tall as her sister, with a serious cast of countenance that made her appear at times of an equal age.

The parents and children still occupied the little house on the shore; it was a very small, poor building, but they had kept patching it up the best they could; and being very happy among themselves, they thought not of its imperfections with any feelings of repining or discontent.

Sam was the delight of them all; parents and sisters hung upon him with an ardor of attachment, looked up to him with a feeling of dependence, confidence, and joy, which made him ever the light of their humble home when present with them, and drew their hearts after him with almost painful interest when absent.

He still wore his sailor's rig; was very neat in his dress; never appearing among business men or at his house, in the same garb in which he stood at the helm. How anxiously would his sisters watch for the first glimpse of his white sail in the distance! and how elastic were their steps, as they bounded from the house to meet him, as soon as they descried their neat, trim sailor-boy, as they called him, turning the angle in the shore near their house.

The day of his return had come, and Mrs. Oakum and Susan were busily employed clearing away the relics of the early meal, and putting, if possible, a brighter polish on every thing, when Mary came into the room, arrayed in her very best, and in one hand she held a small green bag, and in the other her sun-bonnet.

'Why, sister, whither away so early? Your new dress on too, your hair arranged so neatly, and your best shoes and all. Where are you going to make a call so early?'

'Oh, no call, sister dear! I am only going to the store. You know I lost my thimble the other evening, and I thought I would get another before Sam comes; he might want me to do something, and I should be sorry to say I had no thimble.'

A deep blush spread all over Mary's white neck, and temples, and forehead; the rich rose of her cheeks seemed, of an instant, to have sent its crimson hue in all directions. Had Mary equivocated? Not in the least; she had never learned that art. Was not the errand a lawful one? Certainly it was; she told the truth in all its simplicity. She wanted a thimble, and was going for that, and with no other motive whatever.

It was simply a flash of truth that crossed her mind—it was elicited by the remark of her sister in reference to her dress. Susan meant nothing in particular; nor had Mary, until then, an idea that she meant any thing in particular by what she had done.

We must look into things a little, however, while Mary is on her way to the store; for she smiled, slipped on her bonnet, and was off.

Mary was but a few years since a laughing, little romping girl, and she had grown up in great intimacy with a very staid and rather good-looking boy. She had sat on his lap, walked with him by the shore hand in hand, looking for pretty stones and shells; played hide-and-seek with him, in company with her brother and sister, among the rocks by moonlight, and even kissed him just as she did Sam, and thought no harm of it. She has, to be sure, long since, eschewed all such things, and stands now upon her womanly dignity. But this boy, although grown up to manhood, has not grown out of her interest. When the playfulness of childhood passed away, as by right it should, other feelings began to take its place. A deep respect for his fine character, which shone brighter and brighter as he grew up; an admiration of his manly appearance; a feeling of gratitude for the kind interest he took in her brother; a desire to do whatever she heard him say he liked; in fine, to assimilate her views and feelings, her tastes and pleasures, to his, was the unconscious desire of her heart.

But did any body know this? Not a human being. A mother's searching eye may possibly at times have discerned a glimmering of the truth; but if so, she had kept it to herself.

Did Mary know this? No, not as the truth itself must say she did; it was a secret, within what she could see of her little heart, into which no human eye had yet pried; but there it was. It did sometimes betray itself a little—a very little: that blush which seemed to come without a cause, which sent her off so quickly from observation, was just a token that she was a little conscious—only a little—how the matter stood.

And does he love her? If he does not, he ought to; for, let him look the world over, he cannot find a purer, lovelier object to meet his earthly happiness upon; he cannot find a soul that burns with an intenser ardor towards each friend her bosom cherishes; he cannot find a heart that, glowing with the purest earthly love, holds all its rich and priceless treasures for himself alone, like her's.

But we must stop, for she has reached the store, and quietly walks up to the side of the counter; passes a pleasant word with the few smiling customers who are there before her, and receives a salutation from Edward, who, busily attending upon those immediately before him, was using his hand and his tongue with great skill and rapidity.

'Good morning, Mary, are all well at home to-day?' said James, stepping from his place, and standing before her.

Mary looked up in surprise, for she had not yet glanced her eye to see whether the graver senior partner was at his desk.

'All well—very well, I thank you.' His address, and the reply, were delivered in a low tone, and he was leaning over the counter when he spoke.

'Any demands to-day?'

'Nothing but a thimble;' and she smiled and held up her hand, preparing to take off her glove. James immediately produced a little case, and placed it before her, but she shook her head—

'These are silver—a common kind will answer me.' Another case was brought, and James leaned over again, and began to select what, in his judgment, should be about the size; but somehow he picked out of the silver case alone.

'Just try this, Mary; none of those seem to fit you well;' and he gently took the little hand, and placed the thimble on the taper finger.

'You will hardly do better than to keep that.'

'But it is silver, and I cannot afford to lose it; I am for ever losing them.'

'You may be more fortunate with this, for it is a present.'

'Oh—thank you—thank you; it is a beautiful thimble. I shall be very choice of it.'

'Because it is silver?' and James looked at her with rather a meaning glance.

'Oh, no, not altogether; to be sure I should be sorry to lose this, because — because it is more valuable,'—and seeing James beginning to color—'it is not only silver, but it is a keepsake.'

All this passed in a tone that could not be heard amidst the din which Edward and his customers kept up.

'I have news to tell you, likewise, and was on the point of walking to your house to let you know that the owner of that building near you, and about which there has been so much curiosity, is expected to arrive to-day.'

'Then you have known who was the owner?'

'I suppose I may as well confess it.'

'And never told us?'

'You never asked me. The family I have long known; I esteem them highly, and I think you will be much pleased with them, especially with the eldest daughter.'

Mary was silent; she wished to ask several questions, but that *eldest daughter*—somehow the words struck a chill to her heart; she was all at once very thoughtful.

'Your brother and I are anxious to have things arranged before they get here, and Sam particularly wishes that his father and all of you should be there when they arrive, and I think,' said James, 'as you are to be such near neighbors, it would be well to show them all kindness.'

'Oh, by all means; certainly, we will do every thing we can to welcome them, as they are friends of yours; but —'

'But what, Mary?'

'Oh, you cannot be sure that they will wish to be very intimate with us, our circumstances will be so different.'

'They are a family, Mary, that do not regard such distinctions. You will love them—I know you will. I hope to enjoy their society much, and I am sure you will too.'

'I will be there, as soon as I can, with the key; and if you are all willing, we will go to work, and arrange things a little for them.'

'Oh, certainly; we will go with pleasure. Good morning.'

James accompanied her to the door.

'In an hour or so, I will be at your house. Good morning.'

'And I suppose he thinks the thimble will be a bribe to induce me to be very polite to that *eldest daughter*; but he need not fear. I shall do every thing I can to make it pleasant. The thimble I shall return when I have an opportunity, and shall tell him that Mary Oakum could be kind to his friends without—'

She could not say any more, and this she did not say—she only thought it; and then she began to be very much ashamed that she had even thought it. But there was a tumult in poor Mary's heart: at times she would hush it, but then again it would arise, in spite of herself.

James came after a while with the key, but not so soon as he expected. Mrs. Oakum and the girls accompanied him to the house; and as Mary resolved to put down all selfish feelings, and to be very pleasant and agreeable, every thing wore a cheerful aspect; for Mrs. Oakum and Susan were delighted with the idea of seeing and becoming acquainted with their new neighbors, especially as James gave such a favorable account of them. He had to take a little scolding from Susan, but it was done in such a good-natured way, that the harmony was not in the least disturbed by it.

As they had never gratified their curiosity while the house was building, as many had, it was all new to them; great was the admiration expressed at the neatness, taste, and convenience of all its parts; the rooms were so pleasant, and the view so charming.

'And what a sweet place this is!' said Susan, as they entered one of the upper rooms; 'how gracefully those branches of the willow hang before the window, and how beautiful the water looks through them, and the church and the parsonage! It is the finest view from any part of the house, is it not, sister.'

'It is very beautiful,' said Mary; and she sighed.

'Now, sister dear, what was that for? You don't feel sad that we have no such place?'

'My dear sister, do you think I am covetous or envious?' And Susan threw her arms around her neck, and kissed off a tear which she supposed her suggestion had produced.

'Covetous, envious; no, indeed, dear Mary, forgive me, if what I said led to any such idea; but I don't think I ever heard you sigh before. Why was it, sister?'

'Oh, nothing. But we ought not to stay here, ought we, as there is so much to do?'

And down they went, and to work with good-will. Mrs. Oakum was in the kitchen, examining with an eye of one who knew well the comfort of conveniences there; every thing needed was close at hand: a well of water by the door, a shed for the wood, and such a beauty of a milk-room, it almost smelled of cream and butter; and from the kitchen you could look out upon such a love of a garden-spot, large enough to raise all that a moderate-sized family could possibly want; while opening into it and near the house was a neat little stable, of sufficient size for a cow and a horse, with their provender.

'Some one,' said Mrs. Oakum, 'has contrived all this who knows what is needful for the comfort of a family.'

James was very active, and showed great skill in distributing the several articles into the different apartments.

'I guess,' said Susan, smiling archly, 'that one, who seems to know so well where things belong, must have had something to do in getting them: who knows,' said she, winking to Mary, 'but this house is for himself after all; and that *eldest daughter* he talks so much about is to be— —. Dear sister, I know you are not well, you are so pale; you have worked too hard.'

'I am afraid she has,' said James, looking with much anxiety.

'Oh, not at all; I am very well;—but these things, had we not better be putting them in their places?'

'These must be all for one room; they are, you see, painted white and tipped with green,—the chairs, and the table, and washstand, they must be for that little upper room. Don't you think so Mary?' said Susan, catching up a chair.

'I think they would be suitable there,' said Mary.

'There they shall go then,' said James: and soon the little room was furnished.

'Oh, is it not sweet?' said Susan. 'But mother is calling us to help her with the carpet,' replied Mary, and down they went. Here, however, was a difficulty; the carpet was in a roll, and there would be no time to cut it and sew it together.

'It would take us a whole day,' said Susan, 'do our best.'

Mrs. Oakum, however, proposed that she should cut the breadths, and lay them down, and some other day they would come and assist the family in sewing it together; so Mary took out her scissors, and soon the floor was covered; and as this was the best room, the furniture suitable was arranged in it, and to the girls it seemed a grand place.

I've Been Thinking | 163

'And now,' said Mrs. Oakum, 'the rooms seem to be all provided with their furniture, except the kitchen, and I don't see that there is any provision made for that. What will they do?' looking from one to the other. James smiled, blushed, and appeared confused, and was about to say something explanatory, when the door was opened, and Mr. Oakum entered, dressed in his Sunday suit; this he had put on at the request of the girls. He informed them that the sloop was in, and that Sam was on his way up.

Sam had no lack of kisses that day, and Mary even hung upon him more fondly than ever; and Sam thought he saw a tear glistening in her eye, but she wiped it away, and said—

'It was nothing.'

Ah, Mary! the world is full of such *nothings*; it is ever piercing the heart of such sensitive beings as yourself, and forcing out the drops that tell in mute but unmistaking language the aching within.

'So, Mr. Sam, you knew the secret all the time about the house?' said his youngest sister, coming up and hanging on him for a kiss.

'Oh, you know, Susan, secrets are troublesome to ladies; I did not wish to burden you, my dear.'

'Very generous it was in you. Oh, I wish I was strong enough to shake you;' but as she was not, she caught him round the neck, and kissed him.

'But come in, and see how well we have arranged things. Will they be here soon?'

Sam made no reply to Susan's last question, but followed her immediately into the house.

They were all soon collected in the parlor, expatiating on the beauty of the place, and were beginning to ask Sam a variety of questions, when James all at once left the room; and Sam, drawing from his pocket a packet neatly enveloped, his parents and sisters looked at him, expecting some new disclosure.

'My dear parents: I have practised a little deception upon you, for the first time in my life, which I hope you will pardon when you hear the nature of it. This house, which you have been arranging, does not belong to any stranger, as you have been led to think—it is all your own; and here, my dear father, is the deed which makes it and the ground around it your's for ever,' handing to his wonder-stricken parent the paper he had in his hand.

Mr. Oakum took the paper, but was so overcome with amazement, that he could say nothing; he looked at his wife, who, for a moment, sat with her hands clasped before her, her eyes strained in their intense gaze on her darling boy. She then sprang to clasp him in her arms, but the girls were before her, and were hanging around his neck, and fairly smothering him with their fond embrace. Sam put out his arms to receive his mother, and she fell upon his neck, and burst into tears.

'Oh, Sam! my dear Sam! may God bless you for ever and ever.'

His father, overcome by the rush of his own excited feelings and the outburst of affection on the part of the mother and sisters, dropped the paper, and leaning on his hands, could only shed tears of joy. It was not the beautiful gift—valuable as it was—nor the sudden flow of prosperity, that raised them at once from a poor and decayed tenement to a dwelling equal in respectability to the best in the place; thoughts far richer to a parent's heart were thrilling his bosom, and working up his feelings into intense and overpowering emotion. To find in the man who stood before him in his strength and ardor, the same kind, loving, feeling fondness that the boy had manifested—in fine, to know that prosperity and manhood had not changed his boy—it was enough: earth had no better good, heaven could give no richer earthly solace. And could that son have heard the thoughts which rose in gushing ardor to the throne on high, and could his vision but have burst the veil which hides that secret place where thoughts are registered, he would have felt that a recompense already had been treasured for him beyond the reach of venture or decay.

Sam had made but little calculation as to the effect of this surprise, either on his parents or himself. He had often, in boyish days, even when all around was dark and forbidding, amused himself with visions of the future, of all that he might be and do, and in every fancy sketch, his mind portrayed for the comfort of his parents; the joy which, in some unexpected way, might be infused into their spirits, was ever the prominent figure in the scene. This object, now so happily accomplished, had been his aim for years: for this he had resisted his inward impulse to go abroad and visit distant climes, and seek a fortune more genial to his bounding spirit; steadily had he pursued his calling, and faithfully labored and stored away his earnings with almost a miser's care, to gratify this heaven-born, filial love, and in some hour of exquisite delight enjoy his long, long-treasured wish. And now that hour had come. He had opened the floodgates of happiness upon these dear objects of his affection, and was overpowered himself. He sat down beside his mother, and mingled his tears with her's.

But why has Mary left the scene? and why has she gone with such haste to that little upper room? and why does she clasp her hands, and raise her eye to heaven, and shed such tears as now overflow those long dark lids and bathe her lovely cheek? Another token these of that deep feeling which her secret heart so long has nourished; that room is pleasant now, for hither she has come, in this moment of heart-felt bliss, to pour out her heaving thoughts in gratitude to God; and there she hopes, in days and years to come, to send up the incense so pleasing unto Him who loves a contrite heart.

Mary had much to think of; no longer could she hide from herself the fact that she loved James Montjoy; and every word which he had said, and which had caused her so much inward pain, was now a source of new and heart-felt joy, and it was impossible for her to misunderstand those allusions which so plainly pointed to herself; and yet she would say, 'He was only in jest; he knew it must all come out—he meant nothing by it, nothing particular.' Thus ruminating, and with a happy heart, she passed lightly down the little staircase and along the hall, as James was returning from a stroll in the garden, to which, out of delicacy for the feelings of the family, he had retired, just as Sam was about to make the disclosure.

He put out his hand to congratulate her upon the happy surprise; overcome with the scene she had just passed through, and the rush of feelings at the sight of him, she extended her hand, and burst into tears.

As James entered the parlor with Mary, the scene had to be in some measure renewed; for he was so identified with all the prosperity they had enjoyed, that a sight of him under present circumstances but added to the full tide of feeling.

'Oh,' said Mrs. Oakum, 'this has been all your doing.'

'By no means, my dear madam; Sam alone has devised it, and his own honest earnings have paid the cost.'

'Yes, I have no doubt of that, and Heaven's blessing he will have for it; but you first took him by the hand and encouraged him, and—'

'Oh, Mrs. Oakum, we will not go so far back now; and besides, I could no more have done without Sam than he felt he could do without me; but we must clear up our faces and prepare for company, for this matter will fly like the wind when it gets abroad, and you will have the whole town here to see you.'

Commodore Trysail was one of those specimens of humanity with which we occasionally meet, where a rough exterior and a blunt manner conceal a warm and tender heart. In all matters of business he was prompt, correct, and very decided; a little tenacious of authority when he saw any disposition to slight his orders, but allowing great latitude whenever he knew there was a desire to please and obey him.

Old Peter, who had accompanied the family of Major Morris to their new residence, was quite a favorite with the Commodore; and as the two families were but a short distance apart, with the exception that Peter had his hammock slung in one of the Major's out-buildings—he was as much at home at one house as the other.

It was one part of Peter's business to watch the coming in of the mail, and see that the letters and papers for either family were distributed in the quickest possible time; also to attend upon the departure and arrival of the sloop, as there was always something to go or come by that conveyance, it being the only regular one to and from the city. This part of Peter's duty he performed with special pleasure; Sam had ever been a favorite of his, and he never tired of telling over what he knew of him when a boy, and extolling his fine appearance, his activity and his correct conduct in all things, now that he had grown to be a man.

Between the Commodore and Peter Sam was often a subject of conversation, until all that Peter knew of his favorite had been many times repeated.

On this day, so distinguished in the life of his hero, Peter not only brought along from the boat quite a number of parcels, but he had also a weighty cargo of news, which he had gathered on his way back. After giving Lady Morris, as he always styled her, the first of the tidings, he hastened to the Commodore's as fast as his crutches would carry him.

It was a warm afternoon, and the Commodore was seated in his veranda on the shady side of the house, enjoying the cooling view of the expanse of water spread out before him, and the gentle breeze that scarce moved the long branches of the willow that hung above and around him, when he heard the well-known sound of the crutches stumping along the hard gravel path at double quick time. Peter was so much out of breath, and so excited with what he had to tell, that after he had reached the stoop and taken off his hat, and smoothed down his queue and made several obeisances, he could only stammer out,

'Your honor—'

The Commodore looked at him with no little surprise, for the preparation Peter had made betokened quite a long yarn.

'A warm day, Peter.'

'Very, your honor;' and Peter fumbled away at his queue, and twisted his quid to all sides of his mouth.

'You are out of breath, Peter; what is the haste to-day? any news stirring?'

'Great news, your honor, great news.'

'Is war declared, or has the comet lost its tail? let me hear; out with it, Peter.'

'No war, your honor, God forbid: and I guess the comet is whizzing away yet, though we can't see him by daylight; but your honor knows that picture of a house up along the bank there—'

'Ay, ay—what, the house that has no owner? and a pretty box it is; what of it, Peter?'

'But it has got an owner, and who does your honor think it is? Our Captain Sam; he's built it 'spressly for his father and mother, God bless him! and he's rigged it all up for 'em, and he's put 'em in it this blessed day, and there they are, as happy as your honor was in a tight, new ship. And now he says, "Good-by to the old sloop, Peter; I've got the old folks snug and happy, and now I am going to steer my way on the broad ocean, just as you have always been wishing me to do." That's just what he said, your honor. God bless him.'

The Commodore was a match for Peter with the tobacco any day, and whenever a little excited, was sure to clap his finger and thumb into his vest pocket, where there was generally a supply ready cut up of suitable length. As Peter concluded his tale, the Commodore began to fumble for a charge.

'Peter, I'm out; hand me that bit of yarn you are cutting from.'

'Bless your honor, not this; no, no;' and taking out a package that had filled the whole capacity of his jacket pocket, 'here is some, your honor, the boys have put up for me to-day (Peter had the run of the store free), bless their kind hearts. It's bran new, your honor; take it all, and welcome.'

Having untied the roll, cut off a liberal allowance, and given two or three squeezes to the delicious morsel,

'Do you say, Peter, that he has built that handsome place for his father and mother, and furnished it, and given it to them out-and-out?'

'It's God's truth, your honor.'

'Well, Peter, all I can say is, that he has got more of a sailor's heart in him than I thought he had; and do you think that is the reason why he has been shoaling along shore here, when we have all been wondering why such a smart young fellow didn't try to climb a little higher in the world?'

'Nothing else, as sure as that water is runnin' to the ocean. I always tell'd your honor, Capt. Sam would come out bright; he wasn't never made for a land lubber, your honor: his heart is too big, too big for that, I always knowed it was.'

'And I suppose the old folks are very happy. Did they know of it before?'

'Never, your honor, till this blessed day; and when I com'd along by there, Miss Mary came runnin' out; 'Come in, Peter, come in and see our new house;' and so in I goes, and sich a sight your honor never see; there was the mother with the tears a runnin', and the father lookin' as if he had been standin' eight-and-forty hours facing a nor'wester, and the galls and all hold on me, and showing me every thing, and making me eat and drink; it's the happiest family, your honor, I believe there is at this moment on the breathin' earth; I was no better than a baby myself, your honor.'

'Peter, do you go this minute, do you hear?'—Peter had like not to have heard, for he was on his way going somewhere, he knew not exactly for what—'and tell Harry to rig up the carriage, and—do you hear, Peter?'

'Ay, ay, sir.' Peter was hardly within hailing distance.

'Tell Mrs. Morris that I shall call for her.'

'Ay, ay, sir.'

'Bless my soul! he's a fine fellow.' The Commodore was now walking up and down very fast: 'Something must be done for him; he must let that old sloop go to the — —;' the Commodore was not always particular where he sent things, so that they were out of his way.

There are green spots in this world of ours, which tempt us to forget that it is a fallen world, and point us, in their exhibition of true enjoyment, to what it might have been, and what it may yet be. There are pleasures that seem so unalloyed by selfish, earthly dross, we almost feel the breath of heaven fanning our spirits while we mingle in them.

Such was the bright and pleasant scene that Sam had lighted up within that circle of domestic love, his home.

Nor was there any lack of friends that day to greet them kindly, or to sympathize in their joy. The tidings soon spread, as James said they would, and neighbor after neighbor came dropping in, some, no doubt, to gratify their curiosity, but many, many more to give utterance to the joy they really felt.

It was about the middle of the afternoon when the equipage of Commodore Trysail drove up. The old gentleman was a sailor, and not very particular when dealing with men, at least not always so, to polish either his language or his manners; but in the company of ladies he never forgot the respect due to them; he was mild and courteous, no matter how humble the individual or the circle to which he was introduced. Mrs. Morris was no stranger to the family; she had often visited them in their lonely home, and by her affable and kind manners had won their hearts.

No wonder, then, that the girls ran with such haste to welcome her, and conducted her into their new abode with feelings, if not of pride, at least of heart-felt pleasure. She kissed them as they met her at the door.

'I wish you joy, my dear good girls, with all my heart. Mrs. Oakum, I congratulate you on your entrance into such a pretty home; it is a sweet place; but it must be doubly sweet and precious to you under all the circumstances.'

Mrs. Oakum could not reply; tears alone responded to the kind greeting.

'But where is that noble fellow, Sam? I must call him so yet—where is he?'

'He has run away. Do you think, Mrs. Morris,' said Mary, 'he found the neighbors began to come in, and off he went.'

'Do you tell him for me, he's a pretty fellow; and that I shall expect a visit from him expressly in return for this.'

The Commodore had been detained at the door a moment, in offering his whole-soul congratulations to Sam's father. As he entered the room, Mrs. Morris formally introduced him to the mother and sisters. Bowing very low to Mrs. Oakum,

'Madam, I do not wonder that your feelings are excited; he is a noble boy, and you have every reason to be proud of him.'

'He has ever been a dear, good child, sir.'

'Yes; I have no doubt of that, madam; and I suspect he has had a dear, good mother. Ah! it is these mothers that make men what they ought to be. I had a dear, good mother once. I never shall forget her; she taught me a great many good things, when she used to lean over me in my bed. What a different man I should have been had I minded her; but, thank God, I hope I have not forgotten them all.'

A tear might have been seen bedewing an eye that had met the shock of battle, and the rush of the tempest, without a twinkle.

'But, bless my soul! are these two cherubs your daughters?—a kiss, girls; a kiss.'

There was no affectation in their honest hearts, and they received a hearty salutation without blushing any more than might have been expected.

'Do you think, Commodore,' said Mrs. Morris, 'our hero has betaken himself away!'

'The rogue! I wanted to have given him a good sailor's squeeze; and to tell him how happy I am to find that he has a true sailor's heart. But I see how it is; he had rather do a good deed than be praised for it. Will you tell him for me, madam,' turning to Mrs. Oakum, 'that I should be pleased to see him at my house as early to-morrow morning as his engagements will permit? Again, allow me, madam, to wish you much happiness in your new abode, and many, many years to enjoy it in.'

The Commodore bowed to the whole circle, and offering his arm to Mrs. Morris, led her to the carriage.

CHAPTER XV

'Mr. Oakum, good morning to you; you will excuse me for omitting your title; although, if you must have it, I should prefer the one which your old friend Peter has adopted, and call you Captain Sam. I am glad to see you, sir; walk in.'

All this was said at the door of the Commodore's office, and while he was shaking the hand of the young man with great cordiality. This office was a small addition to his handsome mansion, jutting out from one end, and into which was an entrance externally and independent of the passage in the main building.

Sam had made the call at the office door, and was met with the greeting as stated above.

There was a great disparity in their personal appearance, and yet either of them would have been handsome models to represent their different ages and standing in society. The Commodore's large, full, portly form, ruddy face, dark-gray eyes and powdered hair, would well represent the retired commander of sixty-five: while the trim and agile frame, the sun-burnt face, the raven locks, the sparkling, hazel, deep-set and deeply-shaded eye, would have answered well the idea of a young adventurer, ready to commence the untried dangers of the deep. Sam was decidedly a handsome fellow; and whether his sisters had been fixing him out that morning, I cannot say, but he was dressed with much care; too much, some might think, for his calling. It was, however, of the true sailor fashion; and if, when engaged in his work, he was a whole man, we can leave such matters to his fancy.

'You will excuse me, Mr. Oakum, for requesting you to call upon me, or for the inquiries I may put to you; as I have a plan in view, which I should think would be more congenial to a young man of your abilities, than dodging back and forth in that little sloop.'

'I am very happy, sir, to wait upon you, and will very thankfully listen to any views you may please to communicate.'

'First, then, I wish you to state what are your plans for the future. I have heard through Peter—I give you my authority—that you design to leave your present business. If you have no objections, my young friend, make a clean breast to me; I want to hear all about you.'

Sam smiled. 'Why, sir, to tell you the truth, I am really tired, as you say, of "dodging about in the sloop;" but hitherto duty has kept me at the helm very much against my inclination.'

'Glad to hear you say so. Duty, sir, is a glorious master, although sometimes he drives us sadly against our wills. Then you have resolved to start upon a new course?'

'I have, sir.'

'But the sea will be a new business for you. Your cruise along shore cannot have fitted you for what you will meet with there.'

'I have anticipated that, sir; and have already made three short voyages.'

Sam saw that the Commodore appeared much pleased with this information.

'Since you have so kindly requested me, sir, to tell you my past doings and present plans, I will presume upon the permission, and do so.'

'That is just what I wish, sir.'

'The sloop, which seems of late to have been a trouble to many of my good friends, besides the kind-hearted old Peter (Major Morris had not been backward to drop some broad hints in reference to it), was once the object of my highest ambition; but like many objects when attained, seemed only as a stepping-stone to something after which my imagination panted, and for which, I must confess, I have been at times too restless. But an end I had in view, and which I saw I could accomplish by retaining my situation in the sloop, has enabled me to continue at my post, although I must say against my fancy.'

'Yes, yes; and let me tell you, my young friend, it was a noble end, and you will be a gainer, a great gainer by it in the long-run; but'—seeing that Sam was blushing very much, and apparently getting into a state of confusion—'pardon me for interrupting you; please go on, and tell me the whole story.'

'Intending, so soon as that object was accomplished, to launch forth and push my way upon the ocean, I embraced an opportunity afforded me, during a season of the year when our navigation is obstructed, to make a short voyage. Three several times I have been, and the last was of peculiar advantage to me; for, experiencing a hurricane just after we left Havana, the captain and chief mate were washed overboard by a heavy sea that swept our decks, and the second mate did not know enough to keep the reckoning; so at the request of all hands, I took charge of the brig, and, although we encountered two severe gales, brought her safely into port.'

The Commodore rose, and walking across the room, turned, and fixed his keen eye full on Sam.

'You ought to have been handsomely rewarded for that, sir. Was no notice taken of it by the owners or the under writers?'

'Oh, yes, sir'—and Sam drew forth a fine gold watch—'this is their token, but I should have preferred the offer of the brig; she was a fine vessel, but I suppose they had friends who laid a stronger claim than I could.'

'Thus, you have no hesitation as to your ability to take sole command of a vessel to any quarter of the world?'

'I have not, sir.'

'And you are willing to do so?'

'I am very anxious to do so, sir, if I can find any owners willing to trust me.'

The Commodore resumed his seat.

'Mr. Oakum, you must be well aware that our country is at present in a critical situation. War is inevitable. I think so—I am confident of it. The danger, then, in commercial navigation, will be of a very serious nature. I am, as you know, somewhat engaged in the trade to China; two of my vessels are now on the way there; one of these will not return for some time, and the other is to receive a cargo in the usual manner, and will probably be back a little short of one year; but I fear, that before six months come round, we shall be at war. I must make what preparation I can to secure my personal interest against an evil which I foresee. My design is to hasten the return of one of my ships with her cargo, by all possible means. You know that I have just completed a beautiful schooner; she will sail like a witch. I have resolved to send her express to China, and I now offer you the command of her.'

Sam arose, and was about to thank the Commodore for the generous offer.

'Please be seated, Mr. Oakum, you have not heard the end of the story yet. I have business of importance to be attended to in China, and the captain of the ship I design to order back must remain there, and you, sir, will take his place. On your arrival out, you will find yourself master of as fine a ship as swims the ocean.'

Sam could contain himself no longer; he arose from his seat.

'Commodore Trysail, I know not how to express the deep sense I feel of obligation to you—it is the happiest moment of my life, sir.'

The Commodore grasped the hand of the young and ardent sailor, and was delighted to see the flash of joy and pride that sparkled forth from his bright eye.

'You may thank yourself, Mr. Oakum, and the manly efforts you have made to improve your advantages.'

Just then the office door was gently opened, and a shaggy head appeared, nodding very significantly, but saying nothing.

'Well, Peter, any thing new stirring?'

'Why, I thought your honor would be pleased to know that the Major had arrived, and the young lady.'

'What, has Major Morris returned, and Susie with him? that is good news.'

Peter's head was immediately withdrawn, and he was heard stumping it away at a rapid rate.

'It will be no child's play, Mr. Oakum, as you will find, bringing that vessel home; for I am determined, war or no war, that you must get her into port at all hazards, and if I did not think that you would prove a man in the hour of extremity, depend upon it, sir, I should never confide such a trust to you. The risk of loss I expect to run; and after you have done your best, should you fall into the enemies' hands, you will not be in the least to blame. The management of every thing in reference to this matter I leave entirely to yourself. My schooner is ready for you. She is under your command; select your own crew, and hands enough to make a double crew for the ship on her return.'

CHAPTER XVI

Mr. George Rutherford, as I have hinted in a former chapter, was becoming entangled in his pecuniary circumstances. He had no fears as yet that he should not be able to pay every obligation, and have a competency left; but his sensitive spirit was keenly alive to that kind of humiliating deference which is always more or less demanded and received by those who, more calculating in their habits, keep their capital at command, and are enabled to exchange their ready money for the borrower's security.

But whatever annoyance or inward torment he suffered was carefully concealed within his own breast; he could not bear to throw a shade over the bright and joyous heart of his wife.

It was, however, impossible that one who loved with such entire devotedness, should not perceive when some dark and troublous cloud lay upon the object of her affection. Often would she come to him as he sat musing, at the close of day, and ask—

'What is it, George! does anything trouble you? these wrinkles are truly beginning to be permanent. Do tell me, and let me share it with you.'

And then he would smile, and kiss the fair hand, and say—

'Nothing, dear Mary; nothing worth telling; there are a thousand little vexations and cares in life, you know, which help to make the marks upon us, I suppose, and thus show that they have been. Nothing, dear Mary.'

But by degrees accumulated strokes began to bear most seriously upon him; his property melted away by little and little; at one time an unwise act of friendship, at another an unsuccessful negotiation in trade, or may be, a sharper's trick; there seemed to be always some cause at work to drive away his means.

He had become largely implicated in establishing a store near to the property he owned in the barrens, in order to afford an opposition to Mr. Cross, hoping thereby to alleviate the condition of the poor laborers; but the person who managed the business proved to be no match for the wily Cross, and it only served to excite his adversary to bitter revenge.

He had, also, become involved more seriously than he as yet had any idea of himself, with a Company that were engaged in working a quarry.

The prospects held out to him were very flattering, as such things usually are when presented by interested and designing persons; but as each year passed by with no profit realized, and a fresh demand for money to carry on their operations, too confiding to suspect those whose bad management ought to have awakened his doubts, he suffered his purse to be drained, and, worse than all, suffered his name and credit to be used.

Manfully had he borne up under all his reverses, shrinking from no loss nor responsibility, which, however unwisely brought upon himself, was still his own act, and, therefore, sacred as his honor.

At length a storm, he saw, was rising fast, and spreading its dark and gloomy mantle over him. He could not avert its fury; but with fortitude, with a firm determination to maintain his integrity, he awaited the catastrophe.

The first blow which came with much severity was in the failure of Bolton, the individual whom he had established in trade near the barrens. Many were involved in that calamity, and he was compelled, in order to meet the demands which would be made upon him in consequence, to use all his means and his utmost ingenuity to maintain his credit, now become of vital importance to him. Troubles, at times, overtake us like the tiding-bearers to the Patriarch of old; scarce has one sad tale been uttered, when another is ready to begin.

Mr. Rutherford had passed a sleepless night; the long hours had been spent in running over the sad circuit of his misfortunes, and in endeavoring to extricate himself from the tangled maze in which he was involved. His wife would most willingly have been the partner of his cares, and spent the day and night in labor, either of body or of mind. But no—he must not, he cannot disturb the quiet of her bosom; he will yet, he fondly hopes, weather it through, and she shall never know the struggle his spirit has borne. And thus it would have been, and thus his proud and tender heart would have ached in secret, and cloistered all its trials, until it broke beneath the accumulated load; but a kind Providence was watching around his sleepless bed, and knew all that he could bear, and was preparing the way that would, in spite of himself, break open his secret sorrows, and compel him to unbosom himself to her whose gentle spirit would pour out its sweet consolations into his troubled heart, brace up his worn-out feelings, and lay them calmly to rest amid the soothings of love; earthly, it may be, but a bright emblem of that in which the weary soul will sweetly repose when the trials and toils of life are over.

The watching and busy thoughts of the night past were too visible the next morning to escape the eye of love; and as his Mary entered the room where he was seated, waiting for their early meal, she could not help saying to him,

'You are sick, dear George; I know you are.'

Before he could reply there was a knock at the door, and Mr. Rutherford was summoned into an adjoining apartment.

The gentleman expressed his regret for the business upon which he had come; he handed to Mr. Rutherford a paper, which proved to be an attachment upon his beautiful homestead, and the land connected with it.

'You have, no doubt, heard, sir, that the Quarry Company has gone to pieces; and as you appear to be the only responsible one among them, the person named in that paper, and to whom they are largely indebted, feels compelled to take this step, although very reluctantly.'

This explanation was sufficient; Mr. Rutherford perceived the dilemma to which things had at length come. His visitor, having no further business, withdrew; and as he closed the door upon him, he retired again by himself, and was seated by a table with the paper in his hand, when his wife entered the room, and closed the door.

'My dear George, you must let me know what is the matter. You cannot hide from me, that there is some great trouble upon you. Tell me, my dear husband, tell me what it is'—and she threw herself upon her knees before him, and clasping her arms about him, looked up with intense interest beaming from her dark hazel eyes.

'We are ruined, Mary! my property, the inheritance of my ancestors, is all, I fear, to be swept away from me.'

'And you have known this, George, a long time, and have been bearing the trouble all alone in your own breast. Why have you done this, and not let me be a sharer of your sufferings?'

'Oh, Mary, how could I do it? It was out of your power to stop the torrent I have been contending against, and I could not bear to disturb your quiet.'

'My dear George, how little do you understand of a woman's love; bright and pleasant things do not always satisfy its warm desire. I had rather suffer with you, and for you, my dear husband, the sharpest pangs, and feel the direst vicissitudes of life, if I could only prove to you, how much dearer to me is your love than all things else on earth.'

As she said this her eyes were filled with tears, and told so truly with the words she had just uttered, all the meaning of her soul, that he clasped her to his bosom.

'My love, my life, my heart's richest treasure! may God bless you for all the comfort you have been to me, and for all you are now.'

Sorrow, thou child of sin, strong and terrible as is thy power, and crushing as is the weight of thy hand when pressed on no worms of the dust, yet know thou, there is an antidote, a precious gift of Heaven, when by man's sin all blessings which his God had given were justly forfeited — this antidote is love; when fixed on God, it bows the spirit into childlike confidence, clinging closer to the heavenly hand the heavier the blow. And when two kindred souls on earth have merged their hopes, their fears, their interests, their warm desires, their whole hearts' sympathies in one strong true embrace, there is so much of heaven's own happiness in it, that spite of all the anguish under which at times they bow, this sweet and subtile charmer steals within, spreads a calm upon the bosom of the waters, hushes all to peace, and bids them still be happy.

And now she sits beside him, and he tells her all his strange trials, and how dark his prospects are.

'It must all go, Mary.'

'Well, my dear husband, let it all go; your own sweet spirit is unstained by one wrong or mean act; you have never withheld a righteous due; you have never ground the face of the poor; you have never triumphed over those beneath you; you have rather tried to raise them to your own level: and now let poverty come, it cannot sink our spirits, so long as there is no blot on your fair fame, and no stain on your conscience.'

Rutherford was manly in his feelings, but he could not repress his starting tears. His lovely wife, without a sigh, had let go all that wealth could hold out to her, and only thought of her husband's virtues.

'Yes, Mary, that is true. I believe I can truly say with Job: "If I have withheld the poor from their desire, or have caused the eyes of the widow to fail, or have eaten my morsel myself alone, and the fatherless have not eaten thereof: if I have seen any perish for want of clothing, or any poor without covering, then let my arm fall from my shoulder-blade, and mine arm be broken from the bone."'

'I know it, my dear husband, I know it; and as you have acted in the fear of God, his strength will be our refuge.'

CHAPTER XVII

The shades of evening had settled upon that retired spot, the stronghold of Mr. Cross up in the barrens. The doors and windows of his long, low building, were closed; a light was burning on the counter, beside which were seated the owner of the premises and a companion, very unlike him in appearance, whatever similarity there might be in the temper of their hearts—Mr. Cross having rather a round and plump carcass, with cheeks filled out, and bearing the hue which a liberal allowance of gin and water usually imparts. The other was altogether of the mummy order; his body thin and bent over, his limbs long and bony, with a loose furrowed visage, which looked as though it might once have been supplied with flesh, but its substance having melted away, the outer covering now hung flabby and puckered under his chin and beneath his cheek-bones and at the corners of his mouth; his hair was grisly, and stood far off from his wrinkled forehead, which was broad and high enough to indicate the presence of intellect, or at least room for it; the colour of his eyes it would be hard to determine, for they were very small, and the thick, heavy eye-lashes twinkled so continually, it was almost impossible to catch a glimpse of them. A bottle of gin, a pitcher of water and two tumblers stood on the counter, close beside them; and from this we may infer that the two gentlemen were not dissimilar in some of their tastes.

'Now, Squire (for we must know that this gentleman belonged to an honourable profession), 'I think we've done this job up pretty considerably slick—don't you?'

Turning his long face round as Mr. Cross spoke, so as to bring it into a horizontal position, and shaking it very significantly, as each word fell from his lips in a slow and measured tone—

'It has worked, neighbour Cross, like a charm, just as I told you it would. The shoe pinches now, I guess, and more than one foot too—one, two, three, four; only think of it,'—giving Mr. Cross a poke with one of his long fingers—'only think of it—five birds with one stone—only think of it!'—another poke.

'I never thought, Squire, what you could be at, when you wanted me to lend Bolton that money.'

'I knew though, neighbour, what I was about. Jemmy Bolton wanted money bad; he had property enough laying round for you to slap on any time. You and I, you know, have talked about setting Dave up alongside the Montjoys; that, you see, will never work. Bolton I knew, for he told me of it, owed those boys all of three thousand dollars; they had advanced it to him on the timber, thinking, you see, that all was safe, and that it would be coming along. Stop that, says I; trip up Jemmy Bolton—clap on the timber; that cuts the Montjoys three thousand dollars—no small sum for young folks, considering the times too; then down goes Bolton—that gives Bowers & Co., and Jones & Brothers such a pull, you see, down they go too; ha, ha, ha!'—a poke with the long finger—'both of them owe the Montjoys considerable. That, with Bolton's affair, you see, will just about finish the job for them; they can't stand it no how.'

'Poor fellows! I am almost sorry for them.' Mr. Cross was not so sorry but he could smile a little as he said it.

'I am not a bit—I am not a bit sorry, neighbor; they are upstarts, nothing else; and they have made all the folks about them think that they are the end of the law. No, no; let them go down—the sooner the better; and when they are once down on their back, you see, then up goes Dave. You have got the cash, you know—a dash he will make; and the whole country round will be the better for it.'

'Yes; but, Squire, you know these fellows will fight hard to live it through; they are no fancy boys; they have worked their way along by their own efforts; they stand high at the bank. McFall is a great friend of theirs; they will make the bank help them—see if they don't.'

'I have thought of that too, neighbor'—another hard poke—'I've thought of that; and there you have them too.'

'How so, Squire? I have nothing to do with the bank you know.'

'Don't you know a certain man who would not refuse you a favor for a trifle? Bank Directors are not always so independent as they would wish to be thought—ha, ha, ha!'

'Well, what of him?'

'You just whisper in his ear that it would be no particular accommodation to you, that certain folks should receive any favors; that will be enough. One man, you know, in a board is as good as a dozen'—another poke.

'Well, well, I understand.'

'I thought you did—but what was that? There is nobody sleeps here, I hope?'

'Oh no, it is the dog; he is dreaming I suppose.'

'It startled me though, neighbour, for it would not be quite so clever to have any one get the run of what we have been saying.'

'Never fear, Squire; I shut all up myself.'

'I hope you are sure of that; for I was just going to tell you the best of the whole joke.'

'Tell away, Squire; there are no listeners but the old casks; they won't tell any tales.'

'They do sometimes though, neighbour.'

'How so?'

'They tell a little bit, sometimes by the end of our nose, ha, ha, ha!'—another poke—'don't they? ha, ha, ha! Well, as I was saying, the best of it is all to come. Rutherford is clean done up'—one, two, three pokes right off.

'Rutherford done up! What do you mean now, Squire?'

'Why you know I told you that we had killed five birds with one stone, and so we have. Bolton is dead, the other two fellows are kicking, and the Montjoys will be dead soon: and our old friend Rutherford, whom we have been picking at these six years, is down at last, all gone to smash. Think of that, neighbor Cross.'

Mr. Cross made no reply; but turning to the decanter, filled his own glass and the Squire's about half full of the clear stuff, added a little water to his own, and then swallowed the potion at one draught. The Squire did not trouble the water, preferring the good creature in its pure state.

'Your gin is uncommonly strong, neighbour—'ugh, 'ugh, 'ugh—it almost shakes a body—'ugh, 'ugh, 'ugh.'

'Water it then, why don't you? But what is it about Rutherford, and how has that come?'

'Why, you know as well as I do, that Rutherford is an easy body; you know that the quarry folks have been getting round him, and drawing him in more and more every year. He, good soul! thought all was right, while they have been going on, as you know very well, running into debt deeper and deeper. Well, it is only a little pull that is needed to bring down a great weight when it is tottering and ready to fall. This business of Bolton's has upset the whole concern; they only lost a trifle by him, but it touched them just at a delicate time. People got frightened, and the game was up, and Rutherford is in for all their debts; it is thought it will sweep every thing away, homestead and all.

'Now this, I know, is of no consequence to you: it will not give you any title to these barrens; but now that they are in a muss, will be the time to accomplish our great plan. That deed is not on record yet'—a very hard poke—'you know that your deed from old Ross covers the whole ground, when once this claim of Rutherford's is put one side. Old Rutherford, I suppose, thought that the whole tract here was not worth the trouble of looking after, and the young one, no doubt, thinks that all is right; but mind me, neighbour, now is your time, or never. This land, between you and me, which Rutherford owns here, is worth all the rest of his property put together. These Montjoys have, you see, opened a trade for the timber, and there is no telling what its value will yet be. The creditors will be searching the records; it will soon be found out that this deed is not registered, and then your play is out. What you do, must be done at once.'

'True enough, Squire; his deed once out of the way, mine is worth a trifle no doubt; but the question is, has he a deed at all? and if he has, how can we get hold of it?'

'Ah, neighbour, he has got the deed; I have seen it with my own eyes: you see I have not been idle about this matter of yours, although it is a thing that it will not do to say much about. Some time since, I thought I would just call and inquire about some old matters, merely to see what might turn up. He was very polite, you know, handing me a chair, and all that. "You want to look at the old survey, do you, Squire?" "Yes," said I, "if it is not too much trouble, Mr. Rutherford." "Oh no, by no means." And so he out with the old tin trunk; you have seen that trunk in old Rutherford's time.'

'Oh, yes, often.'

'Well, he out with the old trunk; he keeps it just where the old man did, under the secretary; you know as well as I can tell you.'

'Yes, yes, I've seen it, but go on with your story.'

'Well he out with his trunk, as I was saying, and among the very first papers he threw on the table, was this very deed. Thinks I, old fellow, if I had you once in my grip, I guess I know whose fortune would be made.'

'Well, the thing is now, how to get hold of it.'

'That's the thing neighbour;'—one or two good pokes.

'I have a few good fellows that are up to any thing, only let me tell them what to do.'

'Then it can be done, neighbour. What a nice thing it would be to have a little bit of a fire happen, say about midnight. A pretty state of confusion that would make, you know; doors open, everybody running helter-skelter, all frightened to death! Wouldn't that do?'—a hard poke—'but there is no time to lose.'

Cross evidently relished the idea suggested, for he replenished the glasses again, omitting the water this time; then talking in a much lower tone, named the persons—smart fellows, as he called them—arranged time, place of rendezvous, etc.; to all which the Squire assented, every once in a while putting out his long finger and striking neighbour Cross in the ecstacy of his admiration. And thus they devised this deed of darkness, careless of all the terrible consequences which might result, so that their own crafty designs were accomplished.

CHAPTER XVIII

Sam Oakum was indeed very much excited at the close of his interview with Commodore Trysail; the bright prospect before him of soon realizing what his heart had been so long aspiring after, gave a sudden spring to all his feelings, and the spirit of his station seemed already to have taken possession of his mind.

The trifle of news, too, which Peter had communicated, might also have had something to do with the bouyancy of his feelings. Sam longed to see again the little fairy-like creature, with golden locks and dark blue eyes, that once in his early days he occasionally met.

This little fairy, however, is a fairy no longer, for she has grown up to be a fine, good-natured young lady; her golden locks have turned to a rich auburn; her dark blue eyes illuminate, with their bright and pleasant sparkles, her full oval face, on which the rose and the lily have beautifully blended.

Sam has not seen her, however, for four long years, and he thinks of her as she looked then. And if the Commodore had known how much more Sam was thinking about Peter's news, than about the schooner or the ship, it might have injured his confidence, a very little.

As to what this little fairy ever thought of Sam, it would be equally hard to divine. All we know is that when a little girl she used to be very glad to see a little black-eyed boy in blue jacket and trousers, and would frequently smile when she saw him, and perhaps on one or two occasions exchanged a word with him—nothing more.

She is now, I have said, a young lady; and whether she ever thinks of the little black-eyed boy is yet to be known.

Sam had thought all day of the visit which he felt he ought to make to his friends the Morris's. He called there in the edge of evening, and no doubt spent a very pleasant hour, for his friends were rejoiced to see him, and gave him to understand that the Commodore had let them into the secret; and from the kindness with which he was treated, it was very evident that he had not fallen in their estimation.

I said, that he no doubt spent a pleasant hour; but that idea intruded itself rather because there was everything conspiring to make it pleasant, than from its apparent effect upon our hero; for his countenance, as he walked on his way towards home, was sad, and it was some time before the lively, happy circle there could so impart their cheerfulness as to enable him to join heartily with them.

Major Morris and his lovely daughter had reached home, as Peter had said, accompanied by a young lady, who had been a companion of Susan at school, and her brother, a fashionable young man, the parents of whom were wealthy and truly respectable in their standing. And it may as well be told at once, that although not engaged to this youth—for Susan's parents were too careful of her happiness to allow such a step at the age she then was—still there was decided feeling on the part of the young man, and Susan had been perhaps as well pleased with him as with any of those who constantly sought her company. He was not, however, visiting as a suitor, but had been invited with his sister to spend a few weeks at the Major's delightful residence.

Susan Morris was by no means an imaginative girl. She had, it is true, very ardent feelings, but they had always been expended upon real objects; and, in consequence, she was the beloved of every circle where she moved.

Two weeks from the day on which Commodore Trysail gave the appointment, Sam and his beautiful schooner were ready for the ocean.

Partings with near friends are not pleasant scenes, so I shall pass them over. It was a lovely afternoon, one of summer's brightest days; a lively breeze played over the water, and scarcely bending to its power, a small trim vessel, rigged in pilot-boat fashion, was gliding gracefully along, not far from the shore. Every sail was set, and filled just enough to display their graceful cut, the little black hull beneath making them look more white and showy by the contrast. A row-boat, well manned, was by the shore, around which were gathered groups of lookers-on, or friends saying some last words to the youths who held the oars, and whose half serious smiles told plainly that their hearts were not so light as they would seem.

Just beyond the shore, upon the sloping green, a little party stands, eyeing with apparent interest the motions of the schooner and the preparations for departure, which are plainly visible in the gathering crowd that was surrounding the little boat at the water's edge.

'Oh, Susan, what a fine sight that vessel makes; but who would think of venturing to sea in such a craft?'

'Why not, Julia?'

'Oh, she is so small, I should think the waves would ingulf her—but here comes her Captain, I suppose. Your father keeps close to him; and the old Commodore, how proud he seems.'

'Yes, he does, I assure you,' said Mrs. Morris; 'he is proud of his vessel and her Captain too.'

The three gentlemen now approached the ladies, raising their hats, and again replacing them, with the exception of the younger one, who, having removed his light chapeau, kept it in his hand.

There was a seriousness in his air as he immediately stepped up to Mrs. Morris, and received her offered hand.

'May God bless you, my dear fellow! Come, a mother's kiss.'

Sam's heart was brave, but it was very tender. He took the liberty allowed him, but uttered not a word, while Mrs. Morris took no pains to restrain the flowing tears. He bowed to Miss Walton, and then the hand of Susan is within his own. He bowed respectfully, raised her hand, and touched it to his lips. He saw a tear start as he cast one parting glance upon her sweet face, and, without a word on either side, they separated.

The Commodore and Major Morris, each taking an arm, walked with him to the little boat.

'God bless you!' and the Major clasped his hand in both of his.

'God bless you, Captain Oakum—a fine voyage to you!' and the Commodore gave him a sailor's squeeze.

A great many hands were stretched out, and Sam was busy enough for a little while. He was a great favorite, and all were sad at parting with him. Just as he was about to step into the boat, two men were seen hastening along shore.

'There are the two men, Captain, that have shipped to-day.'

'Have you your papers with you?' said Captain Oakum, addressing the men who had just reached them.

'Yes, sir—here they are;' handing them at the same time to the Captain.

'Aboard with you, then.'

They sprang in and tumbled themselves away as they best could. Sam raised his hand; every oar was dropped, and the little boat shot away like an arrow from the strand. As she left the shore, he turned towards the land, and removing his chapeau, waved it towards those who stood on shore, and then raising his eye to the different groups which he saw on the elevated bank, bowed, and at once there was a great waving of handkerchiefs, and some among them had other work to do with theirs, for tears were flowing freely. A fond mother and sisters were there, and there were friends of his early days, hearts knit to him in tenderest friendship. Gracefully the little schooner rounds to, and for a few moments lies flapping in the wind. Her Captain springs upon her deck, again she falls off to take the breeze, the sails swell gently out, and on she goes ploughing her way towards the mighty ocean.

CHAPTER XIX

Sam is now off, and for a season we must bid him adieu. Jim and Ned felt sorely the loss of one with whom they had been so long and happily connected; but matters of the last importance soon demanded their attention, and for the time banished thoughts of friends, and almost all other earthly considerations. Their business had hitherto been prosperous, and they had yet to learn, by their own experience, some of those trials which business men are ever liable to suffer. The advantage which they possessed of receiving supplies immediately from one of the largest marts in our country not only insured to them the trade of individual families, but also that of many stores removed far back into the country; with these they were obliged to deal on liberal terms, allowing them a credit of sufficient length to meet the slow returns of a country trade. They had as yet carried on a successful traffic, settling every six months by an exchange of produce, or a note at short time.

One article of country produce had become a valuable item in their trade—the pine timber from the barrens—and so urgent was the demand for it, in consequence of its excellent quality, and the facility with which it could be floated to market, that they found it necessary to make large purchases beyond what they would receive as an exchange of goods; these purchases had frequently to be made by an advance of one-half or three-fourths of the value, and the balance paid on delivery.

As their orders of late had been much increased, they had exerted themselves to procure funds, and by this method had, as they supposed, secured a very large and valuable lot of timber.

One morning—the very day after the departure of Sam—they were favoured with a visit from Mr. Cross. James, the elder partner, received him politely, but with some reserve; for, to tell the truth, they had no favorable opinion of his character. He had a fine lot of timber for sale, and would be glad to contract with them for it.

'We have already engaged as much as we need at present, sir, and are expecting it every day; in fact, Mr. Bolton promised to deliver it last week, but I presume he has met with some unexpected hindrance.'

'If it is from Mr. Bolton you are expecting the timber, I think you may give up looking for it, as I have been obliged to take all he has on hand, to secure myself for a debt he owed me. I suppose you know that he has gone to pieces?'

As Mr. Cross said this, he cast a very inquisitive glance at young Montjoy—

'I hope you have not advanced much to neighbor Bolton on account of the timber; these are tight times, you know.'

Just then Ned entered the store, and handed his brother a letter, which he had opened and read. Jim saw too clearly that there was a good reason for the very serious air which his brother's countenance assumed, when he handed it to him.

'I believe, Mr. Cross, that we can do nothing about the timber this morning.'

'Good morning, gentlemen.'

No sooner had their visitor left, than they retired to a little back room at the end of their store, where they had held many a pleasant conversation in company with their friend Sam. Heretofore, when they had repaired to this room, it had been with light hearts, and many a joyous hour had they passed there—far different feelings now pressed their spirits. Their trials until now had been of the light and transient kind, which a little youthful energy, a little determination of purpose, or putting forth of physical power, could overcome and scatter. Now they have got a lesson to learn on a new page of life.

When they reached the room, Jim again read over the letter, which proved to be another messenger with bad tidings.

It ran as follows:—

'Gentlemen,—I am sorry to be compelled to inform you that the two notes of Bowers & Co. and Jones & Brothers, which fell due yesterday at the Bank, were protested for non-payment; the note which I hold of yours for fifteen hundred dollars, and to meet which the above notes were left with me, will be due in ten days, and you will be obliged to remit the amount, or otherwise arrange for it, as the distressing pressure at present on the money market will render it utterly impossible for me to honor your note from my own resources. I send this by private hands in advance of the mail, as I wish you to have the earliest notice possible of this event.

'Yours respectfully,
'James McFall.'

To make this letter more intelligible, it may be proper to state that Mr. McFall was a personal friend of the Montjoys, who attended to their banking arrangements—the institution being at such a distance (full twenty miles) as rendered such aid necessary. He received their notes payable at the bank, due from merchants, collected and made payments as they directed, and having facilities, whenever they needed funds for extra service, procured for them what they wanted, either upon their own note, for which he held the business paper as security, or upon the paper itself. In the case of the fifteen hundred dollar note mentioned in the letter, he had procured the money from the bank on it alone, and held their business paper in two notes for about the same amount; these failing to be met, he was obliged to look to them for payment.

To describe the feelings of the two young men, as the alarming news broke upon them, and the calamitous consequences which it threatened, would be a vain attempt. Had an earthquake burst at mid-day, and with its convulsive quiver rocked their building, until they could see the tottering fabric parting at its joints and falling upon their devoted heads, it could not have waked up more intense, more appalling sensations. They had begun by the sweat of their brow; they had exerted every energy; they had advanced step by step; their business had grown by a natural progress; they had not forced it by speculation, nor by an undue haste to acquire wealth; they had abstained from borrowing on the names of others, and from lending their own; they had trusted to none but those who stood well in trade; their yearly gains were such as they had every reason to be contented with; and, but yesterday, they felt firm in their own strength, and buoyant with the fair prospect before them. Now their foundation is gone, and the labor of years that are past, and hope for years to come, alike vanished, as a vision, from before them.

Ned had so long been accustomed to lean upon his brother in every emergency, to have him think out a way for them, that hitherto he had never troubled himself with any further care than faithfully attending to the execution of his plans. Now he saw that the staff upon which he had leaned was broken: the pale features, the knit brow, the clammy sweat that stood upon his temples; the vacant gaze with which he looked upon the letter that lay folded in his hands, told him that James was sore dismayed, and at his wit's end.

'Let us go, Jim, and tell mother all about it.'

But Jim answered him not; he merely sighed and wiped his forehead, and then leaning forward, covered his face, as if he wished to hide even from his brother the agony that was wringing his bosom.

Oh! ye who despise the plodding toil of your daily labor, who think it drudgery to follow the plough, and handle the hoe, and reap the fields, and gather in your scanty gains, and are ashamed of the homely fare and the rude dress that these afford you, could you but have known the bitterness of that trial which was sending its pangs into the heart of that young man, you would prize more highly the freedom you have from distressing care, the independence you enjoy of either the frown or the favor of man, the quiet that is spread over all your humble enjoyments, and the peace of mind which goes with you to your rest and meets your waking thoughts. Depend upon it, that the glitter of wealth is purchased at a higher price than your imagination fancies.

Ned did not venture again to disturb his brother's meditations, and began even to hope that he was devising some plan for their rescue; but for once his clear and business intellect was at fault. The blow was so sudden, that his young mind could only suffer, without being able to wake up its energies to meet and ward off its consequences. Conscious at last that something must be done, and not sufficiently composed to know what that must be, he quietly arose, folded the letter, and placing it in his pocket—

'You are right, Ned; let us go and tell mother. She ought to know how things stand, without delay.'

It was no strange thing for these young men to make a confidant of their mother. She had accustomed them to tell her all their thoughts, and thus had they grown up beneath her fostering care; and opening, as they did to her, the fountain of their soul, she watched each bubble that came sparkling up, cleared all the dross and specks away with sweet maternal care; and still she loved to watch—it was her life's one duty; for well she knew, if all was bright and pure within the living spring, the streams must, in the end, be bright and sparkling too.

Alarmed at once by the appearance of her sons, as they entered the little room, where she sat with their sweet sister, plying their busy needles, she laid aside her task, and turning her anxious eye on James—

'What is it, my children? James, I know you are in some great trouble.'

'We are in trouble, mother, and we have thought it our duty to let you know all about it at once.' And they each took a seat beside her, while Ellen, the darling of their hearts, unused to any thing but smiles from her dear brothers, took Ned's hand in hers, and pressed it in all the warmth of her love, and wept as she looked at the calm yet serious countenance of her light-hearted brother.

In a very straight-forward way, James told his mother the news which had just been brought to them, and ended his communication by saying:

'Thus you see, mother, at one blow, is swept away all that we, have earned by our labors for these six years past; but that is not the worst of it.'

'You are afraid, my son, that it will take more than you have earned; it will leave you in debt?'

'Yes, mother, it will leave us, I fear, one thousand dollars worse than nothing, and that is not all.'

'That is bad enough, James, but I hope you cannot accuse yourselves of any wrong proceedings—any—'

'Nothing wrong, mother, that we can see; but we shall lose—we shall lose our credit, and that, mother, is worse than death.'—And Jim could stand no more; manly as he was, he covered his face, and gave way to a passionate burst of grief.

Mrs. Montjoy spoke not until the violence of it was past, and then, in a very calm and soothing way, gave such counsel as her judgment best dictated.

There is something in the tones of a mother's voice that goes at once to the heart of man. James felt the influence of her sweet words, lulling the violence of the storm within. Calmer views began to break upon him—a juster sense of the responsibility of his present situation. This was his hour of adversity, and he must act the man.

Ned, too, began to feel his heart grow lighter.

'Come, Jim, let us keep up a good heart; things may come round right at last, and if the worst happens, we can go to work again in the old garden.'

'Ah, my son, you will often think of your boyhood's days in that garden: you worked hard, but you were light-hearted and happy, although you sometimes complained of back-aches and blistered hands.'

'Mother, I tell you what,' said Ned, 'heart-aches are worse than back-aches; the one you can sleep off, the other I don't believe we can get rid of in that way.'

'Yes, brother, now that we look back upon them, those were the happiest days, I think, that you and I will ever see; but we did not think so then. Now we cannot go back; we must, therefore, as mother says, meet this trouble like men, and urge our way along the best we may. Mother, I thank you for your dear good words, they have revived my spirit'—and he stooped and kissed her. 'And now, Ned, we have a great deal to do; let us be about it.'

As soon as the brothers were alone, Jim showed that he was himself again, and in a very calm and business-like manner prepared for action.

'The first thing we must do, Ned, will be to see exactly how we stand. While you are attending to customers, I will make an abstract of our books. Then this evening, when the store is closed, we will take an account of our stock; we shall then know better our situation, and what course to pursue. We must put on a cheerful countenance, and keep straight along as usual, for to-day at any rate.'

'I don't know about the cheerful face, Jim, but I will do the best I can.'

CHAPTER XX

Scarcely had Cross and his companion in guilt retired from their dark conclave to carry out their dreadful purpose, when a young man arose stealthily from off a rude mattress upon which he had been lying, listened a moment, then hastily threw on a coat which had served him for a pillow, and with light steps proceeded towards the door; his further progress was now arrested, for the key had been removed, and the lock was bolted. Somewhat alarmed at this hindrance, he cast his eye anxiously along the front windows, and proceeded to undo the fastenings on the inside, when a thought occurred to him, that if he escaped through that opening, it would be noticed on the return of the owner of the store, which, from what he had overheard, would be in a few moments. He therefore replaced the bolt, and hastily retreated to a building connected with the store and running back from it. Here, too, by some unaccountable purpose, he was again frustrated; the door was fastened and the key withdrawn; and, to his consternation, he heard footsteps and voices. Cross, and the gang of wretches he had awaked from their lair, which was in one of the out-houses connected with his establishment, were about to enter the store—he to give his instructions to them, to inspire them with the hellish draught; and they to go hence on their errand of mischief. To remain where he was, and be discovered, his life would not be worth a mention; that he well knew. Above his head was a trap-door, opening into the loft which ran over the store. The covering was removed, he sprang upon a barrel, the nearest article to where he stood; making a desperate effort, his hands grasped the sides of the hole—he heard the key rattling in the lock, exerted himself with an energy the fear of death alone could have inspired, and drew at arms-length the whole weight of his body through the aperture. The door opened, and Cross entered with three of the creatures around whom he had wound the coils of iniquity, until they had become the slaves of his will.

'Now, boys, sit down here. Dick, there's the measure—draw away, and help yourselves.'

Nothing was said in reply; the running liquor alone sounded through the still room, and then the smack of the lips as each in turn gulped down the liquid fire.

'I wouldn't have called you, boys, to-night, but I have a job on hand that must be done now or never.'

'We're ready,' said two of the persons addressed, who were now seated on a bench near the counter.

'You are all ready, I hope,' said Cross, who stood up before them, and eyed the individual who was the youngest of the three, and had not united in the assent. 'No skulking now, Jo.'

'No, no, I'm ready for any thing—that is, I s'pose you don't want no bloody work?'

'You are always afraid of blood, Jo. I've never set you at any such work, have I?'

'No, not exactly—but we have come pretty near it sometimes, you know.'

'"Pretty near it"—never hurt any body.'

'Well, let's have the story,' said the eldest of the gang; 'if there is any thing to do to-night, it's time to be about it.'

'You are the fellow, Dick;'—and Cross laid his hand familiarly on the ruffian, and gave him one or two hearty slaps on the back, in manifestation of his warm approval, and as a stimulant to the performance of his reasonable request.

The demand of Mr. Cross upon their services was made in a low tone, and listened to by them with the deepest attention, each head drooping, and with eyes in a gazing attitude fixed upon the floor.

His directions were given with great clearness; the horses they were to ride, the part of the premises they were to fire, which of them was to enter the house and seize the trunk, and who the individual that should bear it with, the utmost speed to the dark rendezvous, where he, Cross, would be in waiting to receive it.

'And if it goes well, you shall be made men—you hear *that*?'

'Yes.' But they had heard the same before, and were yet the drudges of his will. His power over them they knew—his frown they feared; and his command must be obeyed.

Every word that passed came up with painful distinctness to the ears of the young man who lay above them, almost breathless in his dread lest some sound, even the beat of his heart against the planks, should be heard, and his presence discovered. He knew well the desperate character of the men, and that he must move with wary steps.

Every thing is at length arranged, and he hears them again fortifying their spirits by a deep draught. The door is opened, and one by one they steal out, but apparently with little zest for the work before them. Cross waited a moment on the threshold, until they disappeared amid the dark pines, and then, muttering curses on the men who were about to blacken their souls with a heinous crime for his sake, he stepped back into the store, poured out some gin from his bottle, took a long drink, threw himself into one of the chairs, and, leaning back against the counter, amused himself with swinging his heel against one of the rungs.

Bill Brown—for it was he who had been the providential listener to this vile scheme, had learned more in one short lesson than through his whole life before. Light, as though from heaven, flashed upon him; the dreadful character of his employer was revealed in all its blackness. Fear, likewise, had taken hold upon him; a groan, a movement, even too loud a breath, might place him in an instant on the verge of eternity.

And then, too, the dreadful fate which hung over that family. Bill had been a recreant to the path of duty; his mother's counsels he had set light by, and too often had he ridiculed the interest which she felt in those friends of her early days, and had done his best to persuade Hettie against making her home there: but now he would give half his life for the power of flying to them. How he longed to grapple with the hateful wretch, and then spread the alarm ere their mansion was wrapped in flames, and perhaps some of the family victims to their fury. But he knew that Cross was armed, and a powerful man.

The tramp of horses is heard; his heart sinks within him; furiously they pass the place, and far, far away, the sounds come back fainter and fainter upon the stillness of the night.

How long he thus remained he could not tell, for minutes are hours when the heart is in such an exciting suspense. At length he hears the snap of a watch-case. Cross rises from his seat, opens the door, fastens it from without, and is off. Bill waited not to hear his retiring footsteps; he springs to the floor, hastens to a window, of which he had not thought in his first attempt; it opened on one side of the building, and was seldom used. The sash creaked as he forced it through the mouldy casement, and, quickly letting himself down, carefully closed the shutters, and then looking round as though the avenger of blood might be watching for him, crossed the road, and entered a thick covert of pines. He turned and looked at the long dark building where he had wasted so much of his past life—

'If I once get beyond your reach, good-by to you for ever.'

Distracting were the thoughts which rioted within the mind of this youth. He was sure that the villains were full an hour in advance of him, and the work of destruction no doubt begun ere this. To pursue them, would be fruitless as preventing the catastrophe; to go in the opposite direction and seek his mother's home, would be to fill her soul with unavailable terrors. No house was near, but the one from which he had just escaped—no human being within some miles, to whom he should dare communicate what he knew. It was full nine miles to Mr. Rutherford's. His utmost haste would only enable him, in all probability, to witness the smouldering ruins of their mansion, and, oh, dreadful thought! the ashes of his own sister perhaps. He could think no further; the spirit of vengeance stirred strong within— he groped about for something that might serve him for a weapon, and laid hold of a strong chesnut club; brandishing it in his hand and testing its strength by a blow upon the ground—

'If I can do nothing more, I will make one of them feel the weight of an avenging arm.'

He is resolved to urge on his way towards the scene of mischief. He remembers, too, that in the instructions which Cross had given, one of them on the fleetest horse, was to seize the trunk and hasten off. He might meet him alone, and possibly rescue the prize, if nothing more.

Never had the road seemed so interminable, and his utmost speed was to his burning spirit but a snail's pace. Still he presses on—a long hill is before him; when he reaches its summit he will be near the edge of the barrens. He heeds not the ascent—his whole frame is nerved with an energy he never has felt before—it is his first essay in the path of duty. As he reaches the top a faint streak of light seems to tinge the distant cloud—his heart beats with deep emotion—an instant more, and a flush of light suffuses the whole heavens. He could scream in the intensity of his feelings. He thinks he hears a sound—he pauses to listen—it is—it is—the fiendish plot is accomplished, and the villains are returning with the spoil. The tramp of one horse, however, can only be heard as yet; the rider doubtless bears the fatal treasure. The resolution of a whole life fires his breast and nerves him with a fixed determination to grapple with the wretch—the horseman is galloping up the hill—his jaded beast lags as he nears the top. Bill crouches behind some bushes near the travelled path—his eye is on the horseman—it has caught sight of the burden borne in front of him. With a single bound he grasps the rein at the horse's head, and levelling a desperate blow, brings rider and trunk to the ground. The horse, affrighted, tears down the road, and makes directly for his home. Bill stoops to secure the trunk, not knowing or caring whether his victim is dead or not, when his antagonist, who is only stunned by the blow, springs upon him! They know each other well, and have often tried each other's strength in sport; they are nearly matched—both young, and possessed of great muscular power. Bill is now nerved with the energy of right, and the other with the strength of despair, maddened, too, with a desire for revenge. The violence with which they grapple brings both to the earth—it is a death-struggle—each endeavoring to get his opponent under, and each by turns gaining the advantage, until at length Bill lies apparently at the mercy of his adversary, whose hand is fast clenched to his throat, while he exerts his utmost strength to strangle him. Bill feels that his hour has come, for the death-grip which binds his throat is palsying his strength. One arm, however, is free—he clutches in his despair for something that might serve him for a weapon—his club lay within his grasp—hope springs to his heart—he brings down the weapon with a desperate effort, and it fell on the head of his opponent. Bill felt the tight clench relax, and putting forth his last powers, renews the blow. It has done the work. With scarce strength enough to throw off the body of the now helpless man, he attempts to rise, but in his effort to do this, the blood gushed in a torrent from his lungs. He believes that he has killed the wretched being beside him, and that he himself is parting with life. His reason is bright as ever—he takes up the trunk, and creeping as he best can, leaves the road, hoping to reach a hut which he knows is near by, deliver his charge, and then die, if so it must be. But his strength is less than he supposes—he can drag his trembling body but a short distance. Gradually his powers depart—a strange and dreamy sleep comes over him, and soon all earthly sounds and sense of earthly care are gone; and there he lies, still clenching the object for which he struggled so desperately.

Scarcely had this scene transpired when the companions of the wretched being who lay stretched upon the highway came hurrying along; their horse started from the track. Casting their eyes at the object that had caused it, they both sprang to the earth, examined a moment to ascertain who and what it was, and then looking at each other, simultaneously uttered a horrid oath. But there was no time to loiter; the body must not be there to tell a tale.

'He's dead, Dick; so let's throw him across the horse and be off.'

'He's dead enough, Jo; but where is the trunk? we can't go without that. We had better not meet the old man, if that is gone.'

Uttering all kinds of imprecations on their own souls for having had anything to do with the business, and wishing old Cross all manner of evil, as they groped about in vain for the prolific cause of all this mischief, in utter desperation they caught hold of the body: a groan caused them to drop it instantly—

'Ned, are you alive? Can you tell us where the trunk is?' There was no reply; but the body was warm, and of course life was in it. How to proceed they knew not; and their guilty consciences urged them to do something with speed. In their dilemma, they sent forth again on the still night-air curses too profane for human ears; the light, too, of that foul deed they had committed was growing brighter and brighter; far over the murky sky it spread, and its blood-red glare came down upon them, exposing to their strained eyes the first tokens of the avenger's rod.

At length, in their desperation, they determined to place the wounded and dying man astride the horse, between them. It was no easy matter to accomplish this, and more than one groan escaped the sufferer; but the strait they were in was urgent; they could not be deterred by trifles.

Not far from the dwelling of Mr. Cross, about half a mile in a direct line, a great change was visible in the size of the timber and the aspect of the woods: the fine tall trees, with no undergrowth, and scarcely a bush to obstruct the passage through them in any direction, were suddenly exchanged for a thick and tangled mass of scrub pines, intermixed with alder and black birch. The road leading through it, or rather into it, showed clearly its unfrequented condition; the whole tract being left, after the first fine growth of timber had been taken off, to bring forth what it best could, none then living expecting to reap much benefit from it. The soil was sandy, with scarcely any stones to be seen, except occasionally a small boulder, which, as it lay disconnected with any of its species, impressed the mind with the idea that it was out of its place, and was there by accident.

One spot, however, on this lone region, presented a singular contrast to all the rest; a few rods from the only road which passed into it, was an open, clear place, almost a perfect circle in its form, and about a hundred feet in diameter, upon which was neither shrub nor tree; the whole area being a flat granite rock, without seam or crack; it was not, indeed, a perfect level, but the protuberances upon its surface were scarcely noticeable, except as you walked across it.

To this spot had Cross directed his emissaries, after they should have accomplished his purpose. It was lonely and desolate, and well chosen for such a rendezvous.

What were his feelings, as he paced up and down that rock, lighted by the lurid glare reflected from the cloud above him, it would not be very profitable for us to know; nor shall I attempt to uncover the hideous secrets of such a heart. But there he walked and watched for two long hours—long indeed they seemed to him—and as he paused ever and anon to listen for approaching steps, would curse their tardiness, and then resume his lone, heavy tramp.

At length he heard the sound of voices, and the slow tread of a single horse. In his haste to anticipate the accomplishment of his vile wish, he left the rock and hurried to the road; one of them had dismounted, and was about to pass from the road to the trysting-place, the other maintained his place upon the horse, holding the helpless body of his companion.

Their tale was soon told, for there was not much to say; mystery lay upon every thing concerning the wounded man, or the trunk which had been committed to him.

Cross listened awhile to their story, his rage gathering fire, until, bursting through all bounds, it broke forth like a volcano. He caught the one who was standing near him, by the throat, and drawing a pistol from his breast—

'You lie, you villain! you know you lie! Tell me this moment where you have put that trunk, or I will blow your perjured soul from your body—tell me, quick.'

Overcome with fatigue from the great exertion of the night, and with a consciousness of the atrocity of their crime, the young man exclaimed, in broken accents, weeping as he spoke,

'You may blow my soul out, if you please, Mr. Cross; but as there is a God above, I cannot tell you where it is.'

Throwing the young man away from him with a force that brought him to the earth, he dashed the pistol down with maniac rage, tore his hair, foamed at the mouth, and fairly howled in the violence of his anger. For a while the witnesses looked on in apparent apathy, seeming to care but little how much he vented his spite upon himself. At length the one who still retained his seat upon the horse, very coolly asked,

'What shall we do with Ned? If he was dead we might bury him; but seeing there is life in him, it wouldn't be quite so well, may be; he may yet come to, so as to tell who hurt him, and may be some other things had better be seen to, for the night is wearing away, and—'

Cross, enraged as he was, felt that there was reason in this, and, moreover, that it was of the greatest consequence to him that the wounded man should be taken care of, and placed beyond the reach of meddlers.

'You are right. Take him down to the back part of the east swamp—you know who lives there. Tell Meg I sent him; that no one must know he is there; she must do what she can to bring life in him, and as soon as he can speak, to let me know.'

He stooped and picked up his pistol, uncocked the trigger, replaced it in his bosom, and walked on his way, muttering curses, and pondering on the best manner to avert the danger of discovery which these untoward events threatened.

CHAPTER XXI

The trial which had fallen upon the family of Mr. Rutherford was one so new and unexpected, that, with the exception of himself and wife, but little effect was made upon the members of it.

A vague report, indeed, ran through the house, of some trouble that had befallen its master, but what was the nature of it they could not well define. To Hettie alone had Mrs. Rutherford confided the secret; for she felt that her strong attachment, her faithful disposition, and her discreet behaviour, entitled her to confidence. She received the information with a heart bleeding in sympathy, but manifested so much good sense, had so many encouraging things to say, and put on such a calm, peaceful look, that Mrs. Rutherford felt that she had indeed a prop to lean upon in this faithful girl. All that day Hettie went about with an energy beyond what was usual, taking from Mrs. Rutherford all her cares and duties immediately domestic, and exerting every effort to put as bright a face upon the family as if nothing had happened. The servants in the kitchen had whisperings among themselves, but further than that, there was no sign that any change had taken place. They little knew the cause of bitter anguish that wrung the master's heart; every thing to them appeared as heretofore: their beautiful mansion, the pleasant grounds about it, the noble trees, and all the comforts that spread such a satisfying charm over the whole, to them looked as sure as ever; to him they were but shadows of the past—things that had been, but are not—by one fell stroke swept, all swept away.

After the distracting scenes of the morning, Mr. Rutherford prepared to make a journey of some miles, in order to attend to business connected with the peculiar situation of his affairs, and more especially to consult a legal friend, and get such advice as his case demanded.

Not expecting to return until the following day, he bade adieu to his dear family with a sad heart; and as he mounted his favorite horse, and rode away from his much-loved home—now his no more—he felt that he was under the chastening rod—the hand of God was upon him.

It is said that birds of prey can scent their victims from afar, and spy the hidden carcass, however secret the spot where it may fall.

It must have been by some such instinctive power that our old acquaintance, Mr. Richard Tucker, was affected, on the day that witnessed the catastrophe of Mr. Rutherford's concerns. His place of residence was some miles off, and no tidings had he received of any such event; and yet his yellow gig was that day put in requisition, and northward he must go.

'I shall be home by night, may be.'

This was all that he deigned to say, as he left his home, and the old gig squeaked and rattled as his raw-bone mare started off at a round trot; perhaps she scented her master's game.

About a mile from the Rutherford estate there was a small collection of buildings; it bore the title of village however, and comprised a church, a blacksmith's shop, and a tavern, as also a few small and plain tenements. The tavern, of course, was the rendezvous through the week, and the place where all the news and scandal could be enjoyed. It was soon known around that trouble had fallen on the great man of that region, and a larger number than usual was congregated there just after dinner. But, to their credit be it said, a feeling of deep regret was very manifest: not a tongue was loosened against the sufferer, nor was there one among them disposed to take any measures for his own security, although to most of them he was indebted for services of different kinds.

'George Rutherford,' said an aged, portly man, who seemed to be the oracle of the place, and who had taken the large arm-chair on the wide front piazza of the tavern, 'I have known from a boy; and if there ever was an honest man and a gentleman, he is one. Things have been going hard with him for some time, that we all know; he has had cunning chaps to deal with, and may be they have ruined him; but sooner than take the law of him, I will lose all he owes me, at any rate.'

'So would I;' and 'So would I,' resounded on all sides.

'But here comes Dick,' said the first speaker. 'I wonder what he is after?—hunting for a job, I guess.'

And the old yellow gig drove up, and Mr. Tucker, with all the elasticity of a young man, sprang from his seat, and alighted on the lower step.

'Good afternoon, gentlemen;' and Mr. Tucker bowed very stiffly, which perhaps he was obliged to do, for his coat was buttoned up close to the neck—a habit he maintained at all seasons.

'Good day, Mr. Tucker; you seem to be in a hurry, neighbor; the old mare is quite out of breath.'

'Oh no; not at all,' turning at the same time, and eyeing his beast; 'she always breathes so. You may put her under the shed, Jo,' addressing a good-natured looking black, who stood waiting orders at the head of the beast.

'Yes, massa. Any oats, massa?'

'No—well—I don't care—yes. You may give her a mess—two quarts, Jo. Wet them, you hear?'

Jo took the mare by the head, turned his face away from the company, opened his broad mouth, and went grinning along to the shed.

'My golly! two quarts—ha, ha, ha! a half bushel no fill her belly—ha, ha, ha!'

Mr. Richard has not altered much since we last saw him, either in appearance or disposition. Why he had come along that afternoon, no one knew; nor did he seem to be making preparation as though he had a job on hand. He heard the news of Mr. Rutherford's disaster with apparent indifference. I say apparent, for there is no doubt he felt much and deeply; he talked with one and another, making very few remarks, but asking a great many questions, and occasionally shrugging his shoulders, and knitting his dark eyebrows—it was a way he had. What effect his pantomime had upon those with whom he conversed was not very manifest, for they finally dropped off, one by one, leaving no orders behind them.

It is an old saying, 'If one won't, another will.' Mr. Richard, no doubt, had heard the saying, and must have had considerable faith in it; for there was not an individual, either high or low, that escaped his attentions.

The Irish are proverbially susceptible. Whether Mr. Richard knew this as a historical fact, I will not pretend to say, nor whether it led him to make a more direct and positive attack on poor Pat than he had done upon others that day; the result, however, was, that Jerry Malony, a rather good-natured fellow, to whom Mr. Rutherford was indebted for a summer's ditching, and whose pay was as sure as though already in his own hands, was suddenly seized with great terrors, in view of the certain loss of all his hard earnings, and with a distressing anxiety to become possessed, as a means of securing himself, of a pair of fine black horses, then in the possession of said Rutherford.

We will not enter into all the particulars; suffice it to say, that Mr. Tucker and Mr. Malony adjourned from the east corner of the piazza to a private room inside the building, and thence to a justice of the peace, and thence back again to the bar-room; and, finally, the two worthy gentlemen were wishing each other very good health, and confirming their wishes by potent draughts of genuine Monongahela. There were many little arrangements to be made, which occupied them until the shades of evening had settled very decidedly upon the land.

Old Cæsar, the coachman—with whom we once became acquainted on the little journey Mr. Rutherford and his lady took through the barrens some years since—was still alive, and, to all appearance, active as ever. The old black coach-horses, too, had lost none of their strength or fire, for they were never overburdened, and being under the exclusive charge of Cæsar, were daily tended with as much care as though they had been pet horses of a prince; their dark hides shone as brightly as Cæsar's countenance did after a good supper, and all their appurtenances were kept in the most perfect order. To say that Cæsar was fond of these creatures, whom he had tended and driven so long, would not express all his emotions towards them; they were, next to his master and mistress, and their children, the objects that engrossed his feelings—and Cæsar had very strong feelings, too—his life he would have risked, or even sacrificed, to have preserved any of them from harm. He had no wife or children of his own, nothing to love except his master's family; and no wonder then, if for these beasts, who obeyed every expression of his will, and pawed, and neighed, and pranced, and did all but talk to him when they heard his step approaching, he had peculiar feelings. Moreover, Cæsar was very proud of them: for they were acknowledged, far and near, to be a noble pair; and, to crown all, they were looked upon as his own. Mr. Rutherford never claimed any further right to them than the privilege of a drive occasionally.

Cæsar knew very little about his master's troubles; he had, indeed, heard some whispering in the kitchen among the women; but he paid no further heed to it than to bestow a back-handed blessing on their tongues.

'Dey are always a-goin' jabbering about sumpin' or anoder. Massa George know he own business well enough, neber fear.'

As Cæsar's principal employment of late years was to attend to the horses, he had persuaded his master to fit up for him a room in the building where they were kept, so that, in case any accident should occur to them in the night, he could be on hand. A door opened from this room immediately into the stable; and as the whole premises were kept with the greatest care, there might be found much less eligible sleeping apartments in places that made greater pretensions. Cæsar, however, did not sleep there entirely alone. Besides his pets, the horses, he had a dog of the real mastiff breed, that had been trained with much care, and was as completely under the will of Cæsar as the other quadrupeds; he was a large, powerful creature, and unless under the complete control of a master, would have been dangerous; but at Cæsar's word, he would be passive as a lamb, and at his bidding would lay the stoutest man upon his back, and hold him there without doing further violence, unless there was an attempt at resistance.

Mr. Richard and his client Jerry had been sitting on the piazza of the tavern, watching for the return of Mr. Rutherford, who must pass that way to his house; hour after hour slipped by, and they looked in vain.

'It's striking nine, your honour; shall we wait any longer?'

'It is my opinion, my good fellow, that we might as well be on our way. As a matter of form, perhaps, it might be well enough just to make the demand; but as there is no probability, if it is all true that I hear, not the least probability that he can pay it, or will ever pay it, your only chance, my friend, is, as I say'—slapping his hand on Jerry's knee—'clap on to something tangible; and as you say the horses are valuable, they will be about as handy as anything I can think of. They have legs, you know; we can carry them off, or more probably, we can make them carry us off—ha, ha, ha!'

All this was said with his face turned towards Malony, and speaking close to his ear, while his auditor, being rather short and a little worse for liquor, sat very erect, and looked as consequential as any newly made Justice trying his first cause.

'And as we are to walk, I think we may as well be jogging.'

'I think so, your honor.'

The two worthies accordingly walked slowly along, and before a great while found themselves in the broad avenue leading to Mr. Rutherford's mansion.

'You are well acquainted here, I suppose, Malony? The dog you speak of—is he—is he—loose?'

'No, your honor, not just loose; he keeps tight to the nigger.'

'And he, you say, sleeps in the stable?'

'Pretty near it, your honor—close by.'

'I think, my good fellow, that we may as well go at once, then, to the stable; the nigger being there, it will be sufficient to demand them of him, or to leave the attachment with him.'

Mr. Richard, it must be premised, was not over-burdened with law knowledge. The people among whom he labored had taken his word as law enough for them. They found it hard law, to be sure; but, poor souls, they knew no better, and thought all was right.

Jerry had implicit confidence in his adviser, and so walked bravely along. The dog being just then uppermost in his mind, knowing, as he well did, his ferocious character, he cared much more about a proper introduction to him, than any nice point in law.

'Hadn't I better be after strikin' a light, your honor? it's amazin' dark.'

'Not yet, Malony; not until we reach the stable.'

It cost master Jerry no little trouble to strike his light, for his hand was not very steady; and as he gave two blows with his finger against the steel to one with the flint, there was more blood than sparks flying.

'Bloody murther! that was a pealer: it's taken the skin, it has, your honor.'

'Can't you hit it, Malony?'

'I hit it, your honor, but my finger took it fornint the stone.'

Mr. Richard now took matters into his own hands, and while Jerry was blowing and snapping his fingers, he managed to get some sparks into the tinder, and soon had his lantern in trim.

Cæsar was about the middle of his first nap when he suddenly awoke, and found that Trap was growling in a low undertone. Trap never barked, and very seldom condescended to growl, Cæsar knew that there must be something going wrong; he therefore extricated his head from beneath the bed-clothes, and cast his eye round the premises. The lamp was still burning, and so far as his half-opened eyelids would allow him to see, there was no one in his room besides the usual inmates. Trap, to be sure, was out of his place, and sitting close by his master's bed, looking very significantly up at the red night-cap. As soon as he perceived that his master was awake, he ceased growling, like a very sensible dog as he was, signifying thereby that his only design in using his vocal powers was to stop the snoring, and call his master's attention to matters and things in the waking world. After rubbing away upon his eyes awhile, and working things awake there, Cæsar, in a very philosophic manner, by means of his two arms, which he threw behind him and used as levers, first to raise and then to support and brace his body up, attained a sufficiently elevated position to see and hear what was going on. He was afraid of nothing but witches, and for that reason always had a light on hand; it being well known that neither in daylight nor candle-light was any danger to be apprehended from the 'good neighbors.' But something or somebody was stirring, and near by, too, for he evidently heard footsteps and voices, and, as well as he could make it out, they must be in the stable. Being more or less afflicted with the rheumatism, he was very deliberate in his movements. First throwing his somewhat recumbent body into a straight and self-supporting posture, and thereby relieving his arms from their burden; then casting aside whatever impeded his progress, in the way of covering, he turned his nether extremities by the pivot principle, brought himself in position to stand erect on the floor, and proceeded at once to the light, which was safely shut up in an old carriage lamp, through which the rays streamed forth by a small glass, calculated to converge, and throw them far ahead.

Cæsar was somewhat of a gentleman in his feelings, and on the subject of dress quite particular; for he followed the old fashion of small clothes and knee buckles, and broad-skirted coat and vest, with large lappels, and was ever ready, at any short notice, to appear with becoming apparel in the presence of his mistress. These he wore by day; but he made a complete change when he laid these by, and put on his night rig. As he was a bachelor, and ladies, white or black, had no business about his premises at night, he fixed himself as he thought best; and his fancy was, red flannel. Why he chose that color, he never saw fit to communicate; it may have been, however, that his good sense suggested that white, the usual dress, would make too strong a contrast. He had on a red flannel cap, that came pretty well over his ears, and a red flannel frock, or tunic, covering him from the neck downwards to the usual gartering place; below that the bare poles were plainly visible. To those who knew him perfectly, there was nothing very frightful in all this, because it was Cæsar; but to those who might not have had experience on their side, as he then appeared, with his lantern streaming before him, he might have been mistaken for any thing that was not earthly.

As Trap knew that his business was to keep still and remain in his place until called, so soon as he saw his master upon his legs, he was satisfied that all was correct, and nestled quietly down on his own bed.

The only weapon Cæsar ever kept on hand, was a pitchfork, a very ugly sort of a thing to come in contact with; for in the first place, it not only makes two holes where a bayonet or sword would make but one, but it gives great advantage to the one who uses it in its length of handle; this may have been the reason why Cæsar preferred it. At any rate, there was always one standing in the corner of his room; it had very long and heavy tines, and a handle sufficient to keep an enemy at a respectful and safe distance. Feeling that it might be prudent to be prepared for danger, even if there was none, he grasped his weapon in one hand, and with the lamp in the other, drew back the little bolt, and throwing the door wide open by a strong push, stood in bold relief, casting his light round about through the large roomy stable, and straining his eyes to ascertain who or what it was.

His appearance was the cause of considerable surprise; for although Mr. Malony had talked very freely about the *nigger*, as he was pleased to style Mr. Cæsar Rutherford, and although both he and Mr. Richard expected to see him in the course of their proceedings, yet they could have had no very correct idea what shape a mere mortal, especially a black one, could assume; for no sooner did their own light throw its beams upon this sudden apparition, than they both made rapid retrograde movements, Jerry, in his haste, bringing up against the opposite wall, and Mr. Richard stepping back towards the door, as though it would be safe at least to be out of reach of the pitchfork.

Whether Cæsar was alarmed, it would be difficult to say; for he made no motion other than to throw the light of his lamp, first on one and then on the other of his visitors.

Jerry, he thought, he had seen before; in fact, he was quite sure that he could not be mistaken in the little chunky Irishman, who had been so long under his master's pay; but Mr. Richard, Cæsar could not make out; he had never been in these parts, that he remembered.

As Cæsar's appearance did not improve upon inspection, and as the two gentlemen were too far separated to consult as to further proceedings, a long silence would have been maintained had not Cæsar opened a parley—

'What a you want here?'

The tones were not very mild, nor was the address made in very good humor; for Cæsar threw in a few emphatic words which he sometimes used when excited, just by way of seasoning, and which for brevity's sake are omitted; but then it was a human voice, and it gave some assurance to Mr. Richard at least. He therefore advanced one or two paces:

'Ah, that's you, is it, Boss?'

'Git out wid your Boss, and tell me what a you want here dis time a night!'

'Oh, we don't want any thing with you, my good fellow, but we have got a little business here that must be attended to. You know Malony here?'— turning at the same time towards his discomfited companion:—'You know he's been at work here all summer for your master. Here, Malony, step up here; you have nothing against this good man, you know.'

But Malony preferred remaining where he was. Cæsar's eyes, he thought, showed a little too much of the white to be very safe, especially under the circumstances.

'I am sorry to have disturbed you, my good fellow, but as somebody must be notified before we proceed, I will just read the warrant, as I suppose you will hardly be able to make it out yourself;' and Mr. Richard pulled out a bit of paper and began to read rapidly—'Know all men by these presents,' etc. Cæsar, in the mean time, was getting his wrath up. He never liked the Irishman, and had often cautioned his master against him; and Mr. Richard's countenance not being, as my readers will remember, very pre-possessing, together with the fawning manner in which he attempted to get round him, woke up Cæsar's sensibilities:

'Mister, go to grass wid your paper, and tell a me what you want 'sturbing people dis time a de night.'

Mr. Richard being thus interrupted in his proceedings, stopped reading, and looking full in Cæsar's face—

'You know, I suppose, my good man, that Mr. Rutherford has failed?'

'Hab what?'

'Has failed; that is, can't pay his debts.'

'You a big liar.'

Mr. Richard didn't blush; he never had in his life; but he began to pick up a little courage.

'You must take care, old fellow, how you speak; I am an officer of the law, take care, sir. Here Malony, lead out one of these horses, and I will take the other.'

'What dat you say?'

And Cæsar stepped forward, Mr. Richard retreating at the same time, until he came to the edge of the stall.

'Me like to see you touch one of dem horses.'

Mr. Richard had now come in closer contact with Cæsar; and perceiving that he was quite an old man, and walked rather stiff, made a sudden spring, and grasped the pitch-fork.

'Trap, Trap.'

There was a rush from the little room, and in the next moment Mr. Richard was lying on his back, with the fore-paws of master Trap resting one on each shoulder, and his mouth presenting a row of teeth in such dangerous contiguity to Mr. Richard's throat, that he began to fear matters were tending to extremities, and called out 'Murder!' at the top of his voice.

'Hole you lyin' tongue; he be de death of you.'

'Malony, Malony! help, help; kill the dog; quick, take a pitchfork, any thing, do, my good fellow, he'll murder me.'

But Mr. Malony was not so drunk but he had sense enough to see that there was mischief brewing; and no sooner was Mr. Richard on his back, than he bolted and ran for dear life, Mr. Richard's cries only adding wings to his flight across lots for home.

'I tell a you what, mister, you no hole you tongue and keep till, me let de dog take you lights out in a minit. Hold him dare, Trap, till a morning; den we see how he look.'

'Oh, good man! good man!' Mr. Richard spoke now in a whisper—'do—don't go away, don't leave me here; I promise I will go right off; I was only doing my duty as an officer.'

'Me gib a you duty; you 'member Cæsar next time; take care de horses no kick a your brains out.' There was indeed a very dangerous proximity between Mr. Richard's head and the horses' heels, especially as they were pawing and prancing about under the exciting influence of Cæsar's voice.

'Oh do, good Mr. Cæsar, for the love of mercy, just take the dog off, and let me go! I give you my sacred honor'—But Cæsar had no such idea. The insult offered to his master and his horses had steeled his heart.

'I tell a you what, mister; you no lay till and keep a your tongue, your time is short; he only take two mouthful, you be gone chicken, so good night to you;' and Cæsar hobbled back into his room.

The grave and the gay, the mirthful and the sad, are so blended in this world, that in delineating any series of events, we find ourselves constrained to shift the scenery so often and so suddenly, that if we did not know we were sketching from nature, we should fear to be charged with drawing upon fancy, even to extravagance.

Cæsar had bidden Mr. Richard good night, and to all appearance, designed leaving him, as he said, 'to de mornin', to see how he look den.'

He had been sorely disturbed, and perhaps feeling that it would be rather difficult to compose himself to sleep under the existing state of things, he so far arranged himself in his day apparel that he felt ready for any emergency; it was not according to Cæsar's sense of propriety to be caught in just the shape he had been. After fixing things a little, he threw himself on the bed, talked away for some time, and even made one or two broad grins, as though there was something on his mind not very unpleasant, and finally sunk into a dreamy state, conscious, most of the time, of the condition of external things immediately around him, and yet so mixed up with things and places very foreign to them, that it was not the easiest matter in the world for him to be sure whether he was asleep or awake.

How long he had been lying in this state it would be difficult to say, for time, under such circumstances, makes no tracks that are perceptible.

Among other ideas that flitted through his mind, was that of a light which kept flickering across his window, and occasionally brightening up his whole room. For some time even after he was awake, he lay and thought about it. Distinctly beholding the glare, which now had become steadily bright, filling his whole room and absorbing completely the light of his lantern, suddenly he sprang from his bed, his mind awaking to a full consciousness that something was wrong; he hurried through the stable, and calling off Trap from the pitiful object who had been writhing under his surveillance, opened the outer door.

'Fire, fire, fire!' he called at the full extent of his voice—'fire, fire, fire! Oh, my missus and de children!—the lord hab mercy.'

The old man forgot his age, and ran with the speed of youth.

The sight which had burst upon him was enough to have nerved with energy the most sluggish and unfeeling. On Cæsar it broke with most appalling interest.

He could not, indeed, get a full view, for the house was screened by the large trees and thick shrubbery; but enough could be seen to assure him that the dwelling was on fire; and the inmates, if they had not escaped, were in imminent danger, for the flames were flashing up to the tops of the trees, higher than the roof of the main building. In a few moments he was beside the burning pile, and the whole extent of the awful calamity was revealed to him. The fire was raging over the whole of the back part of the house, having already completely enveloped the back building connected with it, and was throwing its forked flames over the high roof, while the pitch-black smoke, which rolled around the whole premises without, gave awful forebodings of what might be the state of things within. No alarm had yet seized the family that he could discern; he listened in vain for any sound but the terrible cracking of the raging fire.

He attempted the nearest door, but found it fastened. The wood-pile was at hand; he seized the axe; at that moment two men came running into the court-yard and calling fire. Cæsar barely glanced at them, they were strangers to him; but he felt encouraged in his efforts; his arm was nerved with the strength of his early days—one blow drove it from its fastenings, and in he rushed amid the heat and smoke.

The two men followed him, but for a very different purpose than to rescue the sleeping family from their fiery envelope.

When Mr. Rutherford left his home, as before related, his expectation was to remain until the following day; but having accomplished his errand early in the evening, he concluded to return to his family. It would occupy much of the night, but he preferred spending it on horseback, so anxious was he to be again with his wife and children; they were all he had now, and his heart yearned after them with a warmth of affection he had never realized before.

A little past midnight, as he was turning the summit of a hill, a sudden flash of light shot up in the distance; he thought it was the glare of a meteor; but painted on the clouds which overhung the western sky, it left a deep-red glow. As he gazed, while slowly descending the hill, he saw the flush extending, and gradually assuming a brighter and more lurid aspect.

'It must be a fire; perhaps some poor sufferers are looking in anguish upon the wreck of their little all.'

And on he went, ever and anon casting his eye at the clouds, and marking their curious forms, as the light in fitful flashes displayed their shape.

At times, across the distant hills, he seemed to think that he could see the position of the fire, but intervening objects would again confine his view, and he could only discern the light on the clouds above him. Coming at length to an angle in the road, from which he could look in the direction of his home, he was startled to find that there was a clear and well-defined streak of light emanating from some burning building, which must be at least in that vicinity.

Without being conscious of any decided alarm, he urged his horse to a faster pace, and kept his eye more constantly on the light. For some miles from where he lived the road ran among the hills; so that, however great had been his anxiety, it could not be gratified until he should emerge into the open country. At length he is ascending the last eminence that intervenes between him and the objects of the affections; the light is still blazing on the clouds above him; he hastens to the summit, and beholds—heart-rending sight—the home of his childhood—the dwelling where all his earthly hopes and love were clustered—a mass of crumbling ruins, from which the forked flames were shooting up and crackling on the still night-air; those demon sounds went in streams of madness to his heart.

'Oh, my God!' he exclaimed; and deep in the sides of his horse he struck his spurs, and the good creature was urged into terrific speed. It was but a mile, and it was passed with a whirlwind's pace. Straight to the burning pile he rode; a few person's he discerned collected as near the fire as the raging heat would permit.

'My wife and children!—for God's sake tell me quick—where are they?' He sprang from his horse, and was in the arms of the faithful Cæsar.

'All safe, Massa George! all safe, tank God!'

'Thank God! thank God!' and he fell upon the old man like a helpless infant. He was carried into an outhouse, which had been spared by the devouring element, and kind hands and hearts were soon about him administering to his relief. As he awoke to consciousness, his beloved Mary was bending over him, and her warm lips pressed to his in the ecstasy of her joy.

'Oh, Mary! my dear wife! where are my darlings? bring them to me; let me clasp you all once more!'

And quick they came. He cast a look on each, a fond, a satisfied look, and then in one warm embrace he held them all.

'Oh God! this is enough—I ask no more. Let me have but these—poverty in any shape may come; we will not fear it.'

'Amen! my dear husband; we will not fear it.'

It is often said by those who look on the dark side of Divine dispensations, that troubles always come in clusters, and one deep sorrow soon gives place to another. This may be true, but not in the sense which these croakers of misery would intimate. As happiness and unhappiness are often but relative terms in our changing world, it needs but the wise Director of events so to time the dispensations of his Providence, that one evil may counteract another, or to hold up before us the certainty that we and every interest near our heart are at his disposal, to bring us quietly to acquiesce in his will; and in that submission there is peace. George Rutherford, as he rode towards his home, amid the solitude of midnight, pondering over his ruined fortunes, felt that he was suffering the severest stroke which could have come upon him; but when he came in sight of the spot where that home had been, when he looked upon the terrible flames, and felt the dread uncertainty which hung over the fate of those dear ones of his heart, he then felt that God, his Sovereign and his Father, had at his command profounder depths of sorrow in which his soul might agonize. The loss of fortune was but a mere sip of the bitter cup, a mere mist from the dark and waste wilderness of mortal suffering; and when he folded his dear wife and children in his arms, he felt, as he said, 'Let poverty come, we will not fear it.'

But he had yet to learn the full meaning which that word conveys. Little could he tell, born as he had been to affluence, the anguish which would at times wring his spirit; his resources drained, his home destroyed, the little comforts to which his family had been accustomed, the gratification of their finer tastes, the elegancies of life—all cut off; it was well for him that he could not know at once the full extent of that change which had passed upon his fortunes.

One bitter ingredient in his cup was, that he could now plainly see that he had been remiss in that watchfulness and care which were demanded of him, over the inheritance that had been bequeathed to him. His kind feelings had been indulged without the exercise of common prudence, and he had permitted a morbid sensibility that shrunk from a just suspicion of those whose delinquencies he was not wholly ignorant of, and last, though not least in the catalogue which he reckoned up against himself, was his gross neglect in regard to some things requiring but a moment's attention, and yet involving serious consequences. The most mortifying and truly disastrous of these was revealed to him a few days after the scenes recorded in the last chapter. It occurred, too, at a moment when his spirits had begun to revive a little from their depression. It had been suggested to him that the time was not far off when his tract in the barrens would be of immense value. Hitherto it had been estimated comparatively as but little worth. The timber was indeed large, and its value, when it reached the market, considerable; but the cost of preparing it and transporting it so far left but a trifling return to the owner. A new demand was about to be created in the successful application of steam for river navigation. As hope began to agitate his bosom, he immediately remembered that he had, but lately, been examining the deed by which he held that property, and had noticed that there was no certificate upon it of its having been recorded, and that he had designed having it placed upon the public register. This design he had not accomplished, and if it was not there, it was gone for ever, as he knew the flames had devoured the original, with all his other papers.

Hoping that it might still have been recorded by his father, and the notice of the fact neglected to be put upon the deed, he immediately ordered his lawyer to make the search. It was in vain; and to add to his chagrin, the gentleman who made the search informed him that a deed which Mr. Cross had received from one of the original proprietors, intended, as was supposed, to convey a title to only a few acres, did, by this discrepancy, possess him of a vast tract of many miles in extent. Terrible indeed was this blow to him; his last hope of retrieving his condition vanished. He must now look abroad upon the wide world for some honest means of supporting his family. How he envied the laboring man, who, accustomed to toil from his boyhood, went forth to his daily occupation with a lively spirit. How gladly would he have taken his place, no matter how severe the work; but his muscular power was not equal to it. Trained to no regular business, stript of all external dependence, he saw before him but a dark and misty wilderness, through which he must grope his way as he best could.

CHAPTER XXII

The influence which Henry Tracy was enabled to exert can only be fully known when all results and causes shall be developed in the clearer, brighter light of eternity; but a vast amount of good was manifest, even to those whose moral vision was not the clearest. Many a young mind was stimulated to exert its dormant energies, and feeling its strength, rushed on to distinction. His pleasing manners were a beautiful accompaniment to his cultivated mind, and gave a decided tone to those of the young who had any taste for what was refined and elegant. Nor was the renovation he was accomplishing altogether hidden from himself; a great change was working—he saw it; it did not fill his heart with pride, it only stimulated him to further progress, and warmed his gratitude to God. One thing was certain: he had entwined himself around the hearts of all, and his own affections were more truly interested than they had ever been before, beyond his parents' roof. It seemed to be the place where God would have him be—'The very niche he was designed to fill.' It was also the means of deciding him as to the calling he should pursue for life. To be suitably fitted to take the spiritual charge of a people, no matter how secluded or unpolished they might be, was now his highest aim; and after a suitable time he made known to the principal men that this was his intention, and that he must leave them, and go where he could obtain the necessary instruction. Little did he realize the hold he had of their affections, until this determination was expressed. Nothing would satisfy their yearning towards him but his promise, that, when through his course of study, he would come and be their minister.

'We will build you a church just on the spot which you have selected, and we will put you up a house, that you shall call your home as long as you live; only promise that you will come and spend your days with us.'

How could he say 'Nay'? Three years in all has he been separated from them, and now for more than a year he has been settled over them as their pastor. They have erected a church, and it stands, as we have seen, on a beautiful knoll that commands a lovely view of the surrounding waters; and they have built the parsonage, and it is near the church, embracing the same enchanting water view, although somewhat obstructed by its embowering trees and shrubbery. It is, however unoccupied, for Henry is yet a single man, and whether his affections are engaged, it matters not. He has made no declaration of them, and retains his old situation with the Widow Andrews.

A favorite resort of his has been the cottage of Mary Brown. He loves to ramble amidst the seclusion of the thick forest, to call in at the poor cottages, give a word of comfort or instruction, and then rest himself at the table of the widow, and listen to her ready converse about the things of a better world. Sometimes, too, he seems not at all unwilling to listen while the widow talks of one she loves most dearly. Henry had met with Hettie Brown occasionally at Mr. Rutherford's. He had been struck with her appearance, and we need not be surprised at this, for she is some years older now than when we last saw her. The pretty girl with sun-burnt face, and curly raven locks, and dark hazel eyes, is now a lovely young woman. Nor was it her appearance alone that surprised him. Hettie had studied nature rather than books, but she had gathered quite a little store; and the ease with which she conversed, and the variety that her mind brought forth, together with the deep interest she manifested as he poured out from his own more enlarged mind the treasures of knowledge, convinced him that she had a desire for improvement, and an appetite for acquiring information that would make her an agreeable scholar.

A warm yet lovely afternoon had tempted Henry to seek the refreshing shade among the pines; and not caring to extend his walk, he directed his steps at once to the widow's cottage.

At that period of the day, he generally expected to see her sitting a little back from the house, beneath the shade of a large white pine, whose thick and spreading branches afforded a cool and pleasant shelter from the rays of the summer sun. Missing her in her usual seat, he entered the cottage; the moment he stood upon the threshold, he raised his hands and remained perfectly stationary, looking in silent astonishment at the scene before him.

His eye met that of the widow; it was mild and calm as ever, but no smile returned his greeting, and she turned away immediately towards the object that then engrossed her heart, and perhaps intending thereby to direct his notice thither also.

It was enough, indeed, to have chained a mother's attention; for on the bed by which she was sitting, lay her only son, for whose sake she lived thus alone, senseless, but still alive; his pallid countenance and sunken eye and cheek, his short faint breathing, all plainly indicated that life was held but by a slender thread—so slender, that a trifle might sunder it for ever. Close by the head of the sufferer stood his sister, gently waving a large fan, and thereby relieving in some measure the closeness of the atmosphere, which, to one so weak as he appeared, must have been oppressive in the extreme. Neither mother nor daughter attempted to offer any explanation of the circumstances; and Henry had too much delicacy, and was too sincerely affected by what he saw, to intrude any questions, or interrupt the perfect silence of the sick chamber.

Gently rising from her seat, the widow touched the arm of her Hettie, who resigned the place and the fan, and turning her sad yet beautiful eyes toward the young minister, and stepping lightly to the door, signified that she wished him to follow.

He offered his arm, and in silence she led him to a shade sufficiently removed, so that the sound of their voices could not reach the cottage. Resigning her arm, he motioned her to a seat.

'Thank you; I cannot sit, but must return immediately. You have heard of my brother's illness?' looking full at Henry.

'Not a word. But tell me what could have brought him so low in so short a period. When I was here a few days since, your mother said nothing of his being sick.'

'He was brought home two days ago in the condition you now see him.'

Hettie was much affected, and it was some time before she could command her feelings so as to give a clear recital of all she knew: 'That he was found lying by the road—that he was at first supposed to be dead—that a litter was made, and upon it he was brought home—that the ground where he lay was covered with blood, and other marks of a violent scuffle—that he had not spoken a word, nor could any one give the least explanation of the matter.'

'Let me go with you to him at once,' said Henry.

Henry entered the cottage with her. Little, however, could be done besides keeping the sufferer as quiet as possible, and administering some slight nourishment; and thus he lay from week to week, living, breathing, barely able to make himself understood by sign or word, and nothing more. But Henry was not the only male friend who clung to them in this their hour of need. David Cross had been almost a constant attendant from the moment William had been brought home. David had always been a visitor at the cottage; he had been invariably kind to the widow, watching over her in her loneliness, seeing to her little wants, calling and sitting many long hours, and apparently not unwilling to listen to her instructions, and ready to do any act of kindness, insomuch that she felt for him almost the affection of a mother. She pitied him, too, in his peculiar situation; he had no mother, or none that he had ever known as such—it was said that she had died many years ago; he had no brother, sister, or other relative beside his father; from him he had never received many tokens of affection. He would no doubt have been proud to see him rise in the world: and, as we have seen, was very willing to accomplish this end at the expense of others; but he was morose in his disposition, often unkind to the young man, supplying him indeed with money, but as often lavishing his curses upon him as any thing else.

Dave was naturally of a kind nature, but had been bred among those who were rough and rude; his manners, of course, were more or less tinctured by his education; his associates were such as would be likely to lead him into wild adventures and corrupt practices. The only counteracting influence had been that which the widow exerted over him; and his conduct towards her evinced a kindness of feeling, and a sensibility to better things, which those who saw him among his wild companions would never have imagined. The heart of the widow yearned over him, and she never lost the hope that David Cross would one day rise above his present ways.

And besides all this, there was in his heart a strong and long-enduring attachment for Hettie; he had been fond of her when but a girl; and his interest for her had become an absorbing feeling of his heart. During her long stay at Mr. Rutherford's, he had never lost sight of her; but having either business to attend to for his father in that region, or feigning it for his own ends, he would frequently take small parcels or trifling errands from the mother to the daughter, and many a precious bundle of good things had he brought from Hettie, through the kindness of Mrs. Rutherford, to comfort and cheer the widow. He was, therefore, by no means an unwelcome visitor at either house; his personal appearance was not unpleasant—a manly, open countenance, a kind manner, mingled indeed with some roughness, and a fearless, straightforward, animated way, calculated to make a favorable impression. Hettie seemed always glad to see him; so much so, that many of the family firmly believed that she had other feelings towards him than mere neighborly kindness. Mrs. Rutherford knew her heart in this matter, and was convinced that such was not the case.

Hettie indeed did not love him, nor did she feel that she ever could; and was careful to do nothing that might give him occasion to indulge a false hope in regard to her. David had, as I have said, sympathized with William on his sick bed; he it was who had brought Hettie home, and day and night, with Henry Tracy, had been untiring in doing every thing for their relief.

William's consciousness returned to him long before he had any ability to hold conversation, and the dilemma in which he found himself involved occupied almost constantly his waking thoughts. The desperate character of Cross; the vile plot that had been executed against the unsuspecting and noble-minded Rutherfords; the fate of the trunk for which he had fought so desperately, the least whisper of which had not reached his ear: all these subjects distracted his weak and flickering senses—a terrible secret lay in his breast, which he had not the power to reveal in any way that would be intelligible, and when revealed, must crush to ruin the hopes of the friend who was watching at his side, by bringing the father to an ignominious end. At times, in the agony of his contending thoughts, he would groan aloud, and the large drops would gather on his pale forehead. Hettie or the mother would bend over him, and say some soothing word, and wipe his clammy face, and inquire 'why he groaned? or where the pain was? or what they could do for him?' but he would shake his head, and closing his eyes, give up awhile his troubled thoughts and fall asleep. Thus day after day and week after week stole on, and still he lay in his feebleness, gaining strength, if at all, by a very slow and almost imperceptible progress.

It was at the close of a lowery day; the shadows of night were deepened by a dark canopy of clouds which hung over the barrens. The Widow Brown had lighted her lamp and placed it on the stand by the bed of her son, wishing to sit as close to him as she could, while plying her busy needle. David Cross was reclining on a low cot-bed; he had taken Hettie to Mr. Rutherford's that day, and expecting to watch part of the night, was anticipating a few hours' sleep. A gentle tap was heard, and as the widow opened the door, a woman, clad in somewhat better garments than was usual among the people of that region, stood panting for breath, and looking with great earnestness, and in much apparent agitation—

'Are you alone, Mrs. Brown?'

'There is no one here, Margaret, but David, besides my sick son.'

'Oh, *do* step out here a moment—*do*, Mrs. Brown;' and the widow closed the door and followed the woman a few paces from the house. She knew her *well*—poor Margaret! and she pitied her too; for Margaret she had heard was once a pretty, happy girl; her home had been far from there. In an evil hour, she had listened to the flattering tale of the deceiver, and now she was a miserable dependant on the will of Cross—his slave to do his bidding.

'I have run all the way, Mrs. Brown, from my house, and I want you to go right back with me.'

'Not to-night, Margaret, surely; the weather looks so threatening, and I don't like to leave William, and Hettie gone too. What has happened, Margaret?'

'You must go, ma'am, this blessed minute, for poor Ned Saunders is dying, and he says he cannot die in peace until he sees you. He has been raving crazy ever since the night he was brought to my house; but this morning he had a long sleep, and when he came out of it, his reason was all straight—but such a distressed creature you never see. He says he cannot live, and that he must see you—as he has something to tell you which he dare not tell to any one else. You don't know, Mrs. Brown, what a worry I am in; for you see Cross has charged me, by the worth of my life, to let him know the moment Ned had his reason. But I am afraid there have been some evil doings, from what Ned says; and if Cross should get there before I return, there is no telling what he might do to me.'

'Well, Margaret, wait here a minute until I put my things on.'

The widow was soon in readiness; and having committed matters to the charge of David Cross, without giving any particulars further than that she had a call to a neighbor's, closed the door and went on her way, dark as was the night and gloomy the errand on which she was bound.

Margaret led the way; and excited by an impulse of some terrible kind, hurried on through the dark forest with maniac impetuosity. Their path was a difficult one to traverse, for it lay through an unfrequented region, and the opening by which they went, it was almost impossible to trace by the feeble light which yet glimmered from the close of day. Guided almost by instinct, Margaret pioneered, and the widow followed with all the speed she could make. For awhile they skirted the side of a thick and tangled swamp, and then turning a little to the right, came at once upon the feeble twinkle of a pine torch from the window of a log hut.

'Anybody been here, Ned?'

'No one. Has she come?'

'She is here.'

And the sick man raised his eyes to catch a glimpse of her he had wished so much to see, while a smile almost lighted up his wild and haggard countenance.

'Oh, Aunty!'—this was the familiar title by which the good woman was generally addressed—'oh, Aunty! I'm so glad you're come. I'm a'most gone.'

'I hope not, Edward.'

'Yes, I am. I thought I couldn't die till I see you. You've often talked to me, you know—and I thought it was all foolish—I don't think so now.'

He had to pause, for his feelings were greatly excited, and his frame apparently near dissolution. She put her hand upon his forehead, and felt that the death-damp was gathering there. She wiped his face with a cloth, and bathed his temples with some spirit: this revived him a little, and apparently in an agony to unburden his mind, he seized the first return of a little strength.

'Oh, I have been so wicked! I shall go to hell—I know I shall.'

'Are you truly sorry, Edward, that you have sinned against God?'

'Oh, yes! I'm sorry—but what shall I do? I know I deserve to be punished; but oh, Aunty! how can I meet God?'

'If you are truly sorry, and pray to God to have mercy on you for Christ's sake, He will forgive you, Edward; for He has said so.'

'Oh, has He said so? Where? tell me quick, Aunty; for I feel the cold creeping over my heart—tell me quick.'

'In the Bible, Edward: it is full of promises to those who repent of sin, and turn to God through Jesus Christ. He came into the world for that very purpose. He hung upon the cross for us poor sinners: and while he hung there, he pardoned a thief that was hanging beside him, and about to die. He says, "Whosoever cometh to me, I will in nowise cast out."'

'You don't think He will save such a worthless sinner as I am?'

'Oh, yes, Edward; if you throw yourself upon His mercy, and ask Him to forgive you.'

The dying man turned his eyes away from the widow, raised them towards heaven, and clasped his trembling hands together,

'God have mercy upon me, a poor sinner—a dreadful sinner! for Christ's sake; for *Christ's* sake, only for *Christ's* sake!'

And the widow wiped away the big drops that stood upon his clay-cold, forehead. Again he fixed his eye upon her—

'But, oh! there's a dreadful load upon my heart—there are—some things—I have done—that must be told—I cannot keep them. Come, lean your head down close to me.'

The widow was by no means anxious to hear his tale of sins and misdoings, but she obeyed his request. He was greatly excited; his breath flew back and forth like a weaver's shuttle, and he could only get the words out by catches.

'You know—Rutherford's house—has been burnt—and I don't know—but some of them were burnt in it. Cross—hired me and two others. We wanted to get a trunk—a tin trunk—I fired the house. They got the trunk—and I brought it along. Your son Bill met me on the road and struck me from the horse—and tried to get the trunk. We grappled—and I thought I'd killed him—but I don't know nothing since then—that's all—oh dear! Why did I go? Cross, Cross, Cross—did it all;—but, oh God!—here it comes—'

He ceased speaking—his lips trembled, his eyes rolled back convulsively—he clutched at the clothing, a spasm shook his frame—it was death's last stroke; and as the quivering limbs settled into rest, breath and pulse were still.

The widow saw that he was dead; and clasping her hands in silent horror, she looked at poor Margaret for an explanation. Margaret shook her head.

'Don't speak; I believe it is all true, but you must not stay here a minute longer. The poor fellow is dead, you can do him no good; and Cross may be the death of me, if he finds you have been here—hark!'

The noise of approaching footsteps was distinctly heard; but before they could make the least effort at concealment, the door opened, and Cross entered.

The widow spoke to him in her mild, pleasant way. He manifested great confusion tried to speak calmly, but his voice choked and trembled greatly. He cast his eye quickly on the bed—

'What! *dead?* Ned is not *dead?*'

'Yes,' said the widow; 'he has just breathed his last. Can I be of any service to you, Margaret, by staying here? If I can—'

'Oh no,' replied Cross, quickly; 'there is no use, we won't trouble Mrs. Brown.'

'Well, then, I will be going, as it is getting late in the evening.' So wishing them good-night, she quietly stepped from the door, walked slowly a few paces, and then hurried along with as much speed as the darkness would permit.

No sooner did Cross perceive that the widow was gone, than his countenance assumed an aspect of the fiercest rage.

'How is this?'—clenching his fist, and shaking it near to the head of the trembling, wretched female—'how is this? How came that old canting hypocrite here?'

'Ned begged me to go for her: he said he could not die in peace until he saw her.'

'Die in peace!' and he stamped his foot with rage—'die in peace! and did not I charge you, by your life, to let no human being see him in his reason, but myself?' And saying this, he caught her by the hair, and dashed her with his utmost power to the floor. She arose, without uttering a word or groan, upon her knees; she caught him by the arm; he endeavoured to thrust her from him, but her hold was the grasp of despair; at once he drew a poniard, that he always carried in a concealed case at his side; she saw it glitter as he held it up in the act of plunging it to her heart.

'Oh mercy, mercy! for God's sake—for the sake of him who calls you father, don't kill me! Remember all I have suffered for you—the mother of your only child, though you have never owned me. Have not I always done your bidding? lost my soul and body for you?'

Pity, or some other motive, unnerved his arm—he could not just then do the deed; but hurling her from him, threw her to the other side of the cabin, like a reptile that he hated.

In an instant she was on her feet—a rifle was in her hand, and it was pointed in deadly aim at her vile oppressor. The gun Cross had not noticed—it always stood loaded; for Margaret (or Meg as she was called) lived alone, and in that wild place had learned how to use it. He had no idea that the poor worm he had so long trodden upon could ever turn against him; but when he beheld her eyes glaring with fury, and the deadly weapon levelled at his breast, his blood curdled at his heart. He made a step towards her.

'One step more, and you are dead!'

'Put that down, Meg; I don't want to hurt you.' The poor craven now began to cower, and thought that a few soft words would obliterate a life of abuse, carried to a point where woman's love turns to the direst hate.

'No, never! Stir but one foot—move but a single limb—and you will lie beside that wretched victim of your hellish arts. Hear me now, David Cross; I am no longer your slave. You have ruined my name; you have defrauded me of the title of wife; you have made me disown my child; you have kept me in poverty, and made me a companion of outcasts; and now you have thrust me from you, like a hideous reptile—but your hour has come; that miserable being, whom you sent here a raving maniac, has let out your secret—it is already on the wings of the wind.'

Cross trembled in every joint; a fiend, with demoniac power, seemed glaring at him in the being whom but a moment before he had so shamefully abused.

'Meg, forgive me. I have wronged you; I know I have. Don't take my life, and I will make it all right. I will say you are my wife; I will do anything you want.'

'*Forgive* you? Yes, I will forgive you, when you bring back my poor parents who went down to the grave mourning for her you ruined; when you can tear from my mind the memory of wrongs none but a woman's heart could ever have borne so long. Forgive you? no, never. Your life you may have! but *go*—before the dreadful feelings which have been burning in my heart blaze up again. Go! go quick—'

He waited not, but moved to the door, stepped trembling from the threshold, and hurried away through the dark forest.

The moment Cross had gone Margaret opened a small trunk, hastily gathered together a few articles of dress, and slipping a little roll of paper containing her stock of money into her pocket, tied up her clothing in a bundle, cast one look upon the dead body, and then quitted the wretched tenement she had so long called her home, firmly resolved never to enter it again.

She hastened at once towards the cottage of the Widow Brown, and so rapidly did she thread her way through the intricate path, that before the widow had passed over half the distance to her home, Margaret had overtaken her.

'Don't be frightened, Mrs. Brown; I did not think to reach you so soon—but stop and listen to me.'

The widow had indeed stopped, for Margaret came upon her so unexpectedly, that she was much alarmed, and deprived of the ability, even if she had the will, to escape.

'I will listen to you, Margaret, but I have heard dreadful things enough to-night. I am almost distracted now.'

'I would not add a straw to your burdens, my dear good Mrs. Brown, but I am a poor distressed creature. The whole of my life for these many years has been one scene of misery; but I can bear it no longer, and this very night will find me many miles from hence.'

'Oh, *do*, don't talk so, Margaret. Come go with me, and rest you for the night at least; it is so dark, and beginning to storm already.'

'This darkness and the rain are no troubles to me; but just listen one moment. You know that I have told you what I have no other human being. One secret more I must commit to you—that young man who is now at your house is my son.'

'David Cross your son, Margaret?'

'It is God's truth, and all I want of you is, whenever you think it best, to let him know what I have told you. I am now on my way to the city. I shall seek a place of service, and when I find a resting-place, if there is any such spot for me on earth, I shall let you know. But one thing I must beg of you—Cross has treated me like a brute, and I came very near taking his life to-night; but for David's sake, spare him—don't reveal the terrible tale you heard to-night. Promise me, now, won't you'—and Margaret fell upon her knees and clasped the arms of the widow—'promise me, you will not reveal it without in some way you are obliged to do it?'

'Why, Margaret, my mind is so disturbed by all these scenes, that I cannot think of things as I should like to before making any promise; but you know I love David, and would be as careful of injuring him, as my own child.'

'That is enough; but oh, do just put your hand upon my head, and say one prayer over me. I shall go lighter on my way, for I have but a heavy heart, and a weary road lies before me.'

'May God bless you, my child, for Jesus Christ's sake, and make a way for you to some place where you will be in peace; and may you yet have some comfort before you die.'

'Amen!' said Margaret; and seizing the hand of the widow, which had rested on her shoulder, she kissed it again and again, and then departed.

CHAPTER XXIII

Mr. Cross was in no enviable state of mind as he hastened along in the darkness, after leaving the hut of Margaret. The disappointment he had suffered in finding that Ned Saunders was dead; the terrible fright he had endured while standing with the rifle at his breast; the mortification of begging his life at the hand of one he had so long triumphed over; and above all, the knowledge that his secret was abroad—all operated with maddening power, and worked up a tempest within, that raged and tossed until he was bewildered by its fury. He passed his own dwelling without stopping, but hurried on, directing his steps to the north, through a by-path amidst the towering pines.

After some miles of rapid walking, he reached the edge of the barrens, or rather that part of them that had been cleared and in some measure cultivated. He here descried the twinkle of lights from a small settlement. To one of these, a little separated from the rest, he soon came, and knocked with some violence at the door.

'Come in.'

Cross tried the latch, but finding it fastened, repeated the knocks in a way that showed he was in earnest to be let in.

'Come in, I say—but stop, may be the door is fastened. Who are you?'

'Open the door, will you? it's me.'

'Aha—that I will;' and the bolt was withdrawn quickly.

'Why, neighbor, is this you? how are you? come in. Well, you are the last man I should have thought of seeing here this dark night—take a chair, neighbor—what's the news?' And as Squire Foster (for he was the gentleman whom Mr. Cross had honored with a visit) said this, he threw away the smile, or rather grin, that had played over his sallow and flabby face, and assumed his naturally sly and mouserly look. 'Any thing good abroad?'

Cross was in no talking humor: so let the gentleman run on, and in the mean time helping himself to a chair, sat down, and leaning back against the wall, fixed his eye, dark and lowry, full upon the little light that stood flaring and smoking on the middle of the table.

'Well, there's the devil to pay now!'

'Where? what, what, neighbor—any news?'

'None that you will want to hear. Ned Saunders is dead.'

'One rogue less, then, neighbor, ha, ha! he won't tell any tales then about here.'

'But suppose he has told the tale already?'

'That would be bad, neighbor; but you don't mean to say that he has?'

'Yes, I do mean to say so; and the question is, what you mean to do about it?'

'What I mean to do about it?' and he looked at Cross with a vacant stare.

'Why you know we are both implicated.'

'Why, neighbor, that is all between you and me. You know I have been but a mere counsellor.'

'Yes, and a pretty scrape your counsel has got me into. Here is one man dead, the two others gone out of reach, and the thing itself nowhere to be found. Like as not Rutherford has got it back again, and we have had our labor for our pains, and may be something beside not so agreeable.'

'Well, now suppose, neighbor, I should tell you that Rutherford has not got it?'

'Do you know that? and how?'

'What would you give if I should tell you that I have got it, safe and snug in my own hands?'

'Give! I have given enough already; but where is it? let's see it.'

And Cross arose from his leaning posture, sat his chair square on the floor, and himself very erect in it, and looked fixedly at the Squire.

Foster noticed the movement and the look of Cross, and without speaking, arose and stepped into a small adjoining room, took something from a case that stood upon an old dressing-table, and thrusting it hastily into his bosom, came back and resumed his 'Have you got it?'

'Got what, neighbor?'

'You know what, well enough—why, the deed. The trunk you may keep, but the deed can do you no good.'

'Nor you, either, neighbor; it is safe—safe enough. I have got it, and I mean to keep it.' And as he said this, he very deliberately drew a pistol from his breast, and laying his hand on the table, leaned back in his chair and looked at the pretty plaything. Cross eyed him keenly, glancing from the pistol, which he saw was cocked, to the calm and almost unmeaning countenance of Foster.

'What do you mean to do about this?'

'I don't know exactly, neighbor; but at present I shall keep it. Something may turn up, you know—and to save a great deal of talk, as it is getting late, matters must stand thus: I have obtained possession of this at some risk; you agreed to pay me well, you know, if the job succeeded. Go on then—slash away at the timber; cut down and sell off as fast as you can—no one can hinder you—hand over half you get to me, and all will go smoothly enough. Do you agree to that?'

Cross knew that Foster was a great villain, but he had never calculated upon the chance of thus getting into his power; he knew now that he was resolved upon a desperate course.

'I suppose I shall be sued as soon as I begin to cut.'

'No fear from that quarter. Rutherford is down, and has no means to contend with; his creditors will get picking enough to satisfy themselves out of his other property; and no lawyer will undertake the job, on his own risk, without more show of a title than he can now claim.'

'Well, if they do prosecute, you agree to see to it?'

'Ay, ay, neighbor, leave all that to me.'

'And suppose there should be trouble about what Ned Saunders has been blabbing?'

'That won't amount to much; it will soon be known that you are the owner of nearly all the barrens now, and they will be careful enough how they raise their tongue against you; a man is not very likely to swear to his own injury.'

As Cross arose to depart, the other gentleman left his seat also, and dropping the hand which held the pistol, let it dangle by his side; the other hand he placed in his bosom, and facing his guest looked at him very complacently; a slight smile and a gentle, inclination of the head, on the part of Foster, were all the greeting that passed, as Cross neither turned his head nor uttered a word, but with a quick step left the house, and went on his way.

The wages of iniquity are sometimes reaped in this world, and Cross was just tasting the bitter fruit.

CHAPTER XXIV

Mr. Rutherford had received his dear wife and children as it were from the jaws of death, but it had been by the almost super-human exertions of the faithful Cæsar, who, for a long time, was disabled by the severe injuries he had received as he bore them through the burning building. The noble beasts for which Cæsar had fought so bravely, with all the luxuries and comforts of his large establishment, were swept away at the demands of creditors, and nothing that he could call his own remained except the faithful old negro—who, although a slave, was too far advanced in life to be liable as property—and those dear objects in which his heart still found some sweet solace amid the drear prospect which surrounded him.

At present he was occupying a small house which had belonged to him once, and used as a tenement for a laborer on his estate. Few were the articles of furniture which sufficed for their use, and those had been, for the most part, loaned for their immediate necessity. His lovely wife still kept her pleasant smile, but her heart was smitten with a stroke that pressed it down heavily. It was not the loss of all, nor the change of abode, nor the rude and scanty furniture, nor all the other aggravating tokens of their change of circumstances—but she saw the struggle that was agitating her husband's mind; she could not relieve him of that load of care; she could not obliterate from his memory past errors, nor could she mark out for him a path that offered any other prospect than the dark one in which they were travelling then. All she could do was to make the best of what they had, to throw into her words the softest tones, and to lighten up her countenance with the semblance of hope she did not feel.

It was not long after they had thus been reduced to the extremity of fortune's change, wearied with the turmoil of his distracted mind, Mr. Rutherford was sitting at the little window that opened from their abode upon the highway; his Mary was beside him, and she held his hand, and fondly pressed it as she oft had done in better days, put it to her heart, and let him feel how true it beat for him. The shades of evening were just setting upon them, held back a little by the young moon which hung out her crescent in the west, when a vehicle stopped at their door, and a gentleman of lively mien alighted and prepared to enter. Mrs. Rutherford went for a light, while her husband repaired to the door to receive the visitor, whoever he might be, although, as he supposed, some messenger of evil tidings, like all of late.

'Mr. Rutherford, I believe?'

'My name is Rutherford, sir; will you walk in?'

The stranger immediately followed, and entered their small apartment, Mrs. Rutherford, at the same time, placing the light on a little stand.

'I expect you have forgotten me, Mr. Rutherford; my name is Andrews. You remember the poor boy you helped some six years since.'

'Andrews—what, William Andrews!'

'The same, sir. A few years make some change in our appearance.'

It had, indeed, made some change, and one which entirely effaced every resemblance to the plain and homely-dressed lad who, six years since, had left his home to seek his fortune among strangers. He was now well-dressed; and had the ease of manner which is acquired only by mingling in society. He had grown in stature also, and was now a tall and slender man; his fresh, healthy countenance had grown pale. He wore his hair long, after the fashion of the South; his eye alone retained its naturally soft and expressive cast, although its brightness was dimmed, and seemed to indicate a want of energy in the physical frame. His own mother could scarcely have found a likeness to his former self; his very voice sympathized with the apparent languor of his frame, and had nothing in it that would recall the lively tone of boyhood.

'It cannot be!' said Mrs. Rutherford, who now approached and took his hand. 'Not William Andrews! Time has indeed made a change—but we are glad, heartily glad to see you.'

'It is not time alone, madam, that has made a change in my appearance, I suspect. I have been, you know, in a southern climate, and that takes severe hold sometimes of us northern men; but I am very happy again to see you, very happy indeed.'

Without the least reference by either party to the great change which had occurred in circumstances, some little time was spent in a general interchange of question and answer about persons and things; when Mrs. Rutherford left the room, perhaps from feelings of delicacy to her husband, who might not wish to refer in her presence to his own peculiar situation.

'You find, Mr. Andrews, that there have been changes here too, which perhaps must astonish you.'

'I have heard of them, sir, a few miles from hence, and have urged on my journey further than I should have done. I need not say to you, sir, that to me it is the most painful event I have yet met with in life. Is it true, my dear sir? Are you as much reduced as report affirms and appearance indicate.'

'I am as low down, so far as property is concerned, as I can be; there is absolutely nothing left.'

And then, with much composure, Mr. Rutherford unfolded the complicated maze in which he had struggled for some time, and the closing of the scene in the last fatal blow. Although apparently unmoved himself, not so was he who listened to the tale of suffering. The southern clime had marred William's beauty, but it had only added to the warmth of his heart. For some time after Mr. Rutherford had done speaking, he sat wrapt in silent thought; his emotion too strong to dare trust the utterance of a single expression. At length he rose, and taking the hand of his friend—

'Mr. Rutherford, the ways of the Almighty are mysterious, but they must be right. When a lone wanderer, you took me by the hand; you gave me counsel, you assisted me with means, you introduced me to influential friends; you made my heart glad then, and gave me an impetus which has led me on to success beyond my expectations. The money I have returned to you, but the debt of gratitude for your kindness to me in that hour will remain an uncancelled obligation while I live. And now, sir, you must take this trifle from me—I demand the right of a debtor to your bounty—take it, and keep it for your present need; it must not, it shall not be that either you or your angel wife know the pinchings of want.'

His voice trembled so violently, that he could scarcely utter the few last words; nor could Mr. Rutherford respond to this warm burst of sympathy; it had gone directly to his heart, and caused a flow of feeling that could find no vent in words.

'I must leave you for the night. God willing, I shall see you on the morrow, and tell you all my story. You then will see that I do not rob myself, and we will devise some other plan together.'

Mr. Rutherford shook his hand with a silent grasp, but it told the young man that his offering of love and gratitude had done its work. Leaving his best respects for Mrs. Rutherford, William departed.

As Mrs. Rutherford entered the room, after their guest had gone, she found her husband seated by the stand, and looking at something which he had spread out upon the table.

'See here, Mary.'

She stepped up to him, and putting her arm around his neck, stooped over beside him.

'My dear husband! what does this mean? Five hundred dollars!' and she looked at him in amazement.

'Yes, my love; it is five hundred dollars given us by that young man whom a few years since we befriended: this is the way, my dear, that God gives back the bread cast upon the waters.'

'Oh, my dear George!' and she threw herself upon his bosom, 'how glad I am for you; you feel that you have one friend now, don't you?'

'Yes, Mary; and you cannot think how my heart leaps at the thought; one sympathising friend in an hour like this, is indeed "cold water to a thirsty soul"; but oh! that better Friend above, shall we ever forget him, Mary? How good! how true! how wise! how unfailing! if we will only trust in Him.'

They said no more: silently they sank together on their knees, and poured out the fulness of their hearts to that Friend—that better Friend above.

In the hour of our deep distress, when the dark clouds are around and above us, the soul is prone to feel that the darkness which oppresses it is the frown of God: we forget that love may be concealed, not turned away.

To Mr. Rutherford's heart this mercy-drop came; a delightful assurance that he was not forsaken, and that still the arm of sovereign love was stretched out over him.

William Andrews had not been, for the few past years, engaged in the active whirl of business to no purpose: he had amassed a few thousands by a happy venture, and his success had been beyond his most sanguine expectations. But this was not all; he had learned to grapple with difficulties, and by energy and determination to accomplish results which the irresolute and fearful could only dream of. He called the next morning, and in a private interview with Mr. Rutherford procured from him a particular statement of his affairs.

In a few days he called again; and there seemed to be a cheerfulness in his air which he had not before manifested.

'I have been looking over your matters a little, my dear sir, and I cannot think they are in such a hopeless case as you imagine. Your property is indeed all attached, and if sold under the present state of things would, to be sure, be dreadfully sacrificed, and might not bring more than the claims upon it: you certainly value your estate beyond the amount for which it is holden.'

'Most certainly; but by our laws an immediate sale can be forced; and in that case, the whole will scarcely meet the demand.'

'You must apply then to some friend who will assume your debts'— Mr. Rutherford shook his head—'and who will take your property into his hands, until better times come round.'

'I have no friends, Mr. Andrews.'

'We once thought,' said Mrs. Rutherford, who was listening with much interest, 'that we had quite a number; but friends do not always stand the test of such a fall as ours has been.'

'But they could not possibly lose any thing, Mrs. Rutherford.'

'Perhaps they might not; still, you know, it is a delicate matter to ask the favor, when not one of all who have been with us in our prosperous days has seen fit to come near us now. My dear husband, until you so generously had poured out your kindness, felt that he was alone in the world.'

For some time each sat musing in silence over the uncertainty of human fortunes and earthly friendships, when Mr. Andrews drew up to the table, and requesting the attention of Mr. Rutherford a moment, began to spread before him certain documents.

'Please to examine these, sir, and say whether they are correct.'

'These are my obligations, Mr. Andrews—I gave them in good faith; and although I cannot meet them now, will own them to the last farthing.' Mr. Rutherford looked with much astonishment, for he perceived that all the responsibilities he was involved in were lying before him.

'Are there any more that you can think of, Mr. Rutherford?'

'There are no more.'

'Then, sir, you may take them and do what you please with them: all I ask of you is, to give me a claim upon your property for this amount,' naming not more than two-thirds the value of the notes. 'The interest of that I am sure you can pay, and your property is once more your own.'

William was well aware that promptness in such matters was of the first moment. He had at once liquidated every claim at a rate which each one was glad to accept, and thus materially reduced the whole amount: this he could be well secured for; the property of his benefactor need not be sacrificed, and his heart was at rest.

Blessings on you, William Andrews! Your frame is slender, and seems to be nurturing some hidden plague that may ere long make it a prey to the worm; but it is the abode of a generous spirit. How its quickened pulses beat with the ecstatic happiness which now plays within! Your eye is on that noble pair; and the overpowering emotion which is thrilling their bosom at this new and unexpected deed of love, is the richest feast you ever tasted. Oh how they will bless you as the years roll by, when in their happy home and on their own paternal soil they tread in freedom, and think of him whose generous friendship snatched them from the brink of ruin, and placed them there! Oh ye lovers of this world's treasures, did you but know the secret charm these treasures can unfold! Go, dry the widow's tears; go, aid the orphan's helpless steps; go, prop the man of pure and noble soul, bowing beneath the weight of penury's heavy load—and you will feel there is a talisman of untold value in your hoards of gold and silver which you never dreamed of.

Mr. Rutherford had no idea of taking advantage of the arrangement Andrews had made, and insisted upon giving a claim for the full amount; but this William would not allow. He had made a fair bargain with the creditors, and would not permit Mr. Rutherford to bind himself further than the amount he had paid.

'You can, my dear sir, as you are able, make good to each one what he has willingly relinquished.'

'And, God permitting. I will do it to the full amount.'

CHAPTER XXV

We left our friends the Montjoys busy in their store, taking an account of their affairs, and preparing to encounter the difficulties they had been thrown into. They found things not quite so bad as they feared. Should the whole loss be realized, all which they had made would be swept off; but there would be enough to pay their debts—that was a great comfort: and if they could but preserve their credit, matters might all come right again. With the promptness which had ever marked his conduct, the morning after the reception of the intelligence which had given them such a shock, James was on his way to his friend McFall.

The statement which he was enabled to make was very satisfactory; and would have been all that was required, could his friend have been able to advance the funds. The pressure was indeed of a most serious kind, affecting individuals and banks alike; and requiring on the part of each the utmost skill and exertion to stem it through. James found that his only resource now to meet the present emergency, was to lay his case immediately before the Bank; if he failed to procure aid from thence, he saw not whence it was to come. The power which by circumstances becomes thus concentrated, can only truly be felt by those situated as was this young man. Whether it be an individual, or a corporate body, and whether they are conscious of it or not, the ability, for the time being, which is at their command to afford or to withhold the life-blood of trade and commercial credit, is the most despotic in its grasp on the mind of man that can be conceived this side of infinite sway. It is not, of necessity, the fault of those who wield it, that it should often press with such sickening, despairing force; so long as enterprise shall stimulate man to go a step beyond the means at his own disposal, must he in some measure depend upon the aid of others; and once dependent, he can never calculate with certainty upon enduring peace of mind. The fluctuations in trade, like changes in the weather, baffle all the skill of the most shrewd and far-sighted: they come at times before any suitable preparation can be made to meet their destructive influence, and the high-minded, honorable man is obliged to stand before the same tribunal with the mean and designing, and for too often compelled to submit to rules which make no allowance for character.

It was the first time that James had known really what it meant to ask a moneyed favor. He had begun life as we have seen, and gone on, hitherto, so much by his own means, that he felt more like a criminal about to be arraigned, than an honest man in the discharge of duty; and nothing but the absolute necessity of doing something to preserve the credit of his house, and upon which every thing now depended, would have driven him to it. He was not personally known to the cashier, and therefore his friend accompanied him to the Bank, introduced him, and left him to tell his own story. Fortunately for James, the person he had now to deal with was a gentleman in every sense of the word; a man of large experience, at home in all the routine of business, a complete financier, and with a large share of true benevolence.

Every unpleasant feeling was, for the time, at once banished by the agreeable, frank, and very kind manner with which this officer received and addressed him. James felt almost sure that his end was accomplished. He very soon, in a brief manner, related the circumstances in which he had been placed by the sudden failure of so many persons, and then handed to the cashier the schedule of his property and liabilities.

After carefully scrutinizing this paper with an air and expression of countenance that showed his business character, the stern and cold features of which damped James's hopes not a little, and at times caused a fluttering at his heart, which he had never felt before—

'You are aware, I presume, Mr. Montjoy, that these are not only precarious times, in which the Bank feel that the utmost caution must be used, but the times are also very difficult. We cannot aid often, where we not only wish to, but should feel safe in so doing. It is as necessary for us to keep our credit unblemished as for individuals. I will, however, lay your proposition before the Board; if you will call again at one o'clock, you shall have the answer.'

Two long hours of intense anxiety were passed, such as James had never before experienced. Not caring to return to the house of Mr. McFall, he repaired to a grove which lined the banks of pretty river that glided through the place; he sat down beneath the shade, and listened to the murmuring stream and the warbling birds—they were sights and sounds which he had always loved; but he now realized how necessary it was to the enjoyment of nature's simple sweets, to have a mind at rest. How often had he, after a weary day, sat in the quiet evening, and with Ned enjoyed its calm serenity, and watched the moonbeams play upon the water, or through the trembling leaves, and the bright stars coming one by one and gemming all the sky! What pure and peaceful thoughts they kindled, and how unalloyed the happiness that spread its soothing, quickening glow through all his frame! How he looked back now, as to an Eden, where he once had dwelt, but from which he seemed to be expelled for ever! Care, that canker of the heart, had come and taken, like a strong man armed, the full possession of his powers; tinging the heavens and the earth with its dark hue, and spoiling all their beauties.

At the time appointed he returned to the Bank; it seemed to him that the interests of the universe were at stake; and as he walked up to the tall, commanding form of the Cashier, the man appeared to be vested with a power that held the very springs of life at his command.

He was received with the same gentlemanly manner as at his introduction, and requested to walk behind the counter and take a seat, and as though he knew the workings of the young man's mind, and wished at once to relieve his suspense—

'The Directors have concluded to accept your paper, sir; sit down, Mr. Montjoy;' and James took the seat with a lighter heart than he had felt for some time. 'They have done it in the confidence that your statement is correct: and I will say further to you, sir, as you are a young man, and have much business yet before you, that the manner in which you have commenced and carried on your trade, has had great weight in determining the decision of the Board. The times at present are very precarious, and you will need much prudence; but, sir, I believe I can assure you, that so long as you confine your operations to the regular run of your business, any facilities you may need will be at your service here.'

The sun shone very brightly to James as he journeyed towards home that day; nature was almost as captivating to him as in the days of childhood; and the joyous shake of Ned's hand, and the calm sweet smile of his mother, as they listened to his story, all made his heart leap in gladness, and send up to Him whose blessing was the burden of his daily petitions, warm and devout thanksgiving.

Thus the storm which had threatened to overwhelm these young men passed with but partial injury. The foundation they had laid in patient industry, prudent management, and stern integrity, bore them proudly on. The wily plots of Mr. Cross were anticipated by the promptness with which James attended to his affairs; and for the present, at least, the young firm is safe.

CHAPTER XXVI

The Widow Brown, in consequence of the disclosure made by the dying Ned Saunders, was placed in no very agreeable situation. She thought that the unhappy man had his reason, but she could not be so very sure as to be willing to publish what might not after all be true, to the certain injury not only of Mr. Cross, who had ever been kind to her, but of her son also, who had wound himself around her heart, and for whom she had been so earnestly entreated by that miserable woman who declared herself his mother.

She comprehended but a very little of the nature of papers of any kind, beyond those solemn legacies from God to man, which daily she perused with love and gratitude. And what Ned Saunders meant by papers which Mr. Cross was anxious to get hold of, she could not conceive.

'The poor, deluded soul,' said she one day, while walking alone, her thoughts too burdensome to be kept in; 'I am very doubtful that he knew what he said when he talked about those papers; and now that the dreadful deed is done, what good end can be answered by publishing it abroad? It will not build the house again, and God will avenge it in his own time and way.'

She wished much, however, for the time when William should be able to make some disclosures as to his share in the terrible transaction. That he was a participator in the crime she could not believe; but that he had attacked Ned Saunders, and that the consequences had proved fatal to one of them, she had too strong evidence to doubt. The whole was altogether beyond the comprehension of the poor widow, and all she could do, at present, was to wait for time to make plain the path of duty.

William, however, could no longer bear the struggle which agitated his mind, and he determined to unburden it. As there were reasons why he preferred to communicate with his sister, he took an opportunity, when alone, to reveal all he knew, and let her into the secret of his own present condition, and the villany of Cross. Hettie's first impulse was to fly at once to Mr. Rutherford.

'He ought to be made acquainted with these facts without a moment's delay.'

'But David, sister; think of him.'

Hettie was silent; she gazed a moment at her brother, then leaned back in her chair, and resting her head upon her hand, was lost for awhile in busy thought.

'David must be told, William; he must know it before any one else; he has had no hand in it, and all his kindness to us demands this confidence in him.'

William made no reply; he was much exhausted, and even the effort of thinking was painful. The mother also now came in, and, wishing a little relaxation, Hettie left the room and sought a favourite spot to which she was in the habit of retiring, sheltered alike from the rays of the sun and common observation—a tumult of distracting thoughts rioted within; again and again she resolved the doubtful question as to her present duty, and the difficulties attending any course which presented itself to her were so great, that she most heartily longed for some experienced counsel to guide her steps.

In the midst of her perplexities, she was startled at the sound of approaching footsteps.

'I thought I should never find you. Your mother said she guessed you was here; but that thick clump of bushes hid you so, that I had almost given it up.'

'I come here occasionally; it is so retired.'

'I should think it was retired enough; but I don't see what you want to get off so alone for; it is lonely enough, I should think, all over these old barrens. But ain't you glad Bill is so much better?'

'He is better certainly, David; more like himself than he has been yet—don't you think so?'

'That he is—but you look sick; you sit by that bed too much, Hettie. You want a ride—come—Bony's at the cottage—go along with me: we will soon bring your color back.'

'Not to-day, David; indeed I have no desire to ride to-day; and besides, since you are here, I want to have some conversation with you upon a matter in which you are deeply concerned.'

'Well, come on—I'm ready for anything—out with it. I'm so glad Bill is better, I don't care what comes now; but look cheerful a little; do, I beg of you; I have dark looks enough at home. The old man is so cross about something or other lately, that he can't give me a civil word. I thought when I came along, what I would give just to live among you here. I tell you what,

Hettie, I had rather live with you and your mother, and have nothing but bread and water, only to hear kind words;—well, you are queer—just now you was so pale, and now your face is red as a rose.'

Hettie felt the flush which David had noticed; he had never spoken quite so plainly to her before, and she began to fear what next might come; so she commenced the unpleasant task of making him acquainted with his father's conduct; but she did not give the account in the order that she received it, for she began at the catastrophe, and told the story as well as she could, without alluding to the main instigator of the plot.

'But what could have induced those men to commit such a deed? and what could they have wanted with the trunk without there was money in it?'

'There was no money in it, but there were papers of great consequence.'

'Papers? what could they know about papers? they can't read, not one of them; what good would papers do them?' said David; his countenance pale, and his lips trembling with emotion.

'There is something more in all this that you have not yet told me, Hettie; some one is at the bottom of it. Who is it?'

Hettie covered her face with her hands.

'Don't be afraid, Hettie; out with it—is it my father?'

Hettie burst into tears, and David sank to the earth, helpless as an infant. Seeing that he was greatly agitated, and that he seemed in need of help, she was about to go for her mother.

'Don't leave me, Hettie. Do you think that this is truth, and that William has his reason?'

'He seems to have it, perfectly; he has given a clear account of things from the first—I fear it is true.'

'Does any one know of this besides you and your brother?'

'No human being as yet.'

'Depend upon it, Hettie, if my father has instigated this act, he has been in some way thwarted in his design; for his temper, never very good, has been outrageous for some time past; so much so, that I have made up my mind to leave him and this region for ever. There is but one thing which keeps me; you and your mother are the only persons in the world that I care much about—and you I love as I do my life. If you will marry me, Hettie, I will get together all I have got; it will be enough to purchase us a place far away from here, and we will take your mother, and Bill, too, if he gets well; and how happy we shall be.'

Hettie was deeply affected, but she felt that she must deal plainly with him.

'You must not talk so, David; you and I can never be married.'

'You are ashamed of me already, Hettie. My father's disgrace, I see, is to be mine.'

'I shall never attach to you, David, any wrong your father has done— but let us say no more about this. You have ever been kind to me and my family; all that a sister can do for you, I will; beyond this, I hope you will not urge me. But there are some things to be thought of that must be done soon. Mr. Rutherford ought not to be kept ignorant of this matter. I have, out of kindness to you, told you what I have heard, and with a hope that you will make an effort to recover these papers, and thus in part frustrate an evil design, and perhaps save your father from a great calamity. William has told me that he has some faint recollection of feeling the trunk taken from his grasp, while he lay in that helpless condition. You think your father has not got it; probably then, it is in the hands of some person who does not realize the value of it, and may easily be induced to relinquish it.'

'I will do what I can, Hettie, to find out; but I caution you to let no person know a word of all this, at least not until I have failed in finding out some clue to it. Should Rutherford know what you do, and make attempts to search, or to expose matters, it would be the very way, as things are here, to have it put where no one can ever be the wiser for it. If my father has not got the trunk or the papers—and I don't believe he has, for the reason I have told you—it is probably in the hands of some one who has taken it from Bill, and is afraid to say any thing, for fear he would be charged with an attempt to murder.'

David's reasoning appeared so plausible, that Hettie coincided with him as to the propriety, at present, of saying nothing further on the subject to any one.

CHAPTER XXVII

There were many things in the circumstances of Mr. Cross, in themselves not very desirable. He had, to be sure, injured Mr. Rutherford; he had destroyed his home; he had by his artifice, brought him to cruel suffering and mortification; and he had wrested from him an instrument of immense value to its rightful owner, although of very doubtful utility to himself. But this very instrument had fallen into the hands of one whom he hated and feared, and was now held over him as a rod of terror, to force him into compliance with just such measures as the dictator chose.

He had committed also a flagrant crime—one that rendered him liable to the severest penalty of the law; and the knowledge of what he had done was not confined to himself and his agents. One at least, besides, held the fatal secret; and although she was a lone widow, and very much under his power, still she might disclose it—perhaps she had already done so.

His situation was no enviable one. He walked by the crater of a volcano; he could see the fires and hear the rumbling beneath him; at any moment he might be engulfed.

The wicked make the toils which entangle and distress them, but they are not the less troublesome on that account. Cross saw that something must be done, and without delay. The first step was, to ascertain what amount of information Ned Saunders had communicated to the Widow Brown, and then by some means, fair or foul, stop it from going any further. There was also a mystery about the disaster which had befallen William Brown; somehow he believed it to be connected with the loss of the trunk and the injury to Saunders, in what way he could not unravel; but he firmly believed that William knew, if he could or would tell, more than any one else. Cross had visited him frequently during his illness, and kept a shrewd eye upon him, at the same time continuing acts of kindness towards the family, as well as encouraging the attentions of David.

He saw clearly, at length, that William was recovering his strength, and even guessed that he had more ability to converse than he felt willing should be known.

It may seem strange that a father could be willing to expose his baseness to a son; but when the heart becomes accustomed to iniquity, it loses the finer feelings, and becomes callous to all sense of shame, or even desire for the respect and love of its nearest kindred. Cross thought he saw how he might, through the influence of his son, keep a hold upon that family, and he scrupled not to make a confidant of him, even to the exposure of his own base purposes.

David had just returned from the cottage. It was at the closing of day; Cross was alone in his store, and sat pondering upon his plans and prospects, and the multitude of dangers surrounding him.

'Have you been at the Widow Brown's?'

'Just come from there.'

'How is Bill?'

'Better; pretty weak though yet.'

'Can he talk yet?'

'Not much.'

'Not much! Can he talk at all? if he can I want to know it. But where are you going now?'

'Not far; up north a short distance.'

'You can't go now; sit down—I want to talk to you.'

David obeyed without making any reply; he did not fancy his father's talks very much, but he feared to offend him.

'I've got into trouble, and you may as well know it: it has all been done to give you a lift, and make you something in the world; but things have gone wrong end foremost, and now we must make the best of them.'

Cross looked at his son and paused, seeming to expect an answer; but David either did not care how things went, or he wished to know more about them before venturing upon a reply.

'You know Rutherford's house has been burned, and that Ned Saunders is dead; he was the one who did that job. He's gone out of the way, to be sure; but he has told a pack of lies to old Molly Brown, and if she should blab it about, we might get into a mess of trouble; but I suppose you know all about it—she has let it out to you, no doubt.'

But David made no signs of acknowledgment as to whether he did or did not know any thing about it.

'Are you dumb, all at once, that you cannot speak when you are spoken to?'

'You haven't asked me any question yet.'

'Yes, I have; has Molly Brown told you what Ned Saunders said?'

'She has not.'

'Has she talked about it that you know of?'

'Not that I know of.'

Cross sat silent for some time; at length making another effort, he disclosed his purpose.

'The fact is, the old woman knows too much for our good. She likes you well enough; you know that I suppose, and she has good reason to do so; you can stop her tongue if you will.'

'I should like to know how.'

'How? Why, by marrying Hettie; she can't hurt us then, without hurting her own child, and she won't be likely to do that. You shall have money enough: the barrens are pretty much all ours now, or they will be when this matter is once quashed.'

'How so?'

'Why, Rutherford's deed for them is burned up, and there is no record of it, and mine covers it all.'

'But suppose I should tell you that Rutherford's deed is not burnt?'

'How do you know it ain't?' and Cross arose from his seat in great excitement.

'Bill Brown has told all about it; he laid on the truck-bed under the counter the night you and old Foster were here together.'

Dave looked at his father for the first time since the commencement of the interview. The dim light that came in through the open door just enabled him to see the ashy paleness that had over-spread his features.

'Get me some gin;' and Cross nearly fell into his chair as Dave stepped up to him.

'Get me some gin, I say; quick!'

Dave immediately drew a tumbler of the clear liquor, and his father taking it with both hands, with difficulty put it to his mouth, so violent was his agitation; he accomplished it, however, and did not stop until the glass was empty. Drawing a long breath, he handed back the glass.

'Go sit down; I'll be better directly.' Some moments elapsed before he could resume the conversation.

'Who has Bill Brown told that lie to?'

'He has told it to his sister; whether it's a lie or not, I can't say. I shouldn't think he would be like to lie just now, with one foot in the grave.'

Cross saw too clearly that his villany was fully exposed; he sat apparently stunned by the perils which now hovered over him. David at last broke silence.

'The best thing to be done is, to give Rutherford back his deed.'

'That can't be done; I have not got it, nor has it ever been in my hands. There is only one thing that can be of any use now, and that is to stop the mouths of that family; you can easily do that by marrying the daughter.'

'It takes two to make such a bargain as that.'

'You don't suppose she would be fool enough to refuse you?'

'Fool or no fool, she has refused me this very day.'

Cross was again silent. It appeared that difficulties arose at every step; but when the end to be accomplished was so important, the means in his view were of no moment. A plan suggested itself to his mind, cruel and base to be sure; but he was in a strait, and what were the feelings of a gentle girl, even should her heart be broken, in comparison with his own selfish ends?

'That is easy to get along with—there ain't half the girls round here that ever give consent at all. Get her over to the old rendezvous; give the boys and girls a wink, as to what you want; have old Goble on the spot—he's used to it. She'll give in easy enough when you're once buckled together; a little kind treatment and plenty of money will soon settle everything; and when you are in the family, and they can't help themselves, all will go right enough; and then, if they try to hurt either of us, they will only be cutting their own heads off; they won't be for doing that.'

In order to the clear understanding of the plan which Cross had suggested, a little explanation will be necessary.

Among these rude people, the subject of marriage, and everything connected with it, was treated in a peculiar manner; from first to last, secrecy seemed to be the main ingredient in the whole business. The courtship was carried on clandestinely, and very seldom was the marriage ceremony completed—it could scarcely be said to be solemnized—without at least a show of resistance and reluctance on the part of the female; she being often fairly forced into the room by the main strength of her companions, and never did the minister expect a reply, or even the sign of assent to his questions from either party. Goble, the character by whom nearly all the matrimonial bonds in this region had been riveted for the last twenty years, was a nondescript minister, who had some good things in his composition, mixed with a great many others of a very doubtful kind. He could preach in a certain way, on any occasion to which he was called, but he was very seldom asked to perform any such duty, and was well content, so far as he himself was concerned, to do nothing at it; he worked for his living at a small trade, and that, with the trifling fees he received for some professional services, satisfied his humble desires.

David Cross listened to these suggestions of his father, outrageous as they were, with no little interest. He loved Hettie, or at least he thought he did; but brought up and educated as he had been, he could have no very correct idea of those pure and delicate feelings which constitute true love: he supposed that he could make her happy, and felt every disposition to do so. His interview with her the day before had not been as satisfactory as he had wished. He had never before doubted that she would willingly accept him, and had always looked upon her as appropriated to himself; to be thus disappointed, was not by any means grateful to his uncurbed will and unsubdued passions. It produced an unhappy effect upon his mind—a sort of determination to get her into his power; and he meant it in kindness too, for he was sure that he could make her happy.

As his father, therefore, unfolded to him a way that his wish could be accomplished, he eagerly caught at it, and even then resolved that she should be his.

The meeting between William Andrews and his mother was almost too much for the old lady; she ever had loved him dearly, even through all her harsh treatment of him. She had heard of his prosperity in his letters home; he had told her that he was doing well, and the supplies of money which he occasionally sent to her confirmed his statement. But she had not expected such a change in his appearance. His manners and style of dress, and the consideration which was paid to him, caused the old lady at times to feel almost sad as well as proud. William, however, was unchanged in his affection, and left nothing undone that could manifest to her his filial respect and love. The old house was refitted in the neatest manner, as she preferred living in that, she said, the rest of her days, to any new one that could be built. She would have been too happy, were it not that too many tokens of disease manifested themselves, for a mother's eye not to discern that there was a worm at the root of her gourd.

The health of William was not benefited by his native air; the languor which oppressed him became more and more distressing, and the sunken cheek and the hectic flush gave sad notice to the hearts that loved him of his fatal malady. But his spirits retained their elasticity, and the hope of returning health seemed to grow stronger in his own breast, as it grew fainter in the hearts of his friends. He thought he should he better soon; and thus from day to day he went about among the neighbours who were now clustered in his native village, and rejoiced in the magic change which every where met his eye. What hours of delightful converse he enjoyed with those whose enterprise had given the first start to all these new and pleasant scenes, and by whose aid he himself had broken the chains of idleness and vice, and arisen to respectability and independence.

Jim and Ned were the brothers of his heart, and between the three there was an interchange of the most entire confidence: Sam only was wanting to have made the circle of his heart's desire complete.

Through the influence of William, Mr. Rutherford had been induced to hire a tenement for the present, not far from the abode of the Montjoys, until time should more clearly develop what course he ought to pursue for his future support.

To this family he daily resorted, there he found another home, and in their friendship he enjoyed a repose that seemed to him a paradise.

Hettie he often met, and treated her like a sister, so far as she would allow him, but he had said nothing to her about love. Perhaps his heart had been drawn far away, or the power of disease had so deadened his feelings, that he could not arouse himself to the effort of attempting to gain her affections, or perhaps he saw—for love is eagle-eyed—that there was one on whom Hettie looked with just such feelings as he would once fain have had her entertain towards himself.

Henry Tracy still retained his situation, and, of course, William and he were thrown together in the same home; a sincere friendship had commenced between them; the mild and social character of both seemed formed upon the same basis. Although there was a vast difference in their mental attainments, yet William had learned much from intercourse with the world, and could impart valuable knowledge of men and things in exchange for the intellectual stores which Henry had at his command, and thus was his spirit beguiled from those dark and depressing thoughts which often attend upon the sinking frame, and even hasten its decay. Friendship met him at every turn in some new form, and her smile cheered his sensitive spirit, and kept up a genial glow; quickening his languid pulse, and animating him with unnatural vigor.

He had been spending the evening at the Rutherford's, and had been more engaged in conversation than usual; it was near the time for retiring, when he was seized with a slight fit of coughing; and on Mrs. Rutherford's asking if he felt more unwell, as she noticed that he was unusually pale—

'I am in some pain;' and he placed his hand upon his chest. She stepped up to him, and found that the handkerchief which he had just taken from his mouth was stained with blood.

The physician was immediately called in, but his hopeless look, as he bent over the poor youth, gave sad presage of what the end would be. His mother and sister were likewise soon with him; but Mrs. Rutherford persuaded them to leave the care of him to her; and faithfully did that kind and gentle lady watch by his sick bed. She and Hettie moved about the apartment in that calm and unobtrusive manner so grateful to the weak and suffering. Every thing was kept in perfect order, and all tokens of a sick chamber were removed, save the chastened light that came in through the drawn curtains, and the noiseless tread of those who waited upon him. Their countenances, when around the bed, or bending over it to administer some food or cordial, wore no gloomy aspect, no anxious knitted brow, no look of sadness from the eye. He loved to gaze upon them both; angels they seemed to him—attendants from a better world, waiting on his frail body here, and soon to bear his soaring spirit to the bright abode which they had left. And when he talked of death, and told them he was going fast, and soon the struggle would be over; sweetly they would speak about the heaven that was beyond, of the pure white robes, and the golden harps, and the everlasting songs, and the bright meeting they would have when care and toil, and sin and death, were passed.

Mr. Rutherford was often by his side, and showed, in every word and look, how much he felt. He could not hide his aching heart beneath a smile; he loved too well the youthful sufferer. Obligations of the tenderest kind he hourly felt. Nor was this all; he could sympathize with him as a man; how full of ardent hopes, with prospects bright for future years, and all earth's winning smiles beaming on his path, and now to die so soon, was hard, he thought, even though an angel beckoned him away. And thus when he stood by that silent bed, and heard the short, hard heavings of his chest, and saw the daily inroads of disease upon that face, which had so lately beamed like hope's bright star upon his troubled way; he felt like one who looks into an open grave, and hears the clod fall heavy on the coffin-lid; 'twas dark, all dark.

And at that bed, by day and night, whenever he could snatch an hour from his varied duties, was Henry Tracy. His friendship had just begun to kindle into warmth, when he saw that it must soon be extinguished. William loved to have him near; he loved to hear him converse about those realities which now alone absorbed his spirit; and well did Henry know how to deal out the precious manna; so soft and clear, in tones that fell like heavenly music on the ear. He talked about the Saviour—for, to Henry, the name of

Jesus was a name to quicken every pulse, and fill the heart with holy joy; and when he spoke of Him, it was as though he talked about a friend whose ardent sympathies beat in unison with his own; a friend who loved, who was now near at hand, feeling for all his woes, smoothing the dying pillow, taking away the sting of death, and preparing a triumphant passage for his soul into his own blest home.

William drank in his words until his spirit rejoiced within him, and longed to depart. He had a strange pleasure, too, in seeing Hettie stand by the side of Henry and listen to his voice, until her face would glow with the holy fire it kindled in his breast; he could read in her glistening eye, perhaps, what few others could. William loved her even in death, and now, more than he had done for years past. He loved, too, Henry Tracy. As he gazed on them by turns, he felt how well suited they were to one another. He murmured something; Henry heard them, but though Hettie caught but a word, the rich colour that spread over her pale face, proved that she understood them. He spoke their names together, and he blessed them.

Short were the hours after this that William struggled with the pains of life; around him were all the dear ones he had on earth; there was no violence of grief to trouble his departing spirit; hearts were bleeding silently, and as the last breath went to heaven, a moment all watched the still, sweet sleeper, and looked on silently while Mr. Rutherford closed his eyes, and then sat down and wept until their burdened spirits found relief.

CHAPTER XXVIII

During all the period of Hettie's confinement around the sick bed of William Andrews, David saw nothing of her; he felt satisfied that she would not disclose what her brother had communicated to her. The efforts which, in the mean time, he was to make for the recovery of the lost document, were much relaxed by the interview with his father, as related in a former chapter. He saw now that his ultimate object might be gained, and suffered his selfish feelings to work their hateful purpose. He continued his attentions to William and his mother, and did much to supply to them the absence of Hettie.

Reports are easily set in motion, and, as every one is willing to keep them moving, it is not strange that they spread so fast. Thus it began to be whispered that Mr. Tracy and Hettie Brown were engaged to be married; and although no one had any license for saying so, nor was it actually the case, yet so it was said, and David among the rest listened to the story. It took him not altogether by surprise, and only confirmed him in his purpose to accomplish the plan proposed by his father.

The effort William had made to communicate the terrible secret which harassed his mind, enfeebled as it was by disease, had nearly proved fatal to him. The excitement produced by the thought of having the matter made public, with all its consequences to himself and others, together with the physical effort he was obliged to make in order to explain things fully to his sister, brought on a recurrence of his unfavorable symptoms, and as soon as Hettie could be spared from the dying room of William Andrews, she was again at her mother's home, although so exhausted in mind and body as to be able to do little else than watch by his bedside.

'I could not come as soon as I expected,' said David Cross as he entered the cottage of the Widow Brown; 'but we shall have time enough for a good ride yet.'

David looked very pale, and his voice trembled as he spoke, but Hettie did not notice it, for she was busy putting on her things. She had made an engagement with him that morning to take a drive; she felt that she needed the recreation, and as she supposed matters were well understood between them, hesitated not in accepting such an act of kindness.

'I think you had better not drive far, David, for it will soon be night, and William has not been so well to-day.'

'No, no, aunty, we shan't go far, or at least we shan't stay long, for Bony is in good spirits.'

Hettie sprang into the buggy, and Dave drove off at his usual rapid pace.

The rendezvous that Cross had spoken of in his conversation with his son, was situated in the midst of the thickest and least frequented part of the pines. It had once been used as a tavern, in days before Mr. Cross set up in his more public situation. Of late years, it became the haunt of all who wished to have a frolic as they called it—in other words, a low debauch; and scenes of riot were enacted there which even Cross himself did not approve. It was a lone place, and far from any settlement; of course no restraint was put upon those who wished thus to degrade themselves. It was also the chosen place for their marriage scenes; these seldom, if ever, taking place at the home of either party. Two old and miserable-looking beings kept the house, such as it was, and on occasion of an assemblage, gave matters up to the company to do as they pleased, their business being merely to deal out plenty of liquor from behind an old counter in one corner of the room.

'I think we have gone far enough, David; I fear William will begin to be restless.'

'I am only going as far as the house you see yonder. I must stop and water Bony, and as he is so restless, if you will step in and talk a moment to the old people, I will hurry all I can, and then we will be home in less than no time.'

As they drove up, Hettie knew that she had not seen the place before; but hesitated not to do as she was requested, although the house was very forbidding in its appearance.

'You've come airly,' said the old hag who sat just within the door, smoking a short black pipe. Hettie, not understanding her allusion, looked at her in some surprise, without making a reply.

'I say you've come rather airly; the folks ain't none on 'em got along yet.'

'What folks do you mean, granny?'

'Ay, ay, I see you're jist like the rest of the galls, you want to keep it secret as long as you can. We know all about it though; but you're goin' to have a smart un; Dave's a good feller.'

Hettie, supposing the old woman to be a little deranged, merely smiled, and walked into the room. David had driven his horse away, as she supposed, for the purpose of watering—Poor girl! she was in a trap, and soon her light and happy spirit would be writhing in agony.

'Are you ready, David? but where is the horse?' seeing that he had not driven to the door, but come into the room where she was, his countenance pale, and with an aspect that alarmed her. 'Has any thing happened, David? You are not well?'

'Come in the other room, Hettie.' She followed, but a strange foreboding of some evil flashed upon her mind, and so affected her in her then debilitated state, that she was glad to sit down on a long low bench, which ran along under the windows, at the same time fixing her penetrating eyes full on the young man. He took a seat beside her, and turning his head from her—

'I want to talk with you, Hettie, on that subject which you and I have had up between us lately.'

'What, David; about the trunk? have you heard of it?'

'No, there isn't much chance of doing any thing about that just now; but you know what I said to you some time ago about our being married.'

'That I supposed was all settled, David. I told you frankly when you first spoke to me, that it could never be; why should you bring it up again? I meant what I said, and I feel just as I did then.'

'But it is not all settled: I have been thinking of you all my life, Hettie, and you know how intimate we have been, and when I think of your marrying some one else, as it is said you are going to do, I can't stand it, Hettie, no how; and there is no use of talking about it.'

'But you surely would not wish to marry me if I did not love you, David; and that I tell you now, as I told you before, I do not as I expect to love the man whom I would give my hand to. You have been always very kind to me, and to my family, and we all think much of you, and would do any thing in our power for you, but on this subject I must beg of you to urge me no further, for it can never be.'

David now rose and stood up before her. He took one of her hands, at which she made no resistance, but he felt that it was cold as marble, and lay in his grasp like a lifeless thing. He saw also that the color had left her cheek, and that her lips were of a purple hue; the eyes alone retained their life, and gazed at him with an earnestness that he had never met from Hettie's eyes before.

'You must listen a moment to me, Hettie. I now ask you, once again, if you will marry me. I can take good care of you. My father has agreed to let me have money enough to purchase a handsome place, and we will go away from these dreary woods. Your mother and brother shall accompany us, if they will, and our home shall be theirs. I have invited the folks round, and the minister is sent for; in a short time they will be here. I want you to consent, and let it all go off smooth; but consent or not, Goble shall marry us when he comes, and then I should like to see the man that will separate you from me.'

Hettie was not prepared for this; she knew well what were the strange and uncouth customs in that region; but little had she dreamed that they could ever be brought thus to bear upon her. A thousand thoughts rushed into her mind of the most appalling nature. She feared that her conduct towards this young man had not been sufficiently guarded. She had mistaken his character, and now that she was in his power it was revealed to her in colors too glaring to be misunderstood. But her courage did not forsake her. She was well aware that resistance would be of no avail: she cast her thoughts to heaven, and prayed most earnestly that God would make a way for her out of this trouble, in comparison with which death itself would be a welcome messenger. She resolved that there should be no misunderstanding of her feelings. She withdrew her hand, and after a moment's pause, replied:—

'Your conduct, David, is as strange as it is ungenerous—unmanly. You have deceived me by coming to this place; you have taken me away from all help of friends. I am a woman, weak, and in your power; but I tell you now plainly, I despise you for your meanness. I shall protest most solemnly in the presence of your pretended minister, that I will never own you for a husband. No: I would sooner suffer the most excruciating torments, and die the bitterest death, than do one thing, by word or deed, that could give you a claim to me.'

David Cross writhed under this address; but Hettie could not have pursued a course more likely to confirm him in his purpose. He was cut to the heart, and resolved upon revenge. He cared not now for her love—she should be his slave.

As evening gathered over them, groups of females began to gather in the room; and as she cast her eye over them, not one countenance did she recognize as having ever seen before. They were arrayed in all sorts of fanciful styles; their dark complexions set off by pink, blue, yellow, and green dresses, according to the taste of the owner. Their untamed characters were too clearly visible in their rude behavior; and as they gathered around the suffering girl, the only sense they manifested of feeling was a hard, unmeaning smile, and a wink at each other, signifying that there was sport at hand. In the outer room, also, began to be heard the boisterous laugh of men, and the rattling of glasses on the counter, mingled with the harsh sounds of a violin, scraped by a negro, who had grown grey in the service, attending upon all the orgies of the country round. Little did Hettie, until that moment, ever think that there could be grouped within a few miles of her mother's dwelling a scene so nearly allied in her mind to the doings of the bottomless pit; and as the merriment increased with the exciting potions that were dealing out, her trembling spirit could only hang its hope on an unseen hand. She had made up her mind as to the course she intended to pursue. Resistance would be in vain; nor would an apparent opposition or repugnance to the performance of the ceremony avail any thing. She should therefore do as requested until the pretended ceremony began, and then would most solemnly protest against the violence done to her, and warn all present that her friends would prosecute to the utmost all who had a hand in the wickedness.

As the groups were coming in, she anxiously looked among them for a face that she knew, and at length espied one that was familiar, dressed in rather poorer garments than the rest; a young woman whom she had in some measure befriended. She soon caught her eye, and beckoned to her—

'Sally, will you get me a drink of cold water?' The young woman flew with alacrity to do her bidding. As she came near with the cup of water, Hettie spoke kindly to her, made a few inquiries, and then whispered in a very guarded manner a few words. The girl appeared much astonished, looked full at Hettie, and then towards David Cross, who was busily engaged at another part of the room. She then carried away the cup, and left the house.

Inquiries now began to be made after the minister.

'Goble ain't so hungry for his job as he is sometimes; he ought to have been here half an hour ago.'

'He's getting old, Joe; he can't move as he once did. He'll be along, though, by and by—no fear of Goble.'

The old negro, after a while, being pretty well warmed up with the liquor, kept up an incessant jingle on his crazy instrument, bobbing his old grey head about, and occasionally stamping violently with his foot, as he became excited by his own melody. In different parts of the room a couple might be seen shuffling away rapidly with their feet, tossing their arms up and down as they held each other's hands, swaying their bodies in all directions, and performing all sorts of uncouth gestures; until, exhausted by the exercise, they would slap their feet hard on the floor, let go of hands, swing round, and with a loud shout which was echoed by an uproarious laugh throughout the room, mingle again with the crowd.

How long these scenes continued, Hettie could not tell, nor did she heed them much; her mind was too painfully oppressed in anticipation of what she might yet be called to go through.

Henry Tracy had just returned from a visit to some of his charge, and was quietly seated in his study, when the Widow Andrews, putting her head carefully around the casement of the open door, said in a very low voice,

'There's two of the Sheldrakes out here; they want to see the minister.'

'Two what, Mrs. Andrews?'

'Sheldrakes—there's two on 'em, and they're round the corner by the big tree; they won't come in, but they say they want to see the minister.'

Henry stepped to the window, expecting to see he hardly knew what; there were, indeed, two uncouth looking figures, but he recognised them at once as inhabitants of the barrens.

'Are those two men the persons you allude to, Mrs. Andrews.'

'Yes, there they are—there's two on 'em; they're the real Sheldrakes, the critters are.'

Without waiting to inquire into the peculiar meaning of the term, he went out immediately to them, and asked in his pleasant manner.

'Were you inquiring for me?'

'We's wanting to see the minister; there's a little job to be done up our way, and as the regular hand is sick we've come to git you.'

Henry had become quite familiar with these rude sons of the forest, and therefore their appearance and manners were not at all surprising to him.

'What kind of a job is it you have on hand, my friends?'

'Oh, it's a little weddin' job; a couple of young un's want hitchin together; and Dave sent us for Goble, but the old crittur's got the rhumatiz, so he can't go no how; and as we thought it warn't no matter who does it, so as it's done, we've come arter you.'

'What David? David Cross! He is not going to be married, is he?'

'But you won't speak of it; so if you will be about dusk at the corner of the north road, we'll be there and show you the way.'

'I will be there; but you must not lose me in your wild country;' smiling as he said it.

'Never fear, sir, we'll take you safe and bring you back safe, and there shan't be a hair o' your head hurt; only you must'nt mind if the boys is noisy a little; but when they see it ain't Goble that's among 'em they'll behave more decenter, for they set store by you, minister, all over.'

At the appointed time Henry was on the spot; a thick fog had settled around as evening approached, and the two guides were obliged very soon to light their pine knots. As Henry followed on through the thick woods, had it not been that he was somewhat accustomed to scenes of the kind, he might have felt no little uneasiness; for the men were wild looking figures, their long streaming hair, rude garments, dark, Indian countenances, together with the flaming brands throwing their pitchy glare upon the huge trunks of the giant pines through which they threaded their way, while all beyond the little circle of light in which they walked was a wilderness of darkness—the whole scene required no little confidence for one to be quite at ease. The men followed no beaten road, but were guided in their course by marks known only to themselves.

The sound of the violin and the hum of voices were at length heard, and lights were seen close at hand.

'Have you got him, Harry?'

'Aye, aye; but tell 'em to stop their noise.' And the tidings could be heard flying from mouth to mouth; the violin ceased, and all was hushed.

The room in which the ceremony was to be performed was spacious enough to contain a large assembly. It was nearly filled; the men and women standing promiscuously in a dense mass, occupied about two-thirds of the apartment, leaving a clear space sufficiently large for those more immediately connected with the performance; within this stood a number of the younger females with their arms locked, and forming a complete ring encircling those who were intended to be the bride and groom.

Hettie had followed, as she had been requested, on the announcement of the ministers approach; but the excitement under which she labored was so great, that it required her utmost energy to sustain herself without assistance, and she would have died before she would have sought it from him who stood beside her; to have lost her physical or mental powers at such a time, she knew would have been the end of hope for her. She stood with her face covered, as the only way she could command herself, and her agonized spirit poured out its terrible necessities to Him, who she believed could alone help her. As Henry Tracy entered the room, a buzz of astonishment ran through the assembly; the circle of girls opened and extended itself, so as to permit him to be immediately before the couple. He smiled, as he looked at David Cross, but casting his eye quickly to her who stood beside him, the smile flew away, and a deadly sickness came over him. He saw not her face, for it was still covered, but those raven locks, and that lovely form, he had seen too often not to recognise at once. For a moment he stood petrified with amazement, unable to utter a syllable, or do any thing but gaze, almost with horror, upon the terrible apparition which had thus risen before him.

Hearing the movement around her, and supposing the ceremony was about to begin, Hettie sent one long, silent cry to heaven for aid, and then uncovered her face. Had an angel from that bright world appeared for her rescue, it could not have been more surprising to her than the sight of Henry Tracy. She clasped her hands together, fixed her eye full upon him, and uttering a scream of delight, flew towards him.

'Oh, save me! save me!'

'Where is she? where is she?' and a woman broke into the room. 'Where is my child?' And Henry Tracy laid the fainting girl in her mother's arms, and assisted in bearing her from the room into the open air.

When David Cross saw Henry Tracy enter the room, accompanied by the two men whom he had commissioned to procure the services of Mr. Goble, he know at once that his design was frustrated. His countenance was deadly pale, and he cast a glance of fury at the two men, but he durst not vent his anger either in words or actions there. The mighty spell which Henry's influence exerted, even in this waste region, was too evident in the perfect stillness which reigned the moment he entered the room, and the looks of reverence that beamed even from those wild and untamed countenances.

As Hettie darted from his side, he made his way through the crowd to an end door of the building, and with feelings which none might envy, was soon on his way towards his father's house. One by one the company slunk away, when they found that the proceedings were at an end, and in silence groped through the darkness towards their several homes.

When Hettie awoke to consciousness, Henry was bending over her, while her mother sat by her side, smoothing her beautiful forehead, and putting back the dark locks which kept falling over it.

All was still; she listened for those terrible sounds which had well nigh driven her reason; but no sound could she hear, except the sweet voice of Henry.

'You feel better now?'

'Oh, yes; but how has it all come about?'

'We must ask you that, my dear?' said her mother; 'it is all a mystery, a great mystery to us.'

'Sally went for you then, mother? I was fearful it would all be over before she could get there.'

'Yes, my dear, and she is now sitting with your brother until we get home.'

'Do let us go, then, for I am so anxious to get away from this terrible place—but there—what is that!' and Hettie darted a wild glance towards the door. Henry and her mother looked at each other.

'There is nothing here, Hettie—no one beside your dear mother and myself.'

'Oh—well—I am so glad!'

Henry said nothing of his fears; but a terrible thought came into his mind; which was more and more confirmed by an occasional wild glance of her eye. 'Her mind has been injured, or she is about to be visited with severe illness.'

The mother probably did not think as far as he did, although she felt that there was need for immediate departure.

'Are you able to walk, my dear? if so, we had better be going.'

'Oh yes, to be sure, mother.' And she quickly rose from the rude bed on which she had been laid; but no sooner did she attempt to stand, than her trembling limbs gave way. Henry caught her, and again laid her to rest: she was evidently ill already, and no time must be lost in getting away from that miserable abode.

The men who had accompanied Henry were still in waiting to conduct him home. By their aid a litter was constructed; and while the anxious mother bore the torch to light them through the gloom, Henry with his two guides carried the suffering girl.

It was a sad journey that for Henry Tracy. The wild and incoherent remarks which Hettie made, the deathly pallor of her countenance, and the quick flashing of her eye, which he discerned as the light occasionally fell upon her features, confirmed his worst fears.

By his persuasion, the widow consented that she should be taken to Mr. Rutherford's, her own humble home offering no suitable convenience for another invalid.

The ways of God appear unequal only to those who judge prematurely, or without taking into the account that this world is not the end. God sees as we do not: His design in all the dealings of His judgments and His mercies here towards those who love Him, is to make them trust in Him, and cast their thoughts, too prone to settle on this vale of tears and be content with earth, upwards, towards that better, purer home in heaven.

CHAPTER XXIX

War is a name that carries in its dreadful meaning scenes of suffering and woe, little thought of, it is feared, by those who, at the helm of power, too easily proclaim the deadly feud.

The widow's tear, the orphan's helpless sigh, the agonizing groans of bleeding victims, the horrible necessities that wait upon the contest for supremacy where man forgets his nature, and hastes with tiger-thirst to seek the life-blood of his fellow man, are all forgotten or unheeded. A little land, not worth a single pang of one fond mother's heart; a little wrong that might by calm remonstrance be redressed, or even borne with, affords a pretext. The herald of defiance is sent forth, and misery, death, and desolation hover on his track.

The event which Commodore Trysail had predicted came to pass, although somewhat sooner than either he or many other shrewd calculators had anticipated. The Commodore, as we have seen, had no misgivings of conscience about the necessity of the measure: he only wished for a better preparation, before engaging in hostilities with the greatest nation on the globe.

As to his own private interests, a few months would have enabled him to place them on a better footing, yet, perhaps, he thought as little about that matter as most men; at any rate, he took a very decided stand for the government, and strongly upheld it in its declaration of war.

With Peter he still held long private talks on Peter's favorite topic; and every new incident of the war seemed interesting to the old sailor, only as it in some way might affect the safe return of Captain Sam. One morning, as Peter handed in the pack of papers at the door of the office, he looked very anxiously at the Commodore.

'There's three more on 'em come, your honor—'

'More what, Peter?'

'Of the blockaders, sir,—a brig and two schooners.'

'What will become of our young captain, now, Peter?'

Peter slipped the quid to the other side, and worked away at it awhile in good earnest.

'I'm a-thinking, your honor, it's a great pity he ain't in a regular man-o'-war's man.'

'What would he do then, Peter?'

'He'd make her talk, your honor, or I'm mistaken.'

'You don't think he'd fight, do you?'

'What for not, your honor?'

'Why, you know he has been dodging along shore here, Peter, all his life—he has hardly smelled gunpowder.'

'Asking your honor's pardon for the freedom, but I must haul off from your honor this time. Captain Sam may be ain't had much experience in the fightin' way as yet; but your honor knows, it's more what's in a man than what he larns—a brave man ashore will be a brave man at sea, that is, a'ter the sickness is over; but if Captain Sam don't face an enemy's bullet with the best on 'em, I'll cut off my pigtail and give it to the cats.' Peter could have made no stronger asseveration; for he highly valued the long appendage to his bushy head, and of all creatures he hated cats.

'Do you think, Peter, if he had a good ship and a dozen guns on board, with a fine crew, he would know what to do with them?'

'If he don't, your honor, I'll give up t'other leg, and go upon stumps the rest of my days.'

'Well, Peter, I believe you; and we think alike this time. You may take these papers, and show them to Lady Morris.'

'Ay, ay, your honor.'

And Peter hobbled away, discharging the old quid as soon as he had fairly left the house; and treating himself to a new one, muttering as he did so, 'Captain Sam will show 'em—see if he don't.'

The Commodore, through the influence of Peter, had also become much interested in the Montjoys; all the story of their boyish days had been so often repeated that they seemed like old acquaintances; and although, for argument's sake, the old gentleman would appear to doubt the correctness of Peter's reasoning on the certainty of their doing well, yet he had great confidence in the young firm, and an earnest desire for their prosperity.

Old Sam Cutter, too, with whom the Commodore was very intimate, had not failed to make him acquainted with the mighty change which had been brought about through the instrumentality of these boys in this place, now so lovely in its appearance. He felt that they deserved his respect as a citizen, and treated them with a consideration which, for the disparity in years and circumstances, was very gratifying to them.

He was therefore a frequent visitor at their establishment—never hindering them at their work if he found them engaged; but bowing respectfully to the young men and those who might be in at the time, would walk straight through the store into the little back room, which was always in perfect order, and there seek for news among their papers which might not happen to be in his.

On this particular day of which we have been speaking, he had an object of some importance in his visit; and as he passed along to the usual place, he politely requested the favor of an interview with the elder partner, when he could be spared from his desk.

'In a short time, sir, I will wait upon you,' said James, who was making an entry in his book.

That morning, the brothers had been spending some time in consultation about business matters. They had, as we have seen, been very kindly treated by the bank, and in consequence were enabled to keep along and meet their difficulties; but the serious losses which they had met, affected them much more than they at first anticipated. They had never before known what it was to be cramped in their means for doing business, because they had only increased their transactions as they found themselves able to do so; but things could not very easily be brought back by the same process—they must either go on, or suspend altogether; and either alternative involved difficulties of no ordinary kind. To continue as they had, they must for years to come, so far as they could see, be constantly devising ways and means to meet engagements, involving anxiety, dependence, watchfulness, and untiring attention: to suspend their operations, would not only be a bitter humiliation to their sensitive spirits, but there would be a sacrifice of property that might leave them without the ability to pay many of their just debts. There was also a difficulty attending their situation which troubled them more than all else beside. They had been in the habit of receiving from many of their customers small sums of money which they wished to secure against a time of need; the unbounded confidence reposed in the young men brought all the loose money of those in moderate circumstances into their hands: they allowed an interest for it, and hitherto had been able to return any sum when suddenly called for. The amount thus accumulated was now about two thousand dollars; and it was due in sums of from ten to three hundred. With many of these depositors, it was the whole of their possession.

The idea of danger from thus receiving funds had never occurred to the brothers, until they found by experience the difficulties which attended the raising money on an emergency with their diminished capital—in fact, with no other capital than their credit. But now they clearly saw that it placed them over a volcano; it might explode at any time, lay their business and well-earned reputation in ruins together, and utterly disable them from giving back this money thus sacredly intrusted to their keeping. And it was on this particular point they had been consulting that morning; their fears were mutually expressed, and they came to the resolution that they would involve themselves in such difficulties no farther.

As soon as James could leave his desk, he repaired to the back-room. After some kind greetings on either side, the Commodore straightened himself in his chair, and resting one hand on his large gold-headed cane—

'I want to talk with you a little, Mr. Montjoy, about money this morning.'

James's heart beat quick; he could not help it, for the Commodore had placed five hundred dollars in his hands a short time previous, and requested him to keep it until he called for it.

'I put five hundred dollars in your hands lately, which I was to have, you know, when I should call for it.'

'Yes, sir, certainly by all means.' Poor James! he knew not where it was to come from, and he secretly wished that he had never owned a dollar, or that there was no such thing as money.

'Well, sir, I have just received advices from the city that certain sum of money, which I suppose—'

Ned stepped into the office, and requested the presence of his brother a moment. The Commodore bade him go, by all means, that he would wait his leisure.

The business for which James was required was to close a very advantageous bargain for some produce, but he was in no state of mind to do business—money, ready money, was the only idea he could cherish; it clung to his spirit like the nightmare; he could neither bargain nor calculate, so he waived the matter, and was back again to the little room; he merely whispered to Ned,

'The Commodore, I suppose, has come for his money.'

'What shall we do?'

'I don't know.'

And he entered the room again, and sat down.

I've Been Thinking | 267

'As I was saying, Mr. Montjoy, when your brother called you away, a certain sum of money, which I supposed had been invested, I learn by my advices to-day is still lying idle, and waiting my orders. These are ticklish times, Mr. Montjoy, and they will be worse before long. I am afraid of stocks at present, and have therefore concluded to draw for these funds, and place them in your hands; you can use them to advantage, no doubt.'

And the Commodore took a long pinch of snuff, which had been for some time in waiting between his thumb and forefinger.

James felt a load fall from his heart, and for a moment was silent.

'I thank you, sir, for your kind offer, and for the confidence reposed in us; but before I can give you an answer, allow me to confer with my brother.'

The character of these two young men had never been so severely tested before. An offer, unsolicited, had been made to them of that which they stood so much in need of, and which would relieve them from embarrassment. Ned clapped his hands, and rubbed them violently together in the ecstasy of his joy.

'But, my dear Ned, ought we to take it?'

'Why not?'

'Because, he doubtless supposes that we are well off, and has no idea of our losses; and I've been thinking that, under the circumstances, we ought not to touch a dollar of it.'

'That, to be sure, Jim;'—and Ned's countenance drooped; he hung his head, and began to kick the counter with his foot.

'We concluded, you know, Ned, that we would take no more money in this way.'

'Well, we had better stick to that, let what will come.'

'How would it answer to tell him just the situation of things with us, and the reasons why we cannot receive it.'

'If you tell him any thing, Jim, you had better tell the whole.'

James's heart was lighter, because he had resolved to act consistently with a sense of duty.

'I believe, sir, we must decline your generous offer.'

James saw that the Commodore seemed surprised.

'We do this, sir, not but that we need the funds—and they would at the present moment be of immense advantage to us—but we have no doubt, that you have made the offer under the impression that we are in very different circumstances from what, I am sorry to say, is the truth. But as you are a man of business, and can appreciate our motives for not having made a general exposition of our affairs, I will communicate to you our true situation.'

And James gave a clear account of their course of business, from its commencement to the time when such unexpected losses at one stroke swept off the hard-earned profits of their youthful enterprise. He also explained to him the unpleasant situation in which they felt themselves placed, by being made the depositaries of so many sums of money, which might be called for at any moment, and especially should the least surmise get abroad unfriendly to their standing.

After he had closed, the Commodore took out his gold snuff-box, and rapping it pretty hard, helped himself freely, and then very deliberately returned it to his pocket.

'Mr. Montjoy, what you tell me surprises me very much; but it shall go no further, I assure you. Can you favor me with pen and ink a moment?'

He then drew up to the table on which James had placed the required articles.

'I believe it is five hundred dollars exactly that I handed you lately?'

'Just five hundred, sir.'

'I have done it now,' thought Jim; 'he is afraid of us, and intends to draw it out; but my duty has been performed, let what will come.'

'Mr. Montjoy, I said that I was much surprised at the statement you have made, but I cannot say that I am sorry for the misfortune you have met with'—and the keen black eye of the Commodore was fixed upon James; he saw that his remark had affected him, for a deep blush mantled his fine countenance—'because, sir, it affords me an opportunity of expressing, as I could not otherwise do, my sense of your invaluable services to this your native place, and my approbation of your noble character. Here, sir, is my draft for five thousand dollars, which, with what you already have, I place in your hands, if you will merely sign this receipt for the amount, payable as you see in ten years, without interest. Don't say any thing, my dear sir'— seeing that James was about to say a great deal—'not a word, if you please; just sit down a moment, Mr. Montjoy; you say that it has been a cause of uneasiness to you, that you have money in your hands intrusted to you for keeping.'

'We shall now pay that off at once, sir; I will not keep it another day.'

'You must do no such thing, sir. It is a great benefit to these people to have their funds in the hands of an honest firm. This you must do; take two thousand dollars of this money, and invest it in a mortgage, on some good property; keep it as a resort, in case of the worst, and hold it sacred for these deposits; the balance use as you please! And now, sir, a good morning to you;' rising, at the same time, and shaking the hand of James very warmly.

'Your kindness, sir—'

'Not a word, Mr. Montjoy, not a word, if you please; good morning, and God bless you.'

The Commodore, walking through the store, saluted Edward, who stood behind the counter, attending upon customers, with a very long face.

As soon as Ned could be disengaged, he stepped up to his brother, who was working away again at his books—

'See here, Ned.'

'What does it mean, Jim?'

'It means that he has loaned it to us for ten years, free from interest, and with a full knowledge of our affairs.'

Ned was deeply affected with this sudden interposition in their favor; he looked full in his brother's face, and Jim, for the first time in many years, saw tears in his brother's eye.

'I hope we shall not forget this.'

'I hope not, Ned.'

The Commodore walked home with a very light heart that day. He must have felt that he had made a good investment, for his step was very elastic, and he gazed upon the pleasing prospect around him, and looked upon the signs of thrift that met his view on every side with so much complacency, that one would have supposed he had a new interest in it all, and felt that he was a partner in the great concern.

It had been a lovely morning, and nature appeared to be in perfect repose; not a cloud to dim the bright sun, nor a motion in the atmosphere to stir even the leaf of the aspen, if there had been any just then to stir, but it was not the season of leaves. A change, however, was about to take place, and the Commodore was sailor enough to guess that it was likely to be a violent one. Seeing Peter occupying his favorite seat (a large flat rock on the brow of the hill overhanging the shore), with the spy-glass in his hand, and perhaps a little curious to take a peep through it himself, he extended his walk to the edge of the hill.

'A sail in sight, Peter?'

The old man hopped down from his perch at the sound of the Commodore's voice, hastily clapped a quid into his mouth, which he had just cut off for that very purpose, doffed his hat, and laid hold of his crutches, all which ceremonies he went through with a celerity quite surprising.

'I was thinking, your honor, that there's goin' to be foul weather outside to-night; them clouds look squally, and they keep growing thicker and thicker.'

'It certainly looks threatening, Peter.'

'It looks very threatening, your honor; and I don't care, for one, how hard it comes, so it will only blow them ugly black craft that are laying off and on there, high and dry somewhere or another.'

'That, to be sure, Peter; they would have an uneasy berth of it in a heavy gale, where they now are.'

'They would, sir, you may depend on it; and I think they're a little uneasy a-ready, for the biggest on 'em have clawed off out of sight, and the others that were at anchor have hauled up, and are starting too. If your honor will look through the glass, you can see all their movements. They'll have a time on it—there, did you hear that, your honor?'

'A gun, Peter, and a heavy one, but at a great distance.'

'I've heard several on 'em, your honor, before; there's something to pay, out there; they wouldn't fire such metal as that for signals.'

'Well, I only wish they were out of the way for a few weeks, Peter. Captain Sam would stand but a poor chance if he should get among them.'

'There would be no chance at all, your honor, there's so many on 'em; I might as well try to run through that picket fence, crutches and all; and as to fightin' it out, your honor knows there's too much odds agin one—they'd blow him out of water.'

'Or sink him under it.'

'Or sink him under it, your honor.'

Peter's prophecy respecting the weather was too truly realized: the heavens, ere the night shut in, were covered with dark and ragged clouds, chasing each other like heaving surges wildly through the air: gusts of wind occasionally swept along, increasing in violence at each succeeding blast; while in the distance, the heavy roar of the ocean told plainly of the tumult that was going on there, and what might be expected when the strength of the tempest should break upon the land. The fitful gusts at length settled into one long-continued, furious blast, increasing gradually its terrible power, until the strongest dwellings rocked and trembled to their base, and even the stout-hearted turned their thoughts to Him whose will the winds obey, and before whose power man shrinks to nothing.

The family of Mr. Rutherford had been long in a state of painful anxiety, watching untiringly around the sick, and, to all human probability, the dying bed of Hettie. The scenes of trial which she had been passing through for several successive months, had imperceptibly weakened her frame; and the terrible ordeal of the mock-marriage proved just the stroke too much for her to bear. In the wildest delirium, her spirit tossed and agonized for weeks; and then, as her nature sunk, worn out with the wrestling of her troubled mind, it required the nicest care and most faithful attendance to stay up her feeble tenement.

Nothing was wanting that love could minister for her benefit; and hope again began to bless the spirits of friends. Her reason was restored, her strength gradually returned, and although confined still to her bed, the signs of recovery were so evident, that cheerfulness once more blessed the countenances of that much afflicted but still happy family.

Hettie had resolved to keep the secret with which she had been intrusted by her brother no longer than she could acquire strength to reveal it; and on this very day that we have been describing, she had told Mr. Rutherford all she knew.

That evening, while the tempest was roaring around his dwelling, he sat alone in the room where his family usually congregated, Mrs. Rutherford and the children having retired to Hettie's apartment, to give what cheer they could to the sick room during the wild howling of the storm. His thoughts, busied with the intelligence which had that day been communicated to him, and agitated between hope and fear, were devising all manner of plans for the recovery of documents of so much value, and the surest way to bring the dangerous men concerned in the transaction to justice, when a loud knocking against an outer door reached his ear. Thinking it might be some benighted stranger, he hurried to admit him, as soon as possible, to a shelter from the peltings of a pitiless storm.

Opening the door, he requested the stranger to hasten in, not waiting to inquire who he was, or what he wanted. The first glance, however, as he turned towards his visitor, made him regret that he had been so hasty; for David Cross, with a wild and haggard countenance, stood before him. Mr. Rutherford had no reason to think that his errand was a good one, but he was resolved to treat him with forbearance. David spoke first—

'A terrible storm, sir.'

'Your business must be urgent, Mr. Cross, that drives you out through such a night.'

'It is urgent, sir. Is Miss Hettie in a condition to be seen?'

'She is not, except by those with whom she feels perfectly at rest.'

'I must see her, Mr. Rutherford, if such a thing is possible. I have done her great injustice, and I wish to make all the atonement in my power. As you value the future peace of an unhappy man, I beg you, sir, to allow me but a moment's interview.'

'It cannot be, Mr. Cross; your presence in her chamber would, in all probability, throw her again into the same horrible condition from which she has but just recovered; and a relapse would be fatal.'

Cross looked away from Mr. Rutherford, and fixed his eye on the door. He seemed in an agony, for occasionally a tremor shook his whole frame, and Mr. Rutherford thought he saw him wipe away a tear. For some moments neither spoke. At length turning, and with a beseeching look addressing Mr. Rutherford,

'Will you allow me, sir, to send a line to her; perhaps she may wish to see me.'

'I will, sir; but I am not at all sure that you will be permitted to see her, even if she consents.'

He wrote a few lines, and handing it to Mr. Rutherford—

'If she refuses to see me after she has read that, so be it; but I will not then be to blame for the consequences which may follow.'

Hettie read the little note, or, more properly, it was read to her. It ran thus: 'Hettie, I want to ask your forgiveness, and to tell you that I have discovered the paper.—D. Cross.'

'I think he had better come in,' said Hettie; 'there is business of great consequence, which it is in his power to communicate.'

As David Cross entered the room, he paused a moment as his eye fell upon the emaciated countenance of the still lovely girl. He then slowly approached the bed, threw himself on his knees, and wept like an infant. As soon as he could speak—

'Hettie,' said he, 'can you forgive me for my cruel wrong?'

'I have forgiven you long since, David; and have prayed that you may be forgiven of God.'

'I can make but little reparation for the past; I have done all I could. That paper is in the hands of Michael Foster; he holds it to extort money from my father. To-morrow night a plan is laid to wrest it out of Foster's power, and then it will no doubt be destroyed. Measures must therefore be taken in the course of to-morrow, or it will probably be too late. Spare my father, if you can; as for myself, Hettie, I leave you now for ever. You and I will probably never meet again.'

Hettie cast a look of kindness at him as he left the room. Mr. Rutherford had witnessed the scene at the bedside, and his feelings were much softened towards the young man.

'You do not mean to go away while the tempest rages thus?'

'The storm is of little consequence to me, sir. I have communicated to Hettie some things which concern you deeply; and all I have to say is, that whatever steps you may take on the information she gives you, cannot be taken too soon.' Saying this, he left the house.

CHAPTER XXX

A change from terra firma to the restless ocean is sometimes pleasant, even for its novelty, if nothing else—although none who try the experiment but are completely satisfied that, so far as everything connected with comfort is concerned, or real quiet of mind or body, there is nothing like the solid earth. I must, however, ask my readers to risk themselves with me for a short time on the ocean, and perhaps they will the more readily do so, when I tell them that we are to be on board the good ship Lady Washington, and under the immediate command of our favorite Captain Sam.

Those who see our ships only as they lie along side of the busy wharves, and are either discharging or receiving their freight, have but a poor idea of the neatness which the deck of a well-regulated vessel presents in her usual sailing trim. It may be that our Captain was peculiar about this matter, but every thing was so snugly stowed away, and securely fastened, that to all appearance nothing would be displaced, should some sudden freak of old ocean roll her bottom upwards. Her deck was flush from stem to stern, and the gangway on each side was clean and clear; every hand on deck was actively employed in the performance of some duty, but it could be seen that they were intent upon some object more engrossing than that in which their hands were busied, for wistful glances were cast towards their young commander, who was standing near the helm, and, with marks of anxiety on his countenance, eyeing through a glass a distant speck upon the ocean.

'Mr. Barnum, this breeze is not going to last; it's a dead calm already a mile to starboard. Hail the maintop; that fellow must be asleep.'

The chief mate—for it was he who was thus addressed—placing his two brawny hands so as to form a speaking trumpet, raised his face aloft, and sent up a blast that would have aroused no common slumberer.

'Hallo, maintop!'

'Ay, ay, sir.'

'What do you make her?'

'Can't make her at all.'

At this reply, the mate sprang into the shrouds with the agility of a squirrel, and was soon far up amid the complicated rigging, and seizing the glass from the one who had been using it, made a satisfactory examination, and then tumbling down as rapidly as he had ascended, was again beside his Captain.

'It is difficult making her out, for she has got her three masts in one; but she looms large, and from the rig should judge she's a bull-dog, with at least two rows of teeth.'

'Ship, ahoy!' from aloft.

'What quarter?'

'On the larboard beam, and coming down with a spanking breeze.'

'Ship, ahoy!!'

'Ay, ay, we see her; there's no mistake now, Captain Oakum; we are in the midst of them.'

'Call the crew aft, Mr. Barnum.'

Soon every sailor on board was standing near the quarter-deck, and, with respectful bearing, ready to hear the will of their Captain. He immediately stepped up before them, and casting his eye over their hardy and cheerful countenances, explained in a few brief sentences the peculiarity of their situation, and what he should require of them.

'We are in the midst of our enemies; three of their frigates are now in sight, and bearing down upon us. We are bound for our port, and shall go there if we can; it will be no child's play, but I am exposed to equal danger with the rest of you. If we succeed, a handsome reward awaits us, and the satisfaction of having done our duty; if we are so unlucky as to fall into their hands, a prison or a life cruise in a man-of-war will be the game on the other side; but if you are all resolved for home or a watery grave, let me know it.'

A loud and hearty huzza burst spontaneously from the whole crew; and at a signal from the mate they tumbled back to their quarters with an alacrity that showed they were ready for any sport their Captain chose.

A steady breeze was yet bearing the vessel along at a moderate pace, and it could be plainly seen that two of the ships were becalmed, as they were fading away in the distance; from them, therefore, but little was to be apprehended, while the one on the larboard beam was rapidly gaining upon them.

Captain Oakum now sprang into the mizzen chains, and marking with intense interest the surface of the ocean, the working of the clouds, and the situation of the different ships—

'Mr. Barnum—'

'Ay, ay, sir;' and the mate was in an instant by his side.

'I think, that by laying her course due north, we shall carry the wind longer with us, and give them a wider berth.'

The necessary order was given, and the Lady Washington was soon ploughing her way in the direction required.

'The breeze is going, Captain; that ship gains on us fast.'

'I see she does, but the probability is we shall both be becalmed soon; she won't hold the wind long after it leaves us; you had better have the boats unshipped, Mr. Barnum, and ready for launching.'

The right good-will with which the sailors sprang to obey each command, gave satisfactory evidence of what their Captain might depend upon in the hour of extremity.

He felt assured that, whatever forty good men could do, at any risk, would be done, but the responsibility of every movement, and of the result, rested upon himself alone. He had provided his vessel with a few guns of large calibre, and one of these occupied the after cabin—it was a long twenty-four pounder. A large port had been made for it in the stern, which was, however, at present closely fastened; four more of various sizes were stationed at different parts of the main deck, and a plentiful supply of pikes and cutlasses was snugly stowed away in readiness for a sudden call. All these he thought might be of service to him in an emergency, but his main dependence was upon the sailing qualities of his ship; he had tested her well, and felt a confidence which, perhaps, most young captains do, that nothing could outstrip his vessel in a good breeze.

Although prepared for the worst, he had not heard of hostilities having been begun until nearing home. A French brig gave him the intelligence, and also that a blockading squadron was strictly guarding the port for which he was bound, part of which he had thus unexpectedly encountered; and now the ability of his ship, and the skill of her commander, were to be put to the test.

Scarcely had the order been executed for unlashing the boats, when the sails flapped heavily against the masts.

'It has gone sooner than I expected. Launch the boats, Mr. Barnum, and let them be manned to their full capacity; if we can move the ship but a few lengths, it may serve to take us out of the reach of their guns.'

With incredible celerity a row of boats was strung ahead of the ship, and every man pulling with determined energy.

'This calm ain't for nothing; I'm of opinion, sir; there's foul weather brewing, depend on it'—and the mate directed the Captain's attention to the threatening aspect of the clouds in the eastern sky. 'We shall have something to contend with soon, besides the enemy's guns, Captain Oakum; that long streak of light under them black clouds, and those scuds flying off and streaking up so fast, and spreading themselves out so, is no good sign; there'll be a north-easter, and a smasher when it comes.'

'Let it come, Mr. Barnum; any thing but lying here and not able to stir, and that frigate almost ready to fire into us.'

The only hope, indeed, which our Captain could indulge, was that the wind might die away as suddenly with their pursuer as it had with them; but her sails were yet well filled, and, of course, she was gaining upon them every moment; the slow and almost imperceptible motion which his own ship made by the power of oars, would have been discouraging to one who was not buoyed up with the consciousness of doing all that was then in his power to do to escape the trouble which had come upon them. He could not control the winds; he therefore neither cursed them, nor himself, nor the noble ship that was bearing down upon them; but he watched her advance with great anxiety, and would turn his gaze occasionally from this object of interest to the ominous-looking clouds that were gathering in heavier masses every moment—a hurricane, or something very near it, would be a great relief; any thing that would give him a chance to bear his much-loved ship out of the immediate reach of her powerful adversary.

'It's a gone case with us, Captain Oakum; her guns will soon be able to reach us.'

'If she keeps the breeze much longer. Call Derrick, will you, Mr. Barnum.'

John Derrick, who now made his appearance at the call of the mate, held the title on board ship of the old man-of-war's-man. He was the only person of advanced age among the crew; he was about fifty, rather taller than was necessary for a sailor, and of slender make. His head on the top was bald, and the locks which hung from the lower part were long and thin; his neck and chin were concealed by a thick bushy beard, very dark, and making a strong contrast with his pale countenance. Sam had selected him for his skill in gunnery, as well as for his ability as a sailor, and in an emergency, felt more confidence in his opinion than in either of his officers.

'Do you think she is near enough to trouble us, John?' and the Captain looked significantly at the frigate.

'She don't think so, Captain Oakum, or we should hear from her; but I've been on the look out a little, and unless her guns are carronades—ay, ay, she speaks now;' and all at once a column of white smoke belched forth from her bow port, and a ball clipped the glassy surface of the water, passing the whole length of the vessel.

'That tells the story, Captain.'

'I suppose it is a gentle hint for us to let them know who we are, before they give us a benefit; so we may as well show them the stars and stripes, Mr. Barnum, and our boys will pull the better when they see them aloft, in the place of that French gewgaw.'

A hearty cheer burst from the whole crew as they saw their native standard flying at the mast-head, and they bent themselves to their oars, until the boat nearest the ship was at times almost out of water.

'Now we shall take it, Captain; she's rounding to; her whole broadside will be the next salute.'

Captain Oakum felt, in all its force, the danger of their situation. In an instant he was at the bow of his ship.

'Pull away, boys—lay to—every foot tells now.' The energy which he threw into his voice, as he gave out these brief directions, added fresh vigor to their willing hearts and pull away it was. As the frigate swayed round, two guns in quick succession sent forth their messengers of death, and evidently intended not as a compliment, for the aim was direct, both striking the ship, although doing but little damage. Scarce, however had they congratulated themselves on their escape, when a volume of smoke enveloped the deck of the frigate, and the waters were ploughed by a storm of bullets; but one of them reached the ship, the others sinking in the deep at her stern. A loud shout went forth from the Lady Washington, as it was now manifest that she was beyond the reach of harm.

'Will you allow me, Captain, just to give them a try with the Long Tom?' said Derrick, stepping up, and touching his cap respectfully; 'just for the honor of the flag, sir.'

'Not yet, John; we must save our fire until we shall be more sure of our mark. You shall have a chance soon, my good fellow, for I see that they are manning their boats for a visit to us; we must give them the best welcome in our power.'

It was evident now that the time of trial was at hand; for two boats, well manned, were seen pulling towards them; the sea was unruffled as a lake, and nothing to prevent their rapid progress.

As Sam did not intend, under such circumstances, to give up his noble vessel and her valuable cargo without a struggle, each gun was loaded, the men were called in from the boats, pikes were brought out and laid in readiness, and each sailor who was not aloft buckled on his cutlass. The faces of the young men assumed a determined yet cheerful expression, and not one on board but felt that the stripes should fly as long as his arm could wield a weapon.

The sky, also, was becoming black with clouds, and spreading the gloom of night around them; and the long swell that occasionally lifted their vessel, told that already the tempest was doing its work in the distance; every sail aloft was taken in and well secured, and suitable preparation made for the emergency.

'They are calculating, I guess, sir, to finish the job, and make a harbor on board the Lady Washington, afore the squall comes on, or surely no commander in his senses would send boats off with such a mess as any one can see is brewing yonder.

'Now John, is your time: take your hands and get all ready. Don't open your port until I pass you the word, and then make sure work with them.'

'Ay, ay, sir.'

And down he tumbled, and the men allotted to him, with as good will as though piped to dinner. As the boats neared the ship, it could be seen that the officers were urging on to greater speed: and good cause had they, for the roar of the coming tempest had reached them, and but an alternative was now left; they must either secure their prize quickly, or perish amid the wild waves: a return in their open boats to their own ship was impossible.

Captain Oakum saw that the time for an effort had arrived.

'All ready below, John?'

'All ready, sir.'

'Now is your time; let them have it.'

The ship trembled as the engine of destruction belched forth its deadly messenger; the thick smoke curled up over the stern, for a moment obscuring the view; but the next, a loud shout came up from below, and was echoed through the ship. Captain Oakum almost shuddered as he beheld what execution had been done, for the whole crew of one of the boats was battling with the waters, while their companions in the remaining boat were using their utmost exertions to rescue the living and the dying from the wreck of the other. But there was not a moment to spare to look at friend or foe, for the blast of the tempest came sweeping over them in its might, and each man flew to his post at the swift word of his commander, and was prepared to meet the contest with the stormy elements. As the gale struck the ship, the sails flew out with a report like the sudden burst of thunder, and the yielding ship lay over with her bulwarks to the water's edge; a moment she seemed pressed down by a weight that must whelm her in the deep, and then, recovering her balance, gracefully she rose to meet the adversary with which a contest for her life was now to be maintained.

'They'll get their deserts now, Captain; those men can never reach their ship in their crowded state.'

'We must save them, Mr. Barnum, if we can; put your helm to lee, and tack ship.'

The gallant vessel bore proudly up against the mighty wind; a moment she seemed to waver in its very eye, and then falling off, and taking its power on her other beam, bore swiftly on towards the enemies who had so lately sought her destruction. As she dashed along to windward of the boat now struggling amid the foaming waves, Captain Oakum seized the trumpet from his mate, and hailed them—

'You can never reach your ship.'

'Not in our present condition,' replied a fine-looking young officer.

'We will do the best we can for you, but leave your arms behind.'

The roar of the tempest forbade any reply; but the officer raised a white handkerchief, and as the ship flew by, a rope was thrown to the boat, and by the united powers of both crews, she was drawn under the lee of the ship. As much care as possible was taken in removing the wounded seamen, and Sam, as yet unused to the horrors of war, felt his heart sicken as he looked at the terrible fruit of his own orders. He felt that there had been a necessity for it, but would gladly have relinquished his own prospective gains by the salvation of his vessel, rather than have heard one groan from the poor mangled sufferers that now lay in agony upon his deck.

The moment the young officer stepped upon the deck, he presented his sword to Captain Oakum.

'It is a singular fortune, sir, that has made me your prisoner; but I cannot mistake the kindness that has brought you to our rescue in a time like this, and when we were seeking your injury.'

'Retain your sword, sir, and your liberty, as well as that of your companion'—a midshipman, who stood beside the Lieutenant, and was preparing to surrender his weapon in like manner—'and of your crew, I only ask your pledge of honor to attempt no rescue while on board my ship. I will do all I can for your safe return, if we outlive this storm.'

Every thing that could be done for the wounded was immediately attended to; a brotherly feeling was at once established between the crew of the Lady Washington and their late enemies, and each seemed to vie with the other in kind attentions.

Successful thus far beyond his hopes, our young Captain now took a station by the helm, and looked upon the scene, and his situation in reference to the vessels from whose power he had feared so much. Far off in the south-east, the frigate from which he had so narrowly escaped was bearing away in an opposite direction to the course she had been pursuing, and far enough off at present to remove all apprehension from her. In the west could be seen the two which had been becalmed, bearing to the south and east, and evidently doing their best to gain an offing from the coast. To preserve himself from a dangerous contiguity, he had two alternatives, either to endeavor to force his way to the north-ward—almost an impossibility, as the wind then held—or to run before the gale, and venture, through the darkness and the storm, to find his way into port. He was perfectly satisfied that his reckonings had been correct, and that he knew his bearings; although to point his bow to land at such a time, with no other guide than his compass and his chart, he felt to be almost a desperate undertaking. He resolved, however, rash as it appeared, to try the dreadful hazard.

As he communicated his determination to his mate, and ordered him to put the ship before the wind—

'It's a harsh night to venture on a lee shore, sir; but your command shall be obeyed.'

The heavy clouds that rolled in huge masses, scarcely higher than the masts of the ship, had hastened the close of day, and gave sure tokens of what the night would be. The coast, however, had been clearly seen before the daylight departed, and soon the hopes and fears which, by turns, were triumphant in the breast of him on whom such immense responsibility rested, would be certain. All danger from armed vessels was now at an end; but his ship was flying on the wings of the wind; the driving clouds above, and the boiling sea beneath and around her. A costly and gallant vessel, a freight of immense value, and a multitude of human beings, were dependent upon the correctness of his judgment and the determination of his will.

Onward and onward, like a chafed charger, rushed the proud ship, her bow at times nearly buried beneath the billows that tumbled before her, and rolled in majestic grandeur by her sides, or rose like mountains at her stern, threatening to whelm her in their deep dark bosom. How like an infant's dream appeared to Sam now all the past experience of his life: every care or sorrow faded into mist before the deep responsibility that weighed upon his heart. The young Lieutenant was not, as may well be supposed, an unconcerned spectator of the passing scene. He had been struck with admiration, not only at the generous conduct of our hero, but at his manly bearing, his prompt and determined action, and the perfect order and discipline that were so clearly manifested in such an hour of trial. He kept a strict eye on the course of the ship, and confirmed, much to the satisfaction of the Captain, the correctness of her bearings.

'The light ought to be seen, however, Captain, by this time—we have been sailing with incredible rapidity, and must be near the land. Can nothing be seen of it yet?'

'I have my ablest seaman on the look-out, but we have no tidings of it yet.'

Captain Oakum left the stern of the ship and placed himself near to the look-out. It was Derrick whom he had especially intrusted with this important duty; although every soul on board might have been included, for not one but kept an eye ranged towards the quarter where it was expected to be seen.

'Any signs of light yet, John?'

'No signs yet, sir; but we must be drawing near land, sir; the roar of the surf can be plainly heard.'

Scarce had the sailor uttered the last sentence, when at the top of his voice he called out,

'Light on the starboard bow, Captain Oakum!'

And as Sam cast his eye in that direction, the first twinkle of the beacon met his view, and in an instant he saw the imminence of their danger.

'Helm to leeward! hard down!' And springing to his station again beside the helmsman, he issued forth his orders to the seamen without waiting to convey them through his mate. With magic speed the sails were braced to meet the new position of the ship, and take the gale upon her beam. Like a thing possessed of consciousness, the noble craft, almost as quick as thought, turned from the roaring surf, and threw the light upon her other quarter. Hope now hung for safety on the strength of her sails and spars. With all the canvas she could carry, it could but be scarcely visible that she made headway. The stout masts bent like whips, and the laboring ship groaned and cracked and trembled as she plunged into the mighty waves, throwing them, through her whole length, high into the air.

'She'll weather it, Captain: if she can hold on so half an hour longer, we are safe.'

The Captain made no reply; that half hour was freighted with consequences of most heart-stirring interest to him, and at no time had he felt so doubtful of what the end might be. His eye was riveted upon the beacon—that token of his danger and his safety too. What thoughts it kindled in his bosom! Oft had he seen it in his boyhood's days, when light of heart he sat with the dear ones of his home, at their old cottage door. Is he again so near them? Is success, prosperity, and honor soon to be fully realized; or disaster, shipwreck, and death? Slowly the light recedes—the struggling ship, battled fiercely by the terrible tempest, still forces her way, and still the good sails and the bending spars hold on and keep her true.

'Don't you think we are far enough north, Captain, to run in?'

'Ease her off slowly, Mr. Barnum, a point or so.'

'She's a noble creature, sir, few ships could have stood it; but I believe you've the luck with you, Captain Oakum.'

'We have had something with us better than good luck, Mr. Barnum. You may venture now, sir; in with her.'

A loud hurra burst from the deck as the light flew past them; and the Lady Washington, bidding adieu to the raging ocean, entered the comparatively quiet waters of the sheltered bay.

CHAPTER XXXI

When clouds, and darkness, and the driving storm are upon us, we cannot realize that their power is but for a time, and they must give place to sunshine and peace. The beautiful morning that succeeded the tempestuous night recorded in the last chapter, was a surprise indeed to those whose trembling habitations had warned them of its terrible power.

'It has been a hard night, Peter,' said the Commodore, as he stepped forth upon his piazza, and saw the old man busy with the eye-glass, peering across the bright waters of the bay.

'Indeed it has, your honor, and mischief enough done; if you will cast your eye, sir, along the south shore,' handing the glass to the Commodore; 'your honor will see a sight. It's my opinion, sir, that the waters have cleared themselves of everything, and thrown them all bodily on the land.'

'Bless my soul, Peter, what a scene! I fear many lives have been sacrificed yonder, but it must have been more terrible still outside. What is that, Peter? a ship ashore?'

'It is a ship, I believe, your honor, but she's not ashore, sir; there is nothing much but her starn to be seen, but being pretty well acquainted with the bearings hereaway, you see, your honor, the land rises considerably north of the point there, and the trees into the bargain, make quite a bluff to look across, and she would be hid entirely before grounding; the channel runs near the shore, your honor. But she has had a narrow chance, sir, and I see one of her masts is by the board.'

'It is not one of your friends, the blockaders, I hope, Peter? they must have had a lively time of it.'

'If it had only sent them all high and dry, your honor! but I think they must have got a good offing afore the worst on it came; and your honor knows that wind and waves ain't apt to hurt a good ship, if there's no land interference no way: but that ship being there is a puzzle to me, your honor.'

'Well, Peter? let me have my letters and papers in good season this morning.'

'Ay, ay, sir;' and Peter hobbled away towards the town, and the Commodore entered his dwelling with a good appetite for breakfast.

He has just finished his morning repast, when Mr. Rutherford entered his office. He met with a hearty welcome, for the two gentlemen had, since Mr. Rutherford's removal, been on terms of intimacy, although this was the first occasion on which any subject bordering on business matters had been introduced. Mr. Rutherford had resolved in his own mind, during the night past, the peculiar circumstances in which he was placed, and the necessity for prompt and efficient action. He felt the need of counsel, and could think of no one who would be so likely to afford it as Commodore Trysail: for this purpose he had therefore now come.

It will not be necessary for the information of the reader to repeat the substance of his revelation to the Commodore. It was a story, however, which excited much interest in the mind of the old gentleman; he listened with profound attention to the whole recital, and when it was finished, gave his box an extra rap, and politely handing it to Mr. Rutherford—'It is, indeed, a singular event, my dear sir; and you are placed in a situation that requires not only very prompt, but very cautious measures. It would be a righteous thing, no doubt, to bring these men to justice; but the first hint they had of such an attempt would inevitably lead to the destruction of your papers! for although this Mr. Foster might find it a profitable business for him to hold them thus, as a rod over his accomplice Cross, yet he would never be so mad as to risk the discovery of them in his possession: they would be destroyed forthwith, sir. And as to bringing them to justice, it is a very doubtful matter, as it appears to me, whether there is evidence sufficient to convict either of them; they are men, it seems, of some standing in society, if I am correctly informed—none of the immediate actors in the scene are living, or at least to be found. The young man Brown, who is very feeble you say, can only testify to the intention of these men; and his mother does not feel qualified to swear that the unhappy man who made a dying avowal of his guilt in this matter had his full reason.'

'It is all just as you say, Commodore Trysail, and the difficulties of the case presented themselves to my mind as I see they do to yours.'

'And they are serious difficulties, Mr. Rutherford. The probabilities, indeed, would be very much against these men, and the public generally might be convinced that they had committed the nefarious crime; yet after all, a jury sworn to judge according to the evidence brought before them, might not be able to convict them.' The Commodore was suddenly interrupted by the entrance of Peter in a state of excitement really alarming; he did not pause as usual at the threshold, and making a low reverence, present his packet of letters and papers, with 'the mail, your honor,' but he bolted straight into the office, crutches and all, threw his hat down on the floor, took his quid from his mouth, and had liked to have dashed that down too; but his senses came to him in season to prevent such an enormity, so he put it back again as quick as possible. He was very much out of breath, and his eyes flashed with a vividness very unusual. The Commodore put his box away, and straightening himself up, looked at Peter with great astonishment, to say the least of it.

'She's come, your honor.' Peter had great difficulty to get the sentence out, his voice trembled so.

'What has come, sir?' The Commodore had evidently departed from his usual temper towards Peter.

'She's come, your honor, spite of blockaders, harricanes and all, God be praised.'

The Commodore began to catch a glimpse of his meaning.

'You do not pretend to say that the ship has come, the—the—Lady Washington?' and the Commodore started to his feet, and looked very fiercely at Peter.

'It's the truth, your honor, she's riding in the outer harbor: the very same we see'd this morning. A boat has just come ashore, your honor, and I've see'd the men, and sich doins as they tell on you never heered, sir. Captain Sam's blowed the enemy, and he's got twenty on 'em prisoners, and he's give 'em leg bail, and has run into port, God bless him, with that north-easter behind him.'

After delivering himself, Peter turned round, and in two jumps was out of the room, and stumping it off at a round rate. The Commodore was somewhat surprised at this last movement, and stepping to the door, was in the act of recalling his excited valet, when he saw him, in a very animated manner, urging along a person dressed in sailor's garb, and whom the experienced eye of the old Commodore immediately recognized as fresh from on board ship; his rolling, unsteady gait showed very clearly that he had not yet got his land legs on.

'Here's a shipmate, your honor,' said Peter, stepping a little in front of his companion, 'that has a word to say to your honor, but he feels backward like.'

'Come in, my boy, come in; are you from the Lady Washington?'

'Just from aboard, sir.'

'Come in, come in, my good fellow.' And the sailor gave a spring up the stoop as though he was about to mount the shrouds, and taking a step into the office, put his hand into his tarred hat, took forth a sealed letter, and handed it to the Commodore, who immediately broke the seal and read as follows.

'Commodore Trysail:

'Respected Sir:—I am very happy to inform you, that through the aid of Divine Providence, I have brought the Lady Washington into port. To prevent her driving on the beach, I was obliged to cut away my masts, but am busy rigging jury masts to enable us to reach the city, as I do not feel it safe to lie in the outer harbor, should the blockading squadron return to their cruising ground. We have received otherwise but trifling damage. I shall do myself the honor of waiting upon you the moment I place my ship in the hands of your consignees.

'The bearer of this will tell you his own story. He has been a fine fellow on board, and whatever may have been his errors in past days, seems to have taken a new turn.

'Your obedient servant,
'S. Oakum.'

The Commodore, having run over the letter, began to put sundry questions to the sailor, who answered in a style that was perfectly intelligible to the Commodore, but which would have been to ordinary listeners very much like a foreign language. Our friend Peter was an attentive listener. He was standing just without the door, with his head bent over, and turned one side, so as to permit his left ear to have a chance at what was going on. His long queue hung down over his left shoulder, and he was pulling away at it in great earnest. Peter could stand considerable in the way of excitement, but it is not in human nature to stand every thing. To hear such a glowing description of the doings of one that he loved as his own soul, given in a dialect that was sufficient of itself to work up the mind of an old sailor; his feelings got the better of his judgment, and no sooner was the tale over, than, swinging his old hat, he gave three hearty cheers, and stumped it away towards the mansion of Major Morris.

The Commodore had too much of the sailor in him to be surprised at this outbreak of feeling. He smiled as he looked through the door, and saw how Peter was excited, and then addressing himself to the seaman—

'Captain Oakum informs me, my good fellow, that you have something of consequence to say to me on your own account.'

'I have, sir, if you can spare a few moments' leisure.'

The Commodore then excused himself to Mr. Rutherford, and taking the man aside into a private apartment, 'Now, my good fellow, tell me your story without restraint. I am an old sailor, you know, and have lost none of my feelings for a shipmate in trouble.'

'God bless you, sir; but it is an ugly story I have to tell, and if you can have patience to hear me out, you may do with the information what you please.'

Ha then began and gave a short-hand account of his career; that he was born and brought up in a place called Barrens, near by—that he had gotten into bad company, and in the employ of a bad man—that at the instigation of this man, he had been guilty of many improper acts, but that one of these, and the last one in which he had taken a part, had stuck in his heart like a dagger from the moment he did it—that he and his companion, in order to escape punishment in case the crime was found out, and to get away from the man who had exerted his power over them for such shameful purposes, had shipped to sea—that his messmate had taken sick and died, and that his last hours were full of misery on account of what he had done.

'I have therefore, sir, made a clean breast of it all to Captain Oakum, and I am on my way to see the man I once injured so much; but Captain Oakum thought how as you, sir, could tell me what was best to do, and that I might let you know, sir, just the whole on it.'

'But you haven't told me, yet, my man, what this crime you speak of was. You have not murdered any one, surely?'

'God only knows, sir; but we fired a house while they were all asleep; the man who hired us to do it wanted a tin trunk which stood in one of the back rooms. We waited round to have folks give the alarm, but it got well a-burning before any one see it. An old nigger then came and broke the door open with an axe: the house was filled with fire and smoke. The old black fellow—God bless him for a true heart as ever beat in a human body,—went right through the flames, up the stairs, calling as loud as his voice could scream, "Oh my missus and the children!" We hurried into the back room, and feeling about found the trunk, but we had like to have smothered afore we got out; but that old fellow's cry, sir, has rung in my head louder than the loudest noise that the wind and the waves have made, since I have been on the ocean. And, sir, I can't live with it any longer.'

'Did you ever see the man whose house you fired?'

'No, sir, nor do I now remember his name; but he had a character, sir, for being a fine man, far and near.'

'The person's name is Rutherford, and he is now sitting in my office; the very gentleman you saw there.'

'The Lord forgive me! may I not see him, sir, just to ask his pardon, and then let him do with me what he thinks best?'

'You shall see him; but first answer me:—Are you willing to go with me, and meet face to face this man Cross, whom you say instigated this act?'

'I will, sir; only I hope I may be restrained from doing him an injury, for there is that in me, when I think of the villain, that wouldn't mind putting his daylight out, and trampling him in the dust.'

'That would do no good now, you know; it wouldn't rebuild the house, nor ease your conscience, nor reform the man. But I am this morning endeavoring to devise a plan with this gentleman, Mr. Rutherford, for the recovery of this very trunk you have been speaking about. It seems that, after all, it never went into the hands of Mr. Cross, but, by some strange accident, fell into possession of as great a villain as he was, one Michael Foster, who keeps it as a rod over Cross to force money from him. Your presence may be of great consequence. Can your Captain spare you?'

'He has let me ashore for this very business, sir. He thought may be I might be of some use to this Mr. Rutherford; and if I can, God knows I wouldn't value my own life a feather, sir.'

The Commodore told the man to be seated, and stepping into the office, communicated to Mr. Rutherford the particulars he had just been made acquainted with.

'This is a most unexpected turn to affairs, Mr. Rutherford; and I think I can see a way now by which we can get hold of these papers, and get rid of these villains at the same time, if you will leave matters to my management.'

'I will, certainly, sir, and feel deeply—'

'Say nothing about that, if you please. I will call for you in about an hour with my carriage. But first will you see this poor fellow, and set him at rest if you can?'

So saying, he led Mr. Rutherford into the adjoining room. The man was still seated, but was evidently in much agitation, for his countenance wore a death-like expression, and he trembled violently.

'Did you wish to speak with me?' said Mr. Rutherford, stepping up to him; 'you seem to be ill.'

'My body is well enough, sir; although I can't tell why it is in such an ague now. I never trembled before through all the dangers I have been in; but my mind is in a sad case, sir;—you see before you one of the men who burnt your beautiful house;'—and the rough sailor burst into tears.

'Do you truly regret having thus injured one who never did you any harm?'

'God knows I do; but tell me one thing, sir, was any of your family—'

'Burned with the dwelling, you were going to say; no, thank God and the faithfulness of my good old negro, they were not injured.'

'Thank God it is so, sir! and oh that my old messmate could have known this before he left the world!—he died, sir, howling like a raving man—"that he was a murderer!"'

The Commodore now took Mr. Rutherford aside, and making some further arrangements for the accomplishment of his plan, the latter gentleman departed, and Commodore Trysail ordered his carriage to be in immediate readiness.

In about two hours after this interview everything had been completed, and the party selected for the occasion was entering the barrens, and Joe, the Commodore's coachman, was urging on his horses at a very unusual speed, and one which the heavy fat beasts did not seem to relish.

It consisted of Commodore Trysail, Mr. Rutherford, James Montjoy and the sailor. The carriage stopped at the Widow Brown's, and some time was spent in a very particular conversation with the Widow and her son, and then off again to the north at the same rapid rate.

'Hold up a little, Joe, before you reach the tavern; and you may stop at Cross's, and let them blow awhile. It will not be best for us to appear to be in haste.' This latter sentence was intended by the Commodore for the company seated with him.

As the carriage drove up to the long low tavern, the Commodore and James Montjoy alighted; and as they stepped upon the piazza, Mr. Cross met them with a polite bow, and welcomed them to his premises.

Mr. Cross had, for a long time, been anxious to get into the good graces of both of them; for when he found that he could not destroy the young firm, he was desirous of their good-will, that he might the better make sales through them of his wood and timber; and the Commodore being so distinguished a personage, that a nod from him in any public place would be no small consideration for a man of Mr. Cross's standing.

Chairs and benches were immediately presented for their acceptance, but as politely declined.

'Mr. Montjoy and I have a little matter of business to talk with you about this morning, Mr. Cross, and would wish to see you in private.'

'By all means, gentlemen,' and the little fat man led them into a small back room, and carrying chairs with him, even against the protest of his visitors, placed them with much care, as to position and then closed the door.

'Since you have taken the trouble, Mr. Cross, to bring us seats, I suppose we may as well use them,' said the Commodore, taking up his chair, and placing it as if by accident near the door. Cross saw the movement, and from the sudden flush that deepened the purple hue of his face, appeared to feel that, at least, it was a singular one. He however took the stool which he had brought for himself, and placing it at a respectful distance, sat down in a composed manner, tilting it back so as to balance himself on two of its legs, and resting his hands one on each of his knees, as they were spread out, the better to maintain his position.

'Mr. Cross,' said the Commodore, 'when we have business on hand, the fewer words by way of introduction the better. I have a serious charge to make against you this morning, and therefore it is that I have chosen to see you alone.'

Cross immediately dropped his stool on its four legs, and straightening up to make the most of himself: 'If we are to be alone, sir, why have you brought company with you?' looking significantly at young Montjoy.

'To set your mind at rest on that head, Mr. Cross, I will tell you that Mr. Montjoy has, at my request, been deputized by the Sheriff, and acts at present as an officer.'

Cross did not turn pale, for that could not well be, but his countenance assumed a livid hue, and he immediately rose to his feet.

'You may as well be seated, Mr. Cross; this business has been committed to me, and it must go forward, sir; but I have no disposition to treat you with harshness—sit down, Mr. Cross.'

Mr. Cross sat down; there was something in the decided tones of the Commodore's voice that carried with them the idea of implicit obedience.

'Without alluding to the serious crime which I have it in my power to substantiate against you, I at once propose to you, Mr. Cross, that if you deliver up to me the papers which were taken from Mr. Rutherford's house by the men employed by you for that purpose, and at the same time make a quit-claim to your son David of all your real estate, you may then have twenty-four hours to make what other arrangements you please in this vicinity, and nothing shall be revealed until the expiration of that time; otherwise I shall immediately have you arrested for robbery and arson. I give you ten minutes in which to make your choice.'

'It is a false charge, sir; the whole of it is a falsehood, started by that old idiot the Widow Brown and her son; and I intend they shall smart well for it—that they shall, sir.'

The Commodore then gave a signal to James Montjoy, who left the room, and turning himself to Mr. Cross: 'It is a solemn thing for you, sir, to violate the precepts of the Almighty, for sooner or later, the hour of just retribution overtakes the delinquent. I am not sitting in judgment over you, Mr. Cross; but I cannot shut my eyes against the marked tokens of an overruling Providence, that have been exhibited in bringing to light what you supposed was beyond the reach of detection.'

At that moment the door opened, and Mr. Rutherford, followed by James Montjoy and the sailor, entered the room. Cross looked at them with intense anxiety until his eye fell on the latter; he started as though pierced by a ball, and then stood transfixed with amazement, until gradually he settled down into his seat, and stared wildly on the floor.

'Your ten minutes has about expired, Mr. Cross; what do you decide?'

'I am at your mercy, gentlemen, do what you think proper. As to the papers, they are not in my hands, nor ever have been.'

'We know that, Mr. Cross; but as you were intending to take possession of them this evening, you cannot be very ignorant where they are to be found.'

'Who told you that?'

'It is sufficient, sir, that we know the fact. As I have just said to you, the searching eye of the Almighty has been upon you through all the windings of your crooked way, and has brought out all your sin. The wretched beings who have been dependent upon you as hirelings, and whom you have ground to the dust, and trained for your wicked purposes; the woman who has been in reality your lawful wife, although not known nor acknowledged by you as such, the mother of your only child, yet treated by you as the off-scouring of the earth; the son who, by your instigation, had like to have been the ruin of a lovely girl—all are ready to testify against you. Under such circumstances, Mr. Cross, the mercy offered you is very tender in contrast with your iniquity.'

Cross was now indeed sensible that his hour of trial had come: large drops of sweat stood upon his forehead, and he trembled like a reed in the tempest.

'Michael Foster has the papers in his possession; but you must take him by surprise and watch him close, for if he suspects what you want, they will be destroyed before you can help yourselves.'

'He is a justice of the peace, I understand, Mr. Cross.'

'Yes.'

'You will please go with us, then, sir; you can execute the deed there, which you know was one of the terms I stated to you. You have one made out, have you not, Mr. Rutherford?'

'I have, sir.'

The Commodore, without further remark, signified his wish to be on the way: and soon Mr. Cross was seated on an easy cushion in a fine carriage, and with such company as he never had the honor of riding with before; but I presume it was a matter of secret rejoicing with him that the journey would be a short one—the soft seat and the good company were thorns and fire to him.

Commodore Trysail alone left the carriage, and as Mr. Foster opened his door, entered without waiting for any ceremony.

'Mr. Foster, I presume, sir?'

'At your service, sir,' making a low bow to the Commodore.

'You are a justice of the peace?'

'I am, sir.'

'Gentlemen,' said the Commodore—calling to those in the carriage—'the Esquire is at home, you can come in.'

Mr. Foster began to be much surprised, not only at the peculiar manner of his visitor in his own abrupt entrance, but at calling, without leave, a coach-load of folks to follow: his looks however manifested something more than surprise, when he found himself honoured with the presence of those who now entered his apartment.

'Mr. Rutherford, that deed, if you please.' The tones of the Commodore's voice assumed a harshness very unusual with him of late years; his keen eye had penetrated into the character of the man he had now to deal with. 'Mr. Cross wishes you, sir,' addressing Foster, 'to witness his signature, and take an acknowledgment of his free act and deed.'

Foster bowed again, and without reply handed the pen and ink to neighbor Cross. He then sat down and wrote very rapidly, although it was impossible for him to conceal the agitation which his nerves suffered.

'And now, Mr. Foster,' said the Commodore, 'this matter being through with, and Mr. Cross's business settled, your turn comes next.' Foster's jaws, as we have seen, were rather long and flabby at best; but as he dropped his chin and drew up his eyebrows in the surprise that came over him as the Commodore turned upon him his keen, searching eye, he made up altogether an expression rather wo-begone. 'You have had in your possession for some time, Mr. Foster, a small trunk of papers, of but little value to yourself, except as you have held them for the especial benefit of your friend, Mr. Cross, here; but as he has wisely chosen to give up doing business in these parts, they can be of no further use either to him or to you; and as we have abundant proof of the guilt and villany of you both, we shall therefore give you an equal chance, provided you immediately surrender those papers. Twenty-four hours, sir, you may have in order to settle up your business in this region; if, after the expiration of that time, you are seen in this vicinity, I pledge you my word, which has never been broken yet, that you shall be arrested as an accomplice in the crimes of robbery and arson.'

Foster cast his eye at the downcast countenance of Cross, and read too plainly in that the sad situation in which their affairs were placed. Evasion would do nothing for his benefit in this case; he therefore, without making the least reply, walked to a closet which opened into the side of the large chimney, unlocked it, and began taking out sundry old boxes, bottles, paper bundles, etc.; these he placed upon the floor, until the whole cupboard was emptied. He then deliberately took from his pocket another key, and applying it to the back of his cupboard, opened another door there; and thrusting his long arm into the hole, brought forth the long-lost trunk.

'What consummate villany!' exclaimed Mr. Rutherford, as he at once took possession of his property.

'Open it at once, sir,' said the Commodore, 'and see that every thing is right; for if but one paper is missing, they shall both swing for it yet.'

But the papers were all correct, and both Foster and Cross felt in no small degree relieved, even with the conditions then laid upon them, when the party which had thus made each of them such an unexpected visit, was again riding away. And here we may willingly, both for ourselves and our readers, take leave of these two characters: they suddenly disappeared—no one, excepting those in the secret, understanding why; they have been blots upon the scene of our story, and we bid adieu to them with pleasure.

CHAPTER XXXII

There are spots in life, like bright days in the year, when all above, around, and beneath, is so full of beauty, that the spirit bathes in the luxurious scene almost to weariness.

Such a spot to Sam was the day of his return to his native village. The cordial welcome of the good old Commodore, testifying his hearty approbation of his gallant conduct by a commission that at once established his independence; the warm embrace of friends who had grown up with him from boyhood, and who exulted in his enviable prosperity; the respectful consideration that was meted out to him on all sides; and above all, the flow of ardent and almost overpowering affection that met him in that home, where parents and sisters poured out into his own glowing bosom the bursting fulness of their hearts—affection, respect, honor, and independence, all in one united band, waiting upon him, and doing all that in them lay, to make this hour of his life bright and happy.

The meeting between Sam and the family of Major (now General) Morris, was all that he could have asked. His old and first friend, the General, was at a distant part of the country, engaged in active service; but Lady Morris greeted him with the warmth of a mother, and Susan, that once retiring and bashful little girl—a glance of whose eye filled the heart of the little sailor-boy with rapture, who had refused bright offers, and turned away from many an ardent lover—met our hero with a manner so cordial, and with all the friendship of her heart unmasked, that he could doubt no longer of the pure delight that awaited him.

Peter was almost beside himself with joy, and kept his crutches going from morning till night, cutting off immense slices from his bundle of "pig-tail," and stowing them away two at a time; talking to every one he met, telling most incredible stories, and sometimes, when he thought he could do it without being heard huzzaing, as though to let off superfluous steam.

The Commodore, however, before the close of the day, damped his ardor for a few moments, by bringing a serious charge against his favorite.

'It is all well, Peter. To be sure, Captain Sam has shown himself a man, but what do you think about his letting prisoners slip out of his hands in that way?'

'In what way, your honor?'

'By letting them go, and giving them one of the ship's best boats; and finding them with compass and stores, and every thing so that they might put off to sea, and hunt up their squadron—that looks too much like comforting the enemy, Peter.'

'Pardon me, your honor, if I can't agree with your honor this time. Captain Sam had good warrant for what he did.'

'Good warrant, Peter—from whom?'

'I heered our minister—God bless him—on the last Sabbath, and your honor must have heered him too, say—and he took it from the good old Book, your honor—"Love your inimies, do good to them that hate you"— and more of the same kind.'

'But, Peter, you don't mean that we should deal with these men, whom you have been so long wishing that the winds would blow high and dry, according to the good Book, do you?'

Peter had to turn his quid over, and chew a little on it, for he remembered having indulged some rather ungenerous feelings—especially towards his blockading friends.

'It is hard, I allow, as your honor very well knows, to make a man's conscience always jibe right when encountering an inimy to one's self, or thinking of one that is dear to us that may be like to git into their clutches; but when a man can catch a chance to show a little Christian spirit towards them that seek his hurt, whether it be inimies to one's country, or inimies to one's self, it will be better, as I take it, in the long run, your honor, and at the last reckoning, that we should do so.'

'Well, well, Peter, it is getting late, and you must be pretty well tired to-day, you had better turn in.'

'Many thanks to your honor, and a long life.'

CHAPTER XXXIII

Time is not only a destroyer; he is a healer too. Sorrow and joy attend his flight; and each in turn commands the passing hour. The family of Mr. Rutherford had laid aside the badges of mourning which, in token of respect for the memory of one they loved, they had put on when William Andrews died. The scene at his bedside had been ratified in secret, and Henry Tracy felt every day more and more satisfied with the one he had chosen. There was some little stir, indeed, when it was known abroad, and some even hinted the idea that he had stooped a little in taking one situated as Hettie had been; but none who really knew her ever thought so. She was a bright star, dimmed awhile by clouds, and now to shine in her true, simple lustre; her husband's heart, her husband's home, and the circle over which his care rested, were now to feel her sweet and womanly influence.

The pressure of trouble had done its bidden work upon the views and habits of Mr. Rutherford; and then, by the same kind hand which brought it, was it taken off. The recovery of his deed at once placed him in possession of wealth; the immense value of the tract of timber was daily becoming more evident, and he was in a few months enabled to commence the joyful duty of liquidating the claim upon his homestead. He had resolved, in time, to rebuild upon the ruins of his former house; but prudence was his watchword now, and until every cent of the claim was cancelled, he determined to remain in his present situation. He was, however, for a few months occupying the beautiful mansion of Commodore Trysail, at the special request of the latter, who was about to leave for the south, where he and his lady expected to remain some time.

The pretty parsonage, which has been so long waiting for an occupant, is at last full of life and bustle. The windows have been opened for some days, and young female forms are seen moving about in all directions through the house. Curtains are putting up and carpets putting down, bedsteads are coming together, and large flat beds are lying about in readiness to be put upon them; piles of chairs, tied together two and two, are waiting to be released; and crates, boxes, and baskets, all well filled, are being broken open and pulled to pieces, while from them be borne off by nimble hands and feet all sorts of every thing, to be arranged according to their different uses.

In the mean time there is a great stir at Mr. Rutherford's. Old ladies and young ones have been much together there of late; vast quantities of needles and pins and silk and thread have been in requisition; and then the old family recipe-book has been for days lying on the large kitchen table, with heaps of flour and butter alongside of it, and busy hands have been violently engaged beating insides of eggs, and taking out the insides of raisins, and stewing things together in all sorts of ways; while at times a most savory smell would escape to the upper stories, enough to set all the old women and young children running down stairs.

At length the meaning of all this bustle is unfolded. A wedding day has come. Henry Tracy has been putting his pretty cottage in readiness to receive the lovely girl, who has consented to be its mistress; and Hettie, with the aid of her companions, and under the care of Mrs. Rutherford, has been making preparations for the hour when she yields herself in holy wedlock to the man she loves.

It has been a busy day with the family of Mr. Rutherford from early dawn until near its close; and now, as evening approaches, lights are seen glistening from every window in the large building, and through the wide hall, flitting like fairies, young ladies are passing and repassing, and going up and down with light and joyous steps, as though pleasure had come down and shed her quickening charm upon them all. Carriages of various kinds are landing groups of young and old, and then driving off with speed. Attendants at the door in neat array, are leading the new comers to the various rooms assigned for their reception. For a while confusion seems to reign; then all subsides to quiet. The joyous laugh and the lively call are hushed, and within the spacious parlor have all assembled who are to be the witnesses of the solemn rite. Dazzling with lights, scattered profusely round, and trimmed with evergreens and early flowers, it seems a fairy bower; while, circling the room the well-dressed guests, with staid and even solemn faces, are whispering to each other, or eyeing with curious gaze the beautiful festoons that grace the windows or sweep across the lofty ceiling.

It is the wedding day of the young pastor and his gentle bride, and Henry Tracy enters the room, accompanied by his three bridesmen, Captain Oakum, and James and Edward Montjoy. Soon after Hettie appears led by Mr. Rutherford, who is to act as her father, and give away the bride. She is simply dressed without ornament of any kind, but the long white veil which falls in light and graceful folds from her head, and partly hides her dark luxuriant hair. Her bridesmaids follow, Susan Morris, and the sisters of the young Captain, and of James and Edward Montjoy.

'Before I present to you,' said Mr. Rutherford, addressing Mr. Tracy, 'this chief earthly treasure'—and he turned his eyes for a moment to the blushing girl who was leaning on his arm—'I must beg your acceptance of this paper, you will find when you look upon it, that you are not taking to your home a portionless bride. She is as dear to the hearts of Mrs. Rutherford and myself as if she were our own child, and we have given to her the dowry of a daughter of our own. You chose her as a poor portionless girl, and would have loved her as tenderly had she continued so; but we all know that this is an uncertain world, and it is as well to be prepared for its troubles. May God bless you both!'

One wedding, it is said, leads to another. Whether this is so or not, I cannot say, but the signs are ominous; for James Montjoy and Mary Oakum take long walks by moonlight, and Sam spends every evening at General Morris's, and other tokens tell plainly what things are coming to.

But the long road which I and my readers have travelled together, must here end: are you not glad of it?